Around
Lake Michigan

Sault Ste. Marie

M
I
C
H
I
G
A
N

Green Bay

WISCONSIN

LAKE
MICHIGAN

Milwaukee

Grand Rapids

ILLINOIS

Chicago

Gary

INDIANA

SANDERSON

Around Lake Michigan

Jean R. Komaiko
Beverly H. Barsy
Ruth S. Mackelmann

BOSTON
HOUGHTON MIFFLIN COMPANY
1980

Library of Congress Cataloging in Publication Data

Komaiko, Jean.   Around Lake Michigan

Bibliography: p.   Includes index.
I. Lake Michigan region—Description and travel—
Guide-books I. Barsy, Beverly H., joint author.
II. Mackelmann, Ruth S., joint author. III. Title.
F553.K65   917.7   80–12144
ISBN 0–395–29127–5

Printed in the United States of America

AL 10 9 8 7 6 5 4 3 2 1

Maps by Richard Sanderson

*This book is dedicated
with loving thanks to our patient
and supportive families.*

Acknowledgments

The following people helped make this book possible: Lou Asher, Susan Berkson, Gary Besser, Pete Caesar, Margaret Coppess, Bill Diana, Howard Emich, Jinny I. Esser, Commander J. M. Fournier, Emma Goggin, Elmer Gertz, Ed Gray, Bernice Gregorio, Lucy A. Hanson, Tom Hawley, Naomi Hult, John C. Hyland, Ralph B. Josep, Josephine Jones, J. Kosch, Blossom Levin, William McCarthy, Father Duane Mills, Carol Moodie, Ralph Morril, Larry Munro, Louise S. Nathan, Marjorie Perkins, Richard Quick, Richard Robbins, Robert G. Robinson, Bernard and Phyllis Scheras, Roland Schomberg, Jim Smyth, Betty Snydacker, Jane Sooy, Mike Spranger, Bella Steinberg, Carl and June Suhs, Kenneth C. Teysen, Dr. and Mrs. Maurice Tiersky, Robert and Janet Triplett, Anna Ubbink, Willard Wichers, David Williams, and dozens of helpful chamber of commerce people, librarians, and museum personnel.

We wish to thank David Harris and Janice Byer for their decisions, revisions, and patience. We could not have made it without: Sally Scarborough, our marvelous typist and loyal friend; Charles Komaiko, who acted as our counselor and agent; and Kate Ollendorff, whose red pencil kept our Lake and our prose clean.

Foreword

This book began as a love affair with Lake Michigan. Its three authors have lived a stone's throw from Chicago's shoreline for more than 150 years, collectively. We have paddled between its sandbars, sailed over its waves, hiked and biked the paths that parallel it. We are the children of a prairie land and for us Lake Michigan has been the aesthetic and recreational focal point of life: our desert, our rain forest, our great rimmed canyon. Like the mountain that had to be scaled because it was there, we wrote this book because we and our Lake were here.

Lake Michigan is the fifth largest freshwater lake in the world, the only one of the Great Lakes wholly within U.S. boundaries. For centuries visitors have gazed at the Lake in amazement and called it the Inland Sea or Saltless Sea. More people vacation around Lake Michigan and the other four Great Lakes than any place in the country, if not the world. Sooner or later all of them realize that this is one of the most fickle bodies of water anywhere, capable of faster and more frightening change than the ocean. Some of the worst disasters in marine history have taken place on these bodies of water, and yet they can be as calm as a tub before a child's bath. Lake Michigan commands respect. The Lake had a long gestation and a difficult birth; its everchanging contours, its varied topography and climate have had a profound effect on the settlements along its shores. Numerous ethnic groups have wandered its banks, lonely and seeking an area resembling home. The Dutch found their new-old land in Holland, Michigan; the Belgians in Brussels, Wisconsin; the Icelanders on Washington Island off the Door Peninsula; and the Lithuanians discovered a new Baltic in Beverly Shores, Indiana.

European farmers and orchardists have settled in clusters along the

Lake's eastern shore, because there the winds pile up sand at the mouths of rivers and natural harbors, sealing them in to make protected inland waters. Men with industrial skills have moved toward the western shore where the natural harbors of Chicago, Waukegan, Milwaukee, and Green Bay invited the development of shipping and industrial growth. Industrially, Lake Michigan cannot be fully appreciated unless one realizes the enormous population it sustains. And so we have suggested, for those interested, roads that lead to steel mills in Indiana, boat yards in Wisconsin, paper mills in Michigan. Watching the train ferries from Wisconsin cities arrive in ports in Michigan gives firsthand information about the Lake's importance to transportation. Watching ore carriers pass through the Straits of Mackinac, one senses the strategic and historic importance of this great water highway that is vital to American life. And some of the Lake's cities now are international seaports, thanks to the St. Lawrence Seaway.

Around Lake Michigan is not only a guidebook to over one hundred communities on the Lake, but it is a Baedeker to the water itself — its storms and treacherous seiches, its mirages and mysteries, its races, recreation, fishing, diving, and swimming. We list the Lake's marinas, boat repair yards, charter boats, beaches, and waterfront carnivals. Because we believe that the present is better understood if you understand the past, the book contains a mini-history of each lake community, not only of the past it shares with other communities, but also of the unique way it has handled its portion of the Lake.

The book begins with Chicago — the mightiest of the Lake cities, but far from the oldest — and goes clockwise . . . up to Milwaukee, through Door County, on to Escanaba and Mackinac, and down the eastern shore via Charlevoix, Traverse City, and Benton Harbor. It swings through the Indiana dune country, the great industrial valley of the Calumet, and back once again to Chicago. It is a journey of nearly 1000 miles, encompassing four states and six islands that can be toured, two national parks, and many state parks (most with camping facilities). You can rush through the route in two days, or you can mosey along and visit Indian cemeteries, pick cherries till you are dyed juice red, or see a genuine fifteenth-century church that was brought stone by stone to America from the Rhone Valley. The pace is up to you, but we've made it our business to include every point of interest we could, from Architecture to Zoos. (Each city's listings are arranged alphabetically by category with the exception of the category Sources of Information, which, when it appears, is the first listing.) We want this book to be a friend and guide to shoppers, sports enthusiasts, museum and music lovers, wine tasters, and ornithologists. We have listed restaurants where if the cuisine is not haute (and it seldom is), at least the place is (or was when we visited) clean and as close as possible to a good view of the water.

Around Lake Michigan is a "shunpike" book, written for the traveler who loves to rubberneck along the road. It hugs the Lake's shoreline whenever possible, beautiful view or not. We believe this is the way to unlock the combination to the 6000-year saga of life on this great body of water.

We emphasize the tough and resourceful pioneers who founded the villages and towns of the Lake. We urge you to visit any of their homes that have survived.* Castles, mansions, and log cabins (today frequently converted to museums), recapture the era and the aura in which these redoubtable souls lived. So too the churches, they memorialize a cultural heritage of an ethnic and ecumenical mix so great that most of the world's religions have houses of worship along the Lake's shores. And perhaps after you have thought about pioneers and padres you will enter into the great Marquette controversy, for almost every village boasts of a visit from the Jesuit padre, and quite a few claim he breathed his last along their beach.

Around Lake Michigan is primarily a linear trip, but in a few instances we take you farther afield. The Horicon Marsh, the Soo Canal, the music camp at Interlochen, and a few other places seem so significant that we thought they merited the extra mileage.

Though this book is full of off-beat things (such as a mausoleum that hints of black magic, an Indian cemetery with animal-shaped mounds, and a carpenter who fashions furniture out of shipwrecks), we also list chambers of commerce so that you can keep up with changes and new schedules that no guidebook can manage. We provide a small bibliography for travelers who want to explore the Lake further through their own reading and a glossary of terms that belong to the Lake and its history. And we urge our readers to become writers

*An asterisk before the names of buildings or places indicates a listing on the National Register of Historic Places. We have provided architect's(s') name(s), immediately following the building's name, where available and appropriate.

by letting us hear about places or events we might have overlooked.

Above all, we hope you have as much fun as we have always had going around Lake Michigan.

Caveat: Many museums and state parks have admission fees. We have not listed them, but we have given phone numbers.

J.K.
B.B.
R.M.

Contents

vii Acknowledgments
 ix Foreword

ILLINOIS: From Chicago to Winthrop Harbor

  3 CHICAGO
 48 EVANSTON
 58 WILMETTE
 62 KENILWORTH
 64 WINNETKA
 67 GLENCOE
 70 HIGHLAND PARK
 75 HIGHWOOD
 77 FORT SHERIDAN
 79 LAKE FOREST
 82 LAKE BLUFF
 84 GREAT LAKES NAVAL TRAINING CENTER
 85 NORTH CHICAGO
 86 WAUKEGAN
 90 ZION AND WINTHROP HARBOR

WISCONSIN: From Kenosha to Marinette

 97 KENOSHA
104 RACINE
111 MILWAUKEE
128 PORT WASHINGTON
133 HORICON MARSH

135 CEDAR GROVE AND OOSTBURG
137 SHEBOYGAN
148 MANITOWOC AND TWO RIVERS
157 KEWAUNEE
161 ALGOMA
166 STURGEON BAY
173 DOOR COUNTY
    175 JACKSONPORT
    177 BAILEY'S HARBOR
    179 SISTER BAY
    181 ELLISON BAY
    183 GILL'S ROCK
    185 WASHINGTON ISLAND
    188 ROCK ISLAND
    189 EPHRAIM
    192 FISH CREEK
    194 EGG HARBOR
    195 BRUSSELS
197 GREEN BAY
203 SUAMICO
206 OCONTO
210 PESHTIGO
213 MARINETTE

MICHIGAN: FROM MENOMINEE TO GRAND BEACH

221 MENOMINEE
226 ESCANABA
233 GLADSTONE
235 RAPID RIVER
237 STONINGTON PENINSULA
237 NAHMA
237 GARDEN PENINSULA
238 FAYETTE
240 FAIRPORT
240 THOMPSON
241 MANISTIQUE
245 GULLIVER

Contents **xv**

248 ST. IGNACE

251 THE SOO CANAL

252 THE MACKINAC BRIDGE

255 MACKINAC ISLAND

259 MACKINAW CITY

263 CROSS VILLAGE

267 HARBOR SPRINGS

271 BAY VIEW AND PETOSKEY

277 CHARLEVOIX

282 BEAVER ISLAND

286 EAST ARM OF TRAVERSE CITY BAY

    286 EASTPORT

    287 KEWADIN

    287 ELK RAPIDS

    288 ACME

290 TRAVERSE CITY

299 WEST ARM OF TRAVERSE CITY BAY

    299 BOWER'S HARBOR

    300 OLD MISSION PENINSULA

    301 SUTTONS BAY

    302 PESHAWBESTOWN

    303 OMENA

    303 NORTHPORT

305 LELAND

308 NORTH MANITOU ISLAND

309 SOUTH MANITOU ISLAND

310 GLEN ARBOR

313 EMPIRE

314 SLEEPING BEAR DUNES NATIONAL LAKESHORE PARK AND FRANKFORT-ELBERTA

324 ARCADIA AND ONEKAMA

326 MANISTEE

332 LUDINGTON

338 PENTWATER

342 MUSKEGON

349 GRAND HAVEN

355 HOLLAND

364 SAUGATUCK AND DOUGLAS

371 SOUTH HAVEN
376 BENTON HARBOR AND ST. JOSEPH
384 STEVENSVILLE
385 BRIDGMAN
386 SAWYER
387 HARBERT
387 LAKESIDE
388 UNION PIER
388 NEW BUFFALO
390 GRAND BEACH, MICHIGAN, AND LONG BEACH, INDIANA

INDIANA: FROM MICHIGAN CITY TO HAMMOND

393 MICHIGAN CITY
399 BEVERLY SHORES
401 CHESTERTON
405 INDIANA DUNES NATIONAL LAKESHORE PARK
412 JOHNSON BEACH AND DUNE ACRES
413 PORTAGE
415 BURNS WATERWAY HARBOR AND OGDEN DUNES
417 GARY
420 EAST CHICAGO AND INDIANA HARBOR
425 WHITING
427 HAMMOND

431 Past and Present Lake Michigan Terms
433 Lake Michigan Statistics
438 U.S. Coast Guard Stations
439 Harbors and Marinas
443 State and National Parks with Camping Facilities
446 Index

Illinois

FROM
CHICAGO
TO
WINTHROP HARBOR

WISCONSIN

Winthrop Harbor •

Zion •

Waukegan •

North Chicago •

□ Great Lakes Naval Training Center

Lake Bluff •

Lake Forest •

□ Fort Sheridan

Highwood •

• Highland Park

LAKE
MICHIGAN

Glencoe •

Winnetka •

• Kenilworth

Wilmette •

• Evanston

ILLINOIS

Chicago •

INDIANA

SANDERSON

Chicago

Population: 3,266,200   Area Code: 312
Chicago Convention and Tourism Bureau: 332 S. Michigan Avenue; telephone: 922–3530

Chicago is a series of miracles, set in a perfect location, blessed with a glorious lake, and promoted by loyal boosters who have always talked in superlatives. They will tell you that Chicago has: the world's busiest corner (State and Madison), most active airport (O'Hare), tallest building (three of the five highest in the world), most beautiful skyline, greatest number of Nobel Prize winners (forty-four), finest symphony orchestra, biggest American Catholic archdiocese, richest heritage of modern architecture, and largest grain exchange.

Chicago was the birthplace of nuclear fission, the cafeteria, the mail-order catalogue, *Playboy* magazine, Benny Goodman, Gloria Swanson, modern sociology, jazz, the UN, the steamboat, the boxer short, and toothpaste (the last five being examples of excessive, if inaccurate, loyalty).

Enthusiasm has always run high. The bleat, the brag, and the blow have characterized the city from the beginning. As a matter of fact, the nickname Windy City had less to do with prevailing westerlies than with local politicians with a gift for gab and brag. All Chicago politicos have had intense enthusiasm for their city, from the first mayor, William B. Ogden, to the present one, Jane Byrne. "Hizzoner," the late Richard J. Daley, five times mayor, was even invited to Harvard University to tell them how a modern city works.

Boosterism probably began in the seventeenth century with Louis Joliet, who, returning from his trip into Illinois country with Father Marquette, found the vital portage that made a continuous waterway from the Mississippi to the Chicago River and Lake Michigan. He believed a canal was necessary, and he wrote in his journal, "Here will someday be founded one of the world's great cities."

After the great Chicago fire of 1871, when almost everything had been destroyed, a booster was asked, "What next?" His reply, "In five years there will be more people and more profits than if the fire had never burned." He was right.

Father Marquette with voyageurs and Indians in 1673. *Chicago Historical Society*

Remains of the second Fort Dearborn sketched by artist Dwight Benton. *Chicago Historical Society*

Even the great Sara Bernhardt said, "Chicago is the pulse of America, I adore it." And "Big Bill" Thompson, last Republican mayor in memory (1922) bellowed at the critics, "Throw away your hammer and get a horn."

Daniel Burnham, who turned the Lakefront into a series of glorious parks, and in 1909 wrote the famous Burnham Plan, gave the city its credo. "Make no little plans," he wrote, "they have no magic to stir men's blood, and probably themselves will not be realized. Make big plans. Aim high in hope and work . . ." Fortunately at important junctures in the city's life there were always visionaries with large dreams, and men with money to back them. It wasn't always easy, however, because Chicago's history was rough.

It began in the mud and wild onions where Michigan Avenue now crosses the Chicago River. The first real settler (after the Indians) was a cultivated black man from Haiti, Jean Baptiste Point du Sable. With his Indian wife, he built a fine house, which in time was sold to John Kinzie, also a trader and the first white settler. Between the time of du Sable and Kinzie, control of the Chicago area shifted from French to American, always with Indians in the background, armed and egged on by irate British. Finally, in 1795, after the Indian wars, a treaty was signed in Ohio giving the Americans a piece of land six miles square at the mouth of the Chicago River. Historian Milo Quaife called this "the most momentous real estate transaction in the city's history." In 1803, the War Department ordered Fort Dearborn to be built on the Chicago River, as protection for settlers going through the area. The security was short-lived for in 1812 there was a dreadful massacre of the white settlers. Four years later the fort was restored, but by then people were thinking about a canal, dredging the harbor, and seeking wood for new houses for new settlers.

By 1833 the last of the Indians had left for areas west of the Mississippi, and the land boom was on. A lot on Lake Street that sold for $300 in the early part of 1835 was sold again for $60,000 by the next year. Chicago was incorporated as a village in 1833, as a city in 1837. By 1848 it had its canal, and, more important for its future, the first railroad. A decade later, 100 trains were entering the city each day, and in short order it became the rail and grain, pork and farm machine center of the country. Within ten years, the population increased fourfold. So rapid was the growth that it was said that men

Chicago River and harbor in days of schooners. *Chicago Historical Society*

with telescopes sat on rooftops, watching the harbor and train yards, and dispatching omnibuses to meet newcomers as they arrived.

Chicago was now called Queen of the Lakes, but all her streets and houses were mired in mud. In 1855, a young engineer named George Pullman supervised the lifting of houses and streets by ten feet, using fill from the newly dredged harbor to accomplish the task. It took 1200 men turning 5000 jackscrews to raise the Tremont Hotel alone.

Raising the city was a miracle eclipsed only by reversing the river, which had always been a source of disease as it drained sewage and refuse into the Lake. Again engineers performed the feat (often called the eighth wonder of the world) by reversing the flow so that the Lake drained into the river, through a complex series of locks.

Chicago, with its I Will slogan, became a convention center early, with the Rivers and Harbors Convention of 1847 and the 1860 Republican Convention that nominated Abraham Lincoln for the presidency.

Today the country's leading convention center, Chicago yearly caters to 2.5 million conventioneers as well as 5 million holiday visitors.

The great Chicago fire occurred on October 8, 1871. (That same day fires devastated Holland and Manistee, Michigan, and Peshtigo, Wisconsin, lost 800 people.) Chicago's fire was awesome: 17,000 buildings lost, 100,000 homeless, 120 dead, $200 million in property loss. No one is sure how it started, but for years Chicago children have sung, "Old Lady Leary left a lantern in the shed/When the cow kicked it over, she clicked her heels and said/There'll be a hot time in the old town tonight." When Chicago finally shook itself out, a remarkable thing happened: the best architects in the country, attracted by the challenge, came to rebuild the city. They kicked off the Chicago School of Architecture, which has become world famous, its skyscrapers altering the look of Chicago and that of other cities around the globe.

Perhaps the brashest undertaking of all was the city's bid for the 1893 World's Fair, the 400th anniversary of Columbus's discovery of America. Seven architects (including Daniel Hudson Burnham, Daniel Sullivan, and Fredrick Law Olmsted, the great landscaper) turned 600 acres of marsh on the city's south side into a series of lagoons, canals and parks, creating the "White City" that remains unique among the lasting masterpieces of world's fairs.

The immigrants who arrived for the fair often remained, creating an ethnic and blue-collar mix that has given the city its zest, color, and reputation as a workers' town. Today that mix includes Irish, Germans, Scandinavians, Poles, Italians, Greeks, Lithuanians, Bohemians, Croats, Jews, Spaniards, blacks, Orientals, Eskimos, Gypsies, and 6500 American Indians.

The settlers lived in their own enclaves (mainly in their own houses, for Chicago was and still is a city of bungalows and two-family houses), and worked in the Union Stock Yards, in the rail yards, and on construction gangs. The Tower of Babel of course created many problems, including crime — and the Al Capone era of crime and corruption gave the city a reputation it has had difficulty in erasing.

Helping with this great melting pot, in this most masculine of towns, were a corps of remarkable women led by the great Jane Addams, who won a Nobel Peace Prize for her pioneer social service work at Hull House. She and her professional and socialite colleagues (including Mrs. Potter Palmer and Mrs. Joseph Bowen) battled for

Sears Tower, the world's tallest building, dominates Chicago's downtown skyscrapers. *Hedrich-Blessing*

Chicago's near north lakefront. *Skidmore, Owings, and Merrill*

court reform, for child labor legislation, for women's rights, and a dozen other social causes.

By 1899 almost all the little towns ringing the city had voted to become a part of the metropolis. Thus, within a year, Chicago's population suddenly jumped to 3 million, making it second only to New York.

Chicago has always been a city of great virtues and vices, great troubles and disasters. In 1886, the city was stunned by labor unrest at the International Harvester plant, which led to the bloody Haymarket riots; in 1903, by the terrible toll in lives at the Iroquois Theater Fire; in 1915, by the drowning of 812 in the sinking of the *Eastland;* in 1920, by gangland wars, which reputedly drained $136 billion in potential revenue from the city's coffers. But there were delights as well: in 1890, the creation of the Chicago Symphony Orchestra under Theodore Thomas; in 1892, of the University of Chicago under William Rainey Harper; and in the same decade, the Art Institute of Chicago. When philanthropist Martin Ryerson went abroad to buy art for his home town, superior Easterners quipped that he would probably measure it by the yardstick, but he came back with treasures from all over Europe, including the first El Greco ever owned by an American museum. The early decades of the twentieth century also brought the city writers like Carl Sandburg, Harriet Monroe, Ben Hecht, Edgar Lee Masters, to be followed decades later by poet Gwendolyn Brooks and Nobel Prize–winner Saul Bellow. Famous sculptures also began to dot the city, and taxi drivers now often take visitors down Dearborn Street to show them "our Picasso," "our Chagall," and "our Calder."

But this book is about Lake Michigan, and one cannot write about Chicago without first and last considering the great body of water over which it rules. Chicago was born at the Lake; in many places its shoreline was added to by filling in the Lake. Its commerce began at the water's edges, and today, thanks to the St. Lawrence Seaway, it is a proud prairie port. Many of Chicago's leaders have come via the Lake: Hubbard, Kinzie, Ryerson. Some stopped at Mackinac or at the Straits or Escanaba to trade furs, or to sniff the commercial possibilities between points up north and the growing city to the south.

Big fights have raged over the Lake: over diversification of water (for the Chicago River is the only one that drains out of, not into, the

Lake), pollution, water routes to the Mississippi, standards for the St. Lawrence, and so on. But the greatest fight of all was the one waged by A. Montgomery Ward, father of the mail-order business, often called the human icicle. For thirteen long years, against all odds and every vested interest, he waged a campaign to clean up the Lakefront and to keep the downtown Lakefront and its park forever free and clear. He battled in court; he enjoined; he paid out of his own pocket; and against all odds, he won. When he did, he gave the only press interview of his life. "I fought for the poor people of Chicago . . . not the millionaires." His gift resulted in Grant Park and a shoreline and skyline that are among the most beautiful in the world.

Chicago is spread out with a land area of 228 square miles. It is a long narrow city with 29 miles of shoreline marking its eastern edge. Most of the following activities are concentrated along the Lake and in the downtown area. However, there are sights to see and places to go all over the city. In order for you to use our guide effectively, we have keyed our activities geographically with the following symbols:

(d) — downtown (Michigan Avenue: 1200 south to 1200 north)
(s) — south of downtown
(n) — north of downtown
(w) — roughly, west of the Dan Ryan Expressway (I-94)

The busiest part of the downtown area is looped by the El (elevated tracks); hence its name "the Loop." Within the Loop are major department stores, leading banks, city hall, famous sculptures, and a couple of houses of worship, just to name a few of the listings. Just one block east of the El is Michigan Avenue (it runs north and south), an avenue of hotels, the Art Institute, and elegant shops.

The best way to get around in downtown Chicago is on foot. Park your car in the Grant Park garage, which is under Michigan Avenue with two entrances on Michigan Avenue at Van Buren Street and at Monroe Street. Also a block east of the Grant Park garage on Monroe Street is another city parking lot. For the three museums at 1200 south on Lake Shore Drive, there is a large parking lot right there behind Soldier Field (the Greek-looking stadium), with shuttle bus service to the Loop.

If you are not driving a car, use the Chicago Transit Authority (CTA; see Sources of Information) to see the rest of the city.

U.S. Steel Corporation South Works with ore boat in foreground and blast furnaces in background. *U.S. Steel Corporation*

If you have a car, be sure to drive the length of the city via Lake Shore Drive. It's beautiful and free of trucks but do try to avoid the rush hours. The Dan Ryan Expressway (I-94) is the world's busiest road (lots of trucks!), so use it with care and as little as possible.

The symbol ° before the name of buildings or places indicates a listing as a Chicago Landmark.

SOURCES OF INFORMATION

Organizations

American Sightseeing Tours
530 S. Michigan Ave.; telephone: 427-3100.

The Archicenter (architectural information)
310 S. Michigan Ave.; telephone: 782-1776.

Chicago Convention and Tourism Bureau
332 S. Michigan Ave.; telephone: 922-3530.
Branch in Water Tower Visitor Center, Michigan and Chicago avenues; telephone: 922-3530.

Chicago **Magazine** (for current cultural listings)
500 N. Michigan Ave.; telephone: 751–7100.

Chicago Park District (for public information)
425 E. McFetridge Drive; telephone: 294–2492.

Chicago Public Library
425 N. Michigan Ave.; telephone: 269–2800.

Chicago *Tribune* (for sports bulletins)
435 N. Michigan Ave.; telephone: 222–1234.

CTA Information (Chicago Transit Authority for travel routes)
telephone: 836–7000.

Gray Line Sightseeing (for city tours)
400 N. Wabash Ave.; telephone: 329–1444.

Regional Transportation Authority (RTA) Information (for train travel for 3-state area)
telephone: 836–7000, 800–972–7000 (toll-free).

South Shore Recreation (for travel information)
telephone: 641–5570, 219–926–7561 (information for Indiana).

Ticketron (for tickets and information on in-town events)
200 N. Michigan Ave.; 842–5387.

Books

Ira Bach, *Chicago on Foot* (Chicago: Rand McNally, 1977).
Emmett Dedmon, *Fabulous Chicago* (New York: Random House, 1953).
Jory Graham, *Chicago, An Extraordinary Guide* (Chicago: Rand McNally, 1967).
Guide to Chicago Murals: Yesterday and Today. (Chicago: Chicago Council on Fine Arts, 1978).
H. Hatcher and E. Walter, *Pictorial History of the Great Lakes* (New York: Crown Publishers, 1963).
Historic City, the Settlement of Chicago. (Chicago: Department of Development and Planning, 1976).
Barbara Lanctot, *Walk Through Graceland Cemetery* (Chicago: Chicago School of Architecture Foundation, 1977).

David Lowe, *Lost Chicago* (Boston: Houghton Mifflin Co., 1975).

H. Mayer and Richard Wade, *Chicago, Growth of a Metropolis* (Chicago: University of Chicago Press, 1969).

Bessie Pierce, *History of Chicago* (Chicago: University of Chicago Press, 1975).

Arthur Siegel and J. Carson Webster, *Chicago's Famous Buildings* (Chicago: University of Chicago Press, 1965).

Lois Wille, *Forever Open, Clear and Free* (Chicago: Henry Regnery Co., 1972).

Libraries

Chicago Historical Society Library (n)
Clark and North aves., telephone: 642–4600. Local, Midwest, and Civil War history.

Chicago Public Library (d)
425 N. Michigan Ave.; telephone: 269–2900.

Crerar Library (s)
35 W. 33rd St.; telephone: 225–2526. Technology, science, medicine.

DePaul Library (n)
2323 N. Seminary; telephone: 321–7930. Thomas More collection.

Illinois Regional Library for Blind and Physically Handicapped (sw)
1055 W. Roosevelt Rd.; telephone: 738–9210. Bright-colored, ship-shaped building by Stanley Tigerman.

Leaf Library of Judaica and Spertus Museum (d)
618 S. Michigan Ave.; telephone: 922–9012.

Library of International Relations (d)
660 N. Wabash Ave. (in Furniture Mart); telephone: 787–7928.

Municipal Reference Library (d)
121 N. LaSalle; telephone 744–4992. First-rate collection of government materials.

Newberry Library (d)
60 W. Walton; telephone: 943–9090. Humanities, geology, cartology, genealogy. Serious atmosphere for serious students.

Regenstein Library, University of Chicago (s)
57th St. between Ellis and University; telephone: 753–3468.

Ryerson Library and Burnham Library of the Art Institute (d)
S. Michigan and Adams; telephone: 443–3666. For art and architecture students; advance 'appointment necessary.

Woodson Regional Library (of the Public Library) (s)
9525 S. Halsted; telephone: 881–6900. Black history.

ARCHITECTURE AND HISTORIC SITES

Cemeteries and Tombs

Calvary, 1844–1859 (n)
301 Chicago Ave.; south edge of Evanston, Illinois; telephone: 864–3050. Historically, *the* Catholic cemetery, 10 miles north of Chicago's city hall.

Couch Tomb, date unknown (n)
North Ave. and Stockton in Lincoln Park. Northeast edge of Chicago Historical Society. Last remnant of city's first cemetery.

Graceland, 1860 (n)
Clark St. and Irving Park Rd. (north side); telephone: 525–1105. A Who's Who of early Chicago. °*Louis H. Sullivan's Getty Tomb signals the beginning of modern architecture. Its beauty is overwhelming. Maps and brochures available at office.

David Kennison, Boulder Monument, 1920 (n)
Clark and Wisconsin in Lincoln Park. Chicago's only patriot of the Revolutionary War, who died here in 1846, aged 115 years, 3 months, and 15 days.

Mt. Carmel, 1901 (sw)
Harrison and Hillside, Hillside, Illinois; telephone: 449–6100. Al Capone is buried here; his headstone was stolen in 1972.

Oak Woods, 1853 (s)
1035 E. 67th St.; telephone: 288–3800. Civil War cemetery; Lincoln statue; Union graves; 60,000 Confederate troops (prisoners from Camp Douglas) lie under a high obelisk, which President Cleveland dedicated.

Queen of Heaven, 1930–1976 (sw)
1400 S. Wolf Rd., Hillside, Illinois (near Tri-State and 22nd St.); telephone: 449–6100). Largest mausoleum in the country; 30,000 crypts. Brilliant stained glass and beautiful mosaics.

Rosehill, 1859 (n)
5800 N. Ravenswood; telephone: 561–5940. Castlelike entrance designed by architect of the Chicago Water Tower. Many Chicago greats buried here.

St. James-Sag, 1833–1837 (sw)
Archer Rd. extension (#171) at 106th St. South, in section of Argonne Forest Preserve, one block east of #83, Lemont, Illinois; telephone: 257–7000. Parish cemetery of active parish church. Contains oldest marked grave in Chicago area, 1816.

°* **Stephen A. Douglas Tomb,** 1861–1881 (s)
S. 35th St. and Cottage Grove Ave. Tomb of the Little Giant stands 96 feet high. This state memorial, in a garden setting, is illuminated day and night.

Woodlawn, 1920 (sw)
7600 W. Cermak Rd., Forest Park, Illinois; telephone: 442–8500. Within this cemetery is the circus cemetery, enshrined by the Showmen's League of America, marked by a granite elephant with broken tusks (symbol of mourning) in each corner.

Pet Cemetery, 1926 (sw)
6400 Bentley; Clarendon Hills (Hinsdale), Illinois; telephone: 323–5120. Illinois's oldest pet burial ground. Complete service for animals. Dogs, cats, horses, birds, roosters, skunks.

Churches

Chicago Methodist Temple, 1923 (d)
Holabird and Roche
77 W. Washington; telephone: 236–4548. Chapel in the Sky, highest church in the city, added in 1952.

Five Holy Martyrs Church, 1919 (s)
Arthur Foster; 1963 addition, John Schefke
4327 S. Richmond; telephone: 254–3636. Pope John Paul II visited this church in 1979, and in 1969 and 1976 as Cardinal Wojtla.

Holy Name Cathedral, 1874 (n)
P. C. Kelly; H. Schlacks (1915); C. F. Murphy and Associates (1969)
730 N. Wabash Ave.; telephone: 787–8040. Cathedral of largest Catholic diocese in the U.S.

°* **Holy Trinity Russian Cathedral,** 1903 (n)
Louis H. Sullivan
1121 N. Leavitt; telephone: 486–6064. Eastern-style architecture.

Immanuel Presbyterian Church, 1965 (sw)
Loebl, Schlossman, Bennett, and Dart
1850 S. Racine; telephone: 226–7550. A modern mission church of the Mexican community.

Loop Synagogue, 1963 (d)
Loebl, Schlossman, Bennett
16 S. Clark; telephone: 346–7370. Fine stained glass and sculpture.

Midwest Buddhist Temple, 1972 (n)
Hideaki Arao
435 Menomonee, at Ogden Mall; telephone: 943–7801. This temple of the Shin Buddhist sect emanates serenity.

° **Quinn Chapel, AME Church,** 1891 (s)
Architect unknown
2401 S. Wabash Ave.; telephone: 791–1846. Organized in 1844. Note Martin Luther King's footprints in bronze.

Rockefeller Chapel, 1928 (s)
Bertram W. Goodhue
S. 59th and Woodlawn; telephone: 753–1234. At the University of Chicago. Gothic structure with a 72-bell carillon; liturgical banners by Norman Liberte.

St. Patrick's Church, 1854 (w)
Asher Carter and Augustus Bauer
718 W. Adams; telephone: 782–6171.

°* **Second Presbyterian Church,** 1872 (s)
James Renwick; Howard Van Doren Shaw (1900s)
1936 S. Michigan Ave.; telephone: 225–4951. Mrs. Abraham Lincoln worshiped here. Note Tiffany windows.

Seventeenth Church of Christ, Scientist, 1965–1968 (d)
Harry Weese and Associates
55 E. Wacker Dr.; telephone: 236–4671. Handsome, modern, urban church.

Famous Houses

Atrium Houses, 1961 (s)
Y. C. Wong
1370 E. Madison Pk., Hyde Park. Ultimate in privacy — closed on outside, open on private family court.

°* **Charnley House,** 1892 (n)
Dankmar Adler and Louis H. Sullivan; Frank Lloyd Wright
1365 N. Astor. Sharp contrast to later Prairie period of Wright's work.

°* **Clarke House,** 1836 (s)
Architect unknown
1855 S. Indiana. City's oldest frame house, to be restored as part of Prairie Avenue District.

°* **Glessner House,** 1886 (s)
Henry H. Richardson
18th St. and Prairie Ave. Romanesque style. Opens on interior court. Home of the Prairie Avenue Historic District and of the Chicago Architecture Foundation. Open to public. ,

°* **Heller House,** 1897 (s)
Frank Lloyd Wright
5132 S. Woodlawn. Early Wright, pre-Prairie period.

°* **Hull House,** 1856 (sw)
Architect unknown
800 S. Halsted. Famous settlement house started by Jane Addams in 1889 and in use until 1963; it now belongs to the University of Illinois. Open to public.

°* **Lathrop House,** 1892 (d)
McKim, Mead and White
120 E. Bellevue. Classically beautiful, old Georgian house; now, Fortnightly Club.

°* **Madlener House,** 1902 (n)
Richard E. Schmidt
4 W. Burton Pl. Now the Graham Foundation for Advanced Study
in the Fine Arts.

McCormick House Condominium, 1900 (n)
Stanford White; David Adler (1927)
20 E. Burton Pl.

°* **Nickerson House,** 1883 (n)
Burling and Whitehouse
40 E. Erie. Owned by American College of Surgeons.

°* **Robie House of the University of Chicago,** 1909 (s)
Frank Lloyd Wright
5757 S. Woodlawn. The Prairie House. One of the world's greatest.
Open to the public by appointment.

Sedgwick Street Houses, 1978 (n)
N. Sedgwick, 1800 block (east side). Row of houses on urban renewal
land, built by present-day young architects including Larry Booth and
Stanley Tigerman of the Chicago 7 and Wilbert Rueter.

Modern Buildings

Chicago Civic Center, 1965 (d)
C. F. Murphy Associates; Loebl, Schlossman and Bennett; Skidmore,
Owings and Merrill
Washington, Randolph, Dearborn, and Clark.

Chicago Circle Campus: University of Illinois, 1965 (w)
Skidmore, Owings and Merrill — Walter A. Netsch, Jr.; C. F. Mur-
phy Associates
Harrison and Halsted.

Federal Center, 1964 (d)
L. Mies van der Rohe; Schmidt, Garden and Erikson; C. F. Murphy
Associates; A. Epstein and Sons
219 S. Dearborn.

First National Bank, 1969 (d)
C. F. Murphy Associates; Perkins and Will Partnership
Madison, Monroe, Dearborn, and Clark.

John Hancock Center, 1969 (d)
Skidmore, Owings and Merrill — Bruce Graham
875 N. Michigan Ave.

Illinois Institute of Technology, 1942–1968 (s)
L. Mies van der Rohe and L. Hilberseimer; Friedman, Alschuler and
Sincere; Pace Associates; Skidmore, Owings and Merrill
3300 S. Federal. First of Mies's glass buildings.

Lake Point Tower, 1968 (d)
Schipporheit — Heinrich Associates; Graham, Anderson, Probst and
White
505 N. Lake Shore Dr.

Law School of the University of Chicago, 1960 (s)
Eero Saarinen
S. 60th St. and University Ave.

Marina City, 1964 (d)
Bertrand Goldberg Associates
300 N. State.

McCormick Place, 1971 (s)
C. F. Murphy Associates
S. 23rd St. and the Lake.

Sears Tower, 1973 (d)
Skidmore, Owings and Merrill
233 S. Wacker Dr.

Time-Life, 1971 (d)
Harry Weese and Associates
303 E. Ohio.

Old Buildings

°* **Auditorium Theater,** 1887 (d)
Dankmar Adler and Louis H. Sullivan; Harry Weese and Associates
(1967)
430 S. Michigan Ave. Famous for its acoustics. For information on
group tours, call 922–2110.

Brewster Apartments, 1893 (n)
R. H. Turnock; Mieki Hayano (1972)
2800 N. Pine Grove.

°* **Carson Pirie Scott and Co.,** 1899 (d)
Louis H. Sullivan; Daniel H. Burnham and Co. (1906); Holabird and
Root (1960)
1 S. State. Note Chicago School–style windows and ornamentation at
entrance of building.

°* **Chicago Public Library Cultural Center,** 1897 (d)
Shepley, Rutan and Coolidge
78 E. Washington. Marble walls, sparkling mosaics, Tiffany ceilings.

° **Fisher Building,** 1896 (d)
Daniel H. Burnham and Co.
343 S. Dearborn.

°* **Florence Hotel,** 1880–1894 (s)
Solon S. Beman; Environment Seven, Ltd. — Mike Shymanski (1978)
111th St. and Cottage Grove, South Pullman District; telephone: 785–
8181. One of first planned company towns in the country, now being
restored. Hotel open daily for lunch and Sunday brunch.

°* **Manhattan Building,** 1890 (d)
William Le Baron Jenney
431 S. Dearborn. First sixteen-story building in the world.

°* **Marquette Building,** 1894 (d)
Holabird and Roche
140 S. Dearborn.

°* **Monadnock Building,** 1891–1893 (d)
Burnham and Root, north half; Holabird and Roche, south half
50 W. Jackson.

° **Navy Pier,** 1913–1916 (d)
The Burnham Plan
Grand Ave. and the Lake.

°* **Rookery,** 1886 (d)
Burnham and Root; Frank Lloyd Wright, (1905)

209 S. LaSalle. Precursor of skyscraper. Named Rookery because of pigeons on roof.

°* **Water Tower,** 1867–1869 (d)
W. W. Boyington
800 N. Michigan Ave. New Visitor's Information Center.

ART: INDOOR AND OUTDOOR

Galleries

Artemisia (d)
9 W. Hubbard; telephone: 751–2016. A five-year-old women's cooperative. Tues.–Sat., 10–5.

J. Baruch (d)
900 N. Michigan Ave.; telephone: 944–3377. Medieval Slavic art. Tues.–Sat., 10–5:30.

Construct (d)
233 E. Ontario; telephone: 642–2569. Artist-owned gallery for large-scale public sculpture. Mon.–Sat., 9:30–5:30.

Richard Gray (d)
620 N. Michigan Ave.; telephone: 642–8877. Modern, ancient, primitive art. Mon.–Sat., 10–5:30.

Holland (d)
224 E. Ontario; telephone: 664–5000. Richard Hunt sculpture outside. Mon.–Fri., 9:30–5; Sat., 12–5.

R. H. Love (d)
320 S. Michigan Ave.; telephone: 341–0636. Nineteenth-century American art. Mon.–Sat., 9:30–5.

E. Oehlschlaeger (d)
107 E. Oak; telephone: 787–6779. Midwestern artists. Mon.–Sat., 10–5:30.

Jack O'Grady (d)
333 N. Michigan Ave., 22nd fl.; telephone: 726–9833. Graphic arts. Mon.–Fri., 10–4.

Poster Plus (n)
2906 N. Broadway; telephone: 549–2822. Mon.–Fri., 12–9; Sat. and Sun., 12–5.

South Side Community Art Center (s)
3831 S. Michigan Ave.; telephone: 373–1026. Black American art. Tues.–Fri., 1–8; Sat. and Sun., 1–5.

Van Straaten (d)
646 N. Michigan Ave.; telephone: 642–2900. Original prints and drawings. Mon.–Sat., 10–5:30.

Zolla and Lieberman (d)
368 W. Huron; telephone: 944–1990. Contemporary artists, unusual media and techniques. Tues.–Sat., 11–5:30.

Fountains

Clarence Buckingham fountain, 1927 (d)
Bennett, Parsons and Frost of Chicago and Jacque Lambert of Paris
Grant Park near Congress. Evening show with shifting colors.

Celebration, 1976 (d)
Isamu Noguchi
School of the Art Institute of Chicago, 280 S. Columbus Dr.

Mayor Richard J. Daley fountain 1964 (d)
C. F. Murphy Associates; Schlossman and Bennett; Skidmore, Owings and Merrill
Richard J. Daley Plaza, Washington between Dearborn and Clark.

Pioneer Court fountain, 1965 (d)
Skidmore, Owings and Merrill; Alfred Shaw and Associates
Equitable Building court, 401 N. Michigan Ave. Site of Chicago's first house — du Sable's. Notice names of city fathers on fountain.

Fountain, 1975 (d)
Russell Secrest
Harris Bank Plaza, 111 W. Monroe.

Fountain (interior), 1969 (d)
Harry M. Weese and Associates
Field Museum, 1200 S. Lake Shore Dr.

Fountain, 1960 (s)
Eero Saarinen
Law School of the University of Chicago, S. 60th and University.
Sculpture in pool, *Construction in Space in Third and Fourth Dimension,* Antoine Pevsner.

Fountain of the Great Lakes, 1913 (d)
Lorado Taft
Art Institute of Chicago, south wing, S. Michigan and Adams.

Fountain of the Triton (interior), 1930 (d)
Carl Milles
McClintock Court, Art Institute of Chicago, S. Michigan and Adams.
Outdoor dining around fountain during summer months.

Fountain of Time, 1922 (s)
Lorado Taft
Entrance to Washington Park at west end of Midway.

Storks at Play, 1887 (n)
Augustus Saint-Gaudens
Lincoln Park, in garden south of conservatory, on Stockton Dr.

Sounding Sculpture, 1975 (d)
Henry Bertoia
Standard Oil Building Plaza, 200 E. Randolph.

Monuments and Sculptures

Abraham Lincoln, 1887 (n)
Augustus Saint-Gaudens
Lincoln Park (North Ave. and Stockton).

Arris, 1975 (d)
John Henry (Chicagoan)
Congress St. and Dearborn Ave. (north side).

Batcolumn, 1977 (d)
Claes Oldenburg
Social Security Administration Plaza, 600 W. Madison.

Flamingo, 1973 (d)
Alexander Calder
Federal Plaza, Dearborn Ave., between Adams and Jackson.

The Four Seasons (1974) (d)
Marc Chagall
One First National Bank Plaza, Dearborn and Monroe.

Hymn to Water, 1964 (d)
Milton Horn (Chicagoan) Facade of Central Filtration Plant, E. Ohio
and the Lake. Weekend tours, with reservations.

Lions, 1893 (d)
Edward Kemeys
Entrance, Art Institute, S. Michigan and Adams.

Nuclear Energy, 1967 (s)
Henry Moore
Ellis Ave. between 56th and 57th, °University of Chicago Landmark
site: First self-sustaining controlled nuclear chain reaction.

Slabs of the Sunburnt West, 1973 (w)
Richard Hunt (Chicagoan)
Circle Campus, University of Illinois, south of library, east of Morgan, within brick-walled campus. Dedicated to Carl Sandburg.

The Spearman and the Bowman, 1928 (d)
Ivan Mestrovic
Grant Park and Congress Plaza.

Untitled, 1964–1967 (d)
Pablo Picasso
Richard J. Daley Civic Center Plaza, Dearborn between Washington
and Randolph. Chicago's first modern outdoor sculpture.

° **Union Stock Yards Gate,** 1865 (sw)
Burnham and Root (assumed).
Peoria and S. Exchange (behind bank). All that remains of the mighty
yards.

Murals

Carl Sandburg–Louis Sullivan, 1943 (n)
Harry Varnum Poor
Uptown post office (indoors), 4850 N. Broadway.

Chicago — Epic of a Great City, 1938 (n)
Harry Sternberg
Lakeview post office (indoors), 1343 W. Irving Park Rd.

Clouds Over Lake Michigan, 1976 (d)
Ruth Duckworth
Dresdner Bank (indoors), 141 W. Jackson.

Father Marquette — 1934, 1937 (s)
J. Theodore Johnson
Morgan Park post office (indoors), 1805 W. Monterey.

Great Indian Council, Chicago — 1833, 1938 (n)
Gustaf Dalstrom
Chestnut St. post office (indoors), 830 N. Clark.

History of the Packinghouse Worker, 1974 (s)
William Walker
Amalgamated Meat Cutters Union Hall, 4859 S. Wabash Ave.

In Defense of Ignorance, 1977 (s)
Mitchell Caton and Calvin Jones
8650 S. Ashland.

Leyenda de Bonanpak, 1977 (sw)
Aurelio Diaz, Oscar Moya, and Carlos Cortez
Opposite entrance to Benito Juarez High School, 2150 S. Laflin. One
of a series of brilliant-colored murals on viaducts and buildings by
Aurelio Diaz and his Casa Aztlan helpers.

Murales Culturales de la Islan Puerto Rico, 1973–1978 (nw)
Mario Galan and helpers of the Puerto Rican Art Association
Puerto Rican Congress, 2313, 2315, 2317 W. North Ave.

Roots, 1976 (sw)
Caryl Yasko and Lucyna Radycki
3343 W. 63rd St.

Spirit of Hyde Park, 1976 (s)
Astrid Fuller
57th St. viaduct of the Illinois Central (South Side).

Untitled, 1978 (d)
Sachio Yamashita
N. Michigan and Grand, entrance-exit underground road, under city.
A rainbow of line and design in dazzling color by artist and Indian
youth helpers.

Museums

The Art Institute of Chicago (d)
S. Michigan and Adams; telephone: 443–3500. French Impressionists;
Oriental and ceramic collections; Thorne Miniature Rooms; Children's Museum; Chicago Stock Exchange restoration. Mon.–Wed.
and Fri., 10:30–4:30; Thurs., 10:30–8; Sat. 10–5.

Museum of Contemporary Art (d)
237 E. Ontario; telephone: 280–2660. Daily, 10–5; Thurs., 10–8; Sun.,
12–5.

Smart Gallery (University of Chicago) (s)
5550 S. Greenwood; telephone: 753–2121. Bequest of the founders of
Esquire magazine; a small but excellent gallery. Tues.–Sat., 10–4; Sat.,
12–4

ENTERTAINMENT

Fairs and Festivals

The Chicago Boat and Sport Show (s)
McCormick Place, S. 23rd St. and the Lake; telephone: 791–6000.
January.

The Chicago Automobile Show (s)
McCormick Place, S. 23rd St. and the Lake; telephone: 791–6000. The
largest commercial show in Chicago. February.

Medinah Shrine Circus (d)
600 N. Wabash Ave.; telephone: 642–9300. March.

The Dog Show (s)
International Amphitheater, S. 43rd and Halsted; telephone: 927–
5580. International Kennel Club; all-breed. April.

Brandeis Used Book Sale (n)
Edens Plaza Shopping Center; telephone: 251–0690. Over 250,000 books every year. May.

The Hyde Park Art Fair (s)
Hyde Park Art Center, S. 57th and Kimbark; telephone: 947–9656. The oldest and still most prestigious of the more than 100 art fairs in the area. June.

Fourth of July Fireworks
Soldier Field Stadium, 425 E. McFetridge; telephone: 294–2200. Sponsored by the American Legion.

ChicagoFest (d)
Navy Pier, Grand Ave. and the Lake; telephone: 744–8400. The Lake, sun, stars, and excellent music. August.

Gem, Mineral, Jewelry International Show (nw)
O'Hare Exhibition Center, 9301 Bryn Mawr; telephone: 549–3612. September.

International Holiday Folk Fair (d)
Navy Pier, Grand Ave. and the Lake; telephone: 744–6555. Forty ethnic groups representing thirty countries provide food and entertainment. October. Free admission.

American Indian Powwow (d)
Chicago Armory, 234 E. Chicago Ave.; telephone: 275–5871. November.

Christmas Around the World (s)
Museum of Science and Industry, 57th St. and S. Lake Shore Dr.; telephone: 684–1414. Crèche, trees, choral groups, and ethnic foods.

Museums of Science and History

Adler Planetarium (d)
1300 S. Lake Shore Dr.; telephone: 332–0300. Observatory. Outer space made understandable. The Chicago Society for Space Settlement meets here monthly. Mon.–Thurs., 9:30–4:30; Fri. 9:30–9; Sat. and Sun., 9:30–5. Free except special shows.

Chicago Academy of Science (n)
2001 N. Clark; telephone: 549–0606. Oldest museum in the Midwest (1857). Ecology and geology of Great Lakes. Daily, 10–5.

Du Sable Museum of African-American History (s)
740 E. 56th Pl.; telephone: 947–0600. Du Sable was the first permanent settler of Chicago. Tues.–Fri., 10–4; Sat. and Sun., 12–4.

Field Museum of Natural History (d)
1300 S. Lake Shore Dr.; telephone: 922–9410. Gems, shows, films, self-guided tours for children. Daily, 9–5; Fri., 9–9. Free on Fridays.

International Museum of Surgical Science and Hall of Fame (n)
1524 N. Lake Shore Dr.; telephone: 642–3632. History and progress of medicine; library. Tues.–Sat., 10–4.

Museum of Science and Industry (s)
S. Lake Shore Dr. and 57th St.; telephone 684–1414. Coal mine, submarine, nuclear reactor; Chicago's most famous museum. Daily, May to Labor Day, 9:30–5:30; rest of year, Mon.–Fri., 9:30–4; Sat. and Sun., 9:30–5.

Oriental Museum (s)
1155 E. 58th St.; telephone: 753–2474. Stunning exhibit of ancient civilizations of Near East. Tues.–Sat., 10–4; Sun., 12–4.

Polish Museum of America (n)
984 N. Milwaukee; telephone: 384–3352. Daily, 1–4.

Shedd Aquarium (d)
1200 S. Lake Shore Dr.; telephone: 939–2426. Ten thousand fish. Fish feeding time, 11 and 2. Daily, 9–5; Fri., 9–9; free admission.

Music

Music of the Baroque (s)
1642 E. 56th St., Suite 206; telephone: 643–9386. Series of eleven Baroque concerts.

Kingston Mines (n)
2356 N. Lincoln; telephone: 525–6860. Blues. Music starts about 9:30 PM, seven nights a week. Small cover charge and minimum.

Chicago Symphony Orchestra (d)
Orchestra Hall, 220 S. Michigan Ave.; telephone: 435–8111. Sir Georg Solti presides over the world's greatest orchestra, Margaret Hillis over the excellent choir.

Chicago Children's Choir (s)
5650 S. Woodlawn; telephone: 324–4100. Christmas concert; June gala concert; other concerts held throughout area. Call for information.

Chicago Public Library Cultural Center (d)
Washington and Michigan; telephone 269–2837. Concerts and recitals. Wed., 12:15. Free admission.

Somebody Else's Troubles (n)
2470 N. Lincoln; telephone: 929–0660. Folk music nightly; open stage Mon. Small cover charge and minimum.

Grant Park Summer Concerts (d)
James C. Petrillo Bandshell, Butler Field (Columbus and Jackson); telephone: 294–2420. Beautiful music under the stars. Late June to late August: Wed. and Fri., 8 PM; Sat. and Sun., 7 PM. Noontime concerts; call for dates.

Jazz Showcase (n)
901 N. Rush; telephone: 337–1000. Nightly at 9, 11, 1. Minimum.

Lyric Opera (d)
20 N. Wacker; telephone: 346–6111. Chicago Opera School takes over in the spring. Late Sept.–early Dec. Curtain 8 PM.

Rockefeller Chapel (University of Chicago) (s)
5850 S. Woodlawn; telephone: 753–3381. Tues. noon lecture-recitals when university in session. Periodic evening concerts; call for times. Dr. Edward Mondello, organist. Free admission.

Old Town School of Folk Music (w)
909 W. Armitage; telephone: 525–7472. Folk singing led by fine folk musicians. Third Sun. of each month, 2 PM.

Ticketron
Telephone: 842–5387. Information on what is playing at the major theaters and where tickets may be purchased.

Parades

Unless otherwise noted, parades are usually held downtown — Michigan Ave. or Clark St. from Wacker to Congress. For details, call Chicago Convention and Tourism Bureau, 922–3530.

Chinese Parade (s)
22nd St. and Wentworth area. Celebration of the Chinese New Year. February.

St. Patrick's Day Parade (d)
Even the river is dyed green. March.

Memorial Day Parade (d)
Part of our Civil War heritage. May.

Bud Billiken Parade (s)
39th St. south on Martin Luther King Dr. to Washington Park. Biggest parade in Chicago in honor of mythical patron saint of black children. August.

Chicago Park District Youth Parade (d)
Hearty show of Chicago's youth. August.

King Neptune Parade (d)
Part of ChicagoFest, Venetian Night, lake shore festival. August.

German-American Parade (d)
In recognition of General Von Steuben who helped Washington at Valley Forge and Yorktown. September.

Mexican Day Parade (d)
Mexican Independence Day celebrated with mounted caballeros, senoritas, and mariachi bands. September.

Columbus Day Parade (d)
Floats, bands, bugle corps, in honor of Christopher Columbus. October.

Fire Department Parade (d)
Fire Prevention Week; anniversary of great fire of 1871. Fire department's marching band; new equipment displayed. October.

State Street Santa Claus Parade (d)
Christmas season. Decorated store windows fascinate young and old.
December

Special Things to Do

Take a Water Trip (d)
Wendella Sightseeing Boat, Lower Level, 400 N. Michigan Ave.;
telephone: 337–1446 One- and two-hour trips with views of river,
locks, skyline.

Be a Lake Watcher (far s)
Calumet Park, 9300 South at Lake. Watch 1000-foot lake boats and
foreign ships move into Calumet River and Lake Calumet. See new
container facility of port authority being developed opposite US Steel.

Explore Navy Pier (d)
East Grand Ave. at Lake; phone: 744–8400. For ship schedules, tele-
phone: 744–4838. Walk the pier that extends 3/4 mile into Lake.
Murals. Renovated theater. Picnicking and view.

Bicycle in Lincoln Park (n)
Bike rentals: Diversey at Lake Shore Dr.; Grand Ave. at Lake Shore
Dr. Marvelous trails along Lake's shore.

Visit a Great Wholesale Market (d)
South Water Market, 14th and Racine. Take in sights and smells of
Chicago's produce market.

Visit an Indoor Market (d)
Chicago's Water Tower Place, 855 N. Michigan Ave. Great shopping;
theater; movies; restaurants (a McDonald's with a maitre d'); endless
shops. Prismatic elevator in atrium mall.

Attend a Meeting (s)
Operation Push, 930 E. 50th; telephone: 373–3366. Marvelous blend
of soul, gospel, speakers, action programs, and Reverend Jesse Jackson. Saturdays, 9 AM.

Spend an Evening Laughing. (d)
Second City, 1616 N. Wells; telephone: 337–3992. Home of topical
reviews and good satire.

Take a Gallery Walk (d)
620 N. Michigan Ave.; Ontario and Oak streets. Everything from Eskimo to American Indian art; old masters; moderns; the whole gamut.

Discover a City Street of Crafts (n)
3300–3400 N. Halsted. Wander in and out of shops where you can learn to warp a loom, attend a knitting class, brush up on cooking techniques, or throw a pot.

See an Urban School (w)
University of Illinois, Circle Campus and environs, Halsted and Taylor. Walk this urban campus. Visit Jane Addams House. Fire Station, 558 W. De Koven, where fire started. Maxwell St. Market (best Sundays). West Side Medical Center.

Twelve Theaters

Apollo Theater Center (n)
2540 N. Lincoln; telephone: 549–1342. First off-loop theater built especially for productions.

Body Politic (n)
2261 N. Lincoln; telephone: 871–3000. Three facilities under one roof: Mainstage, with professionals; Studio Theater, for new playwrights, produced by the Laboratory Co.; Upstairs Theater for mixed events (music, dance).

Court Theater of the University of Chicago (s)
5706 University; telephone: 753–3581. Summer: Outdoor Quadrangle Winter: Mandel Hall

Free Street Theater (d)
59 W. Hubbard; telephone: 822–0460. Summers, tour neighborhoods and parks with "Showmobile"; "Free Street Too" with senior citizens.

Goodman Theater (d)
200 S. Columbus Dr.; telephone: 443–3800. Goodman Stage Two does experimental theater at Wrigley Theater of Latin School, Clark St. and North Ave. Call for schedules and changes.

Kuumba Workshop (s)
2222 S. Michigan Ave.; telephone: 842–2500. Established center for black arts; dance, creative writing.

Old Town Players Workshop — Theater (n)
1718 N. Park Ave.; telephone: 645–0145. Community theater.

Organic Theater Company (n)
Leo Lerner Theater, 4520 N. Beacon; 728–1001. Excellent touring company.

The Puppet Place (n)
2146 N. Halsted; telephone: 871–5011. Only puppet center in the Midwest. Periodic productions for adults. Company also trains students, teaches in universities. Sept.–June, Sat. and Sun. at 1 PM.

St. Nicholas Theater Company (n)
2851 N. Halsted; telephone: 348–8415. Best run of off-Loop theater. Many new plays.

Theater Building (n)
1225 W. Belmont; telephone: 327–5252. Two groups perform here: Travel Light and Pary Production.

Victory Gardens Theater (n)
3730 N. Clark; telephone: 549–5788. Small theater, with Mainstage, Studio and Readers Theater productions.

RECREATION

Harbors and Charters

For general information on harbors, telephone: 294–2270

Belmont Harbor (n)
3200 N. and Lake; telephone: 281–8587.

Burnham Park Harbor (d)
1500 S. Linn White Dr.; telephone: 294–4614.

Diversey Harbor (n)
Fullerton and the Lake; telephone 327–4430.

Jackson Park Harbor (inner, outer, and 59th St.) (s)
2200 E. 65th St.; telephone: 363–6942.

Monroe St. Harbor (d)
Monroe and Lake Shore Dr.; telephone: 294–4612.

Montrose Harbor (n)
Montrose and the Lake; telephone: 878–3710.

Charter Boats, Inc. (d)
Burnham Harbor; telephone: 922–4848. Sportsfishing.

Chicago Sportsfishing Association (d)
Burnham Park; telephone: 922–1100.

Mercury Sightseeing Boat (d)
400 N. Michigan Ave. (south side of river); telephone: 332–1353.

Shoreline Marine Sightseeing Co. (d)
80 E. Jackson (docks at the Shedd Aquarium); telephone: 427–2900.

Wendella Sightseeing Co. (d)
400 N. Michigan Ave. (north side of river); telephone: 337–1446.

Picnic Areas

Belmont spit (n)
3200 N. Sheridan. Enter from 4000 north, go south to the end. View of harbor, dock and boats.

Burnham Park (d)
Between 47th and Adler Planetarium.

First National Bank Plaza (d)
Dearborn and Monroe. Brown bag it at noon. Sit on steps; people watch; summer entertainment.

Buckingham Fountain (d)
Grant Park near Congress. Watch the geysers bubbling. Great view of yacht basin.

Indian Boundary Park (n)
2500 Lunt Ave. A nice place to stop when far north.

Lincoln Park (n)
Between North Ave. and Diversey. Particularly nice on Sundays. Every ethnic group is eating al fresco, and one can smell everything from soul food to chicken teriyaki. Food can be purchased in park.

Montrose Beach and Harbor (n)
4500 N. Sheridan and the Lake. Swim, eat, watch the boats, and snooze.

Olive Park (d)
Surrounds the E. Ohio St.–Lake Shore Dr. Filtration Plant, across from Navy Pier. New and lovely. In honor of a Vietnam War hero.

The Point (s)
5600 S. Lake Shore Dr. To Hyde Parkers, the Point is the place.

South Shore Country Club à la Community Park (s)
7100 S. Shore Dr. Beach and park in prime location.

Sun Times Plaza (d)
401 N. Wabash. Approach through street level on Michigan Ave. through Wrigley Building courtyard entrance, or by stairs from Wabash Ave. Fountains, trees, flowers, benches for brown bagging. River view.

Washington Park (s)
Between 51st and 59th. Frederick Law Olmsted's famous park, landscaped garden. Site of 1893 World's Exhibition. Playground and Du Sable Museum.

Sports (Participatory)

For general information, contact the Chicago Park District (CPD), 425 E. McFetridge Dr.; telephone: 294–2492.

Bicycling
Lakefront trails from 5800 north to 6700 south. For maps and specific information, telephone: 261–8400

Boating
Launching ramps: Burnham Park, Burnham (d); Calumet Park, 95th St. Harbor (s); Jackson Park, 59th St. Harbor (s); Lincoln Park, Diversey Harbor (n); Lincoln Park, Wilson (n); Rainbow Beach, 79th St. (s). For information, call CPD (see above).

Bocce Ball
Thirteen city courts open during daylight hours. For information call CPD (see above).

Canoeing
American Youth Hostels, 3712 N. Clark; telephone: 327–8114.

Fishing
Licenses (either for season for residents or one-day for nonresidents) obtainable for anyone over sixteen years old at the city clerk's office, 121 N. LaSalle; telephone: 744–6882. Fish on piers, sea walls, jetties, Lakefront lagoons and harbors.

Frisbee
Bring your own Frisbee to any of the parks, with or without your dog. For information, call CPD (see above).

Golf
Jackson Park, 18-hole (s), 6401 Stoney Island; Lincoln Park, 9-hole (n), 3800 N. Sheridan Rd. and the Lake. For more information, call CPD (see above).

Hiking
Prairie Club, 6 E. Monroe; telephone: 236–3342. For Illinois and Indiana group walks.

Running
Joggers are everywhere. Races sponsored at parks (CPD, see above); America's Marathon/Chicago in the fall; "Run for Lake Michigan," sponsored by Lake Michigan Federation (telephone: 427–5121).

Soccer
National Soccer League of Chicago sponsors competition. For information, call CPD (see above).

Swimming
Thirty beaches on Lakefront; swimming June through Labor Day. Major North Side beaches are Foster (5200), Fullerton (2400), Montrose (4500), North (1600), Oak (1000); on south side, Calumet (9500), Jackson Park (4700–6700), and 31st St. For information, call CPD (see above).

Tennis
Six hundred and fifty courts; major courts are at Lincoln, Jackson, Garfield, Burnham, and Marquette parks (8 AM–10 PM). For information, call CPD (see above).

Sports (Spectator)

For general information on games and races, contact the Convention and Tourism Bureau (telephone: 922–3530), the last page of the Chicago Yellow Pages, or the newspapers.

BASEBALL

Chicago Cubs (n)
Wrigley Field, 1060 W. Addison; telephone: 281–5050.

Chicago White Sox (s)
Comiskey Park, Dan Ryan and 35th St.; telephone: 924–1000.

BASKETBALL

Chicago Bulls (w)
Chicago Stadium, 1836 W. Madison; telephone: 346–1122.

FOOTBALL

Chicago Bears (d)
Soldier Field, 425 E. McFetridge Dr.; telephone: 663–5100.

HOCKEY

Chicago Blackhawks (w)
Chicago Stadium, 1836 W. Madison; telephone: 733–5300.

HORSE RACING

Maywood Park Race Track (w)
North Ave. and River Rd., Maywood, Ill.; telephone: 626–4816.

Arlington Park Race Track (nw)
Euclid Ave. and Rohling Rd., Arlington Heights; telephone: 775–7800.

Hawthorne Park Race Track (w)
3501 Laramie, Cicero, Ill.; telephone: 652–9400.

Sportman's Park (w)
3301 Laramie, Cicero, Ill.; telephone: 242–1121.

POLO

Chicago Armory (d)
234 E. Chicago Ave.; telephone: 943–4074. In the summer games are
at Oakbrook; telephone: 654–1550.

SOCCER

Chicago Sting
Soldier Field or Wrigley Field; telephone: 558–5425.

SAIL BOAT RACES

Chicago Yacht Club
Belmont Harbor; telephone: 477–7575. Biggest race on Lake, Chicago
to Mackinac in July from Monroe Harbor near Lighthouse. Glorious
sight. For information, telephone: 861–7777.

Zoos, Conservatories, and Gardens

Brookfield Zoo (sw)
8400 W. 31st, Brookfield, Ill.; telephone: 242–2630. Daily 10–6.

City Garden (d)
Wrigley Building Plaza and Sun Times Plaza, 400 N. Michigan Ave.

Garfield Park Conservatory (w)
300 N. Central Park; telephone: 533–1281. Orchids, cacti, palms. Garden for the blind. One of the great botanical gardens of country. Daily,
9–5.

Grant Park Gardens (d)
Between Michigan Ave. and the Lake, Randolph and 12th St. Flowering trees at different seasons, rose gardens.

Indian Boundary Park Zoo (n)
2500 W. Lunt; telephone: 274–0200. Small neighborhood zoo.

Lincoln Park Conservatory (n)
Stockton Dr. south of Fullerton in Lincoln Park; telephone: 294–
4770. Daily, 9–5.

Lincoln Park Zoo (n)
2200 Cannon Dr.; telephone: 294–4660. Urban zoo, being modern-

ized. Map. Feeding schedule. Don't miss Great Ape House, the nursery, penguin house. Daily, 9–5; children's zoo, 10–5.

Morton Arboretum (w)
Rt. 53, Lisle, Ill.; telephone: 969–0074. 1500-acre botanical and arboreal wonderland. Picnic area. Hiking. Watch an ancient prairie being grown under modern horticulture. Daily, 8–sunset.

Perennial Garden of Jackson Park (s)
59th St. and Stoney Island.

Rainbow Garden (s)
Adjoining Rainbow Beach at 78th and 79th Sts.

Senior Citizen Gardens (n)
6040 N. Sheridan. One of 1500 flower and vegetable gardens in the city. Children also grow plants for the Big Tomato contest.

Victory Gardens (s)
Adjoining Rainbow Garden, 78th and 79th sts. and Lake. George Beadle, president emeritus of the university, grew his Nobel Prize–winning hybrid corn here.

RESTAURANTS

Expensive

The Bakery (n)
2218 N. Lincoln; telephone: 472–6942. Tues.–Thurs., 5–11; Fri. and Sat., 5–12.

Binyon's (d)
327 S. Plymouth Ct.; telephone: 341–1155. Mon.–Sat., 11:30–10.

Cape Cod Room, Drake Hotel (d)
140 E. Walton; telephone: 787–2200. Daily, 12–12.

Casbah (n)
514 W. Diversey; telephone: 935–7570. Sun.–Thurs., 5–11; Fri. and Sat., 5–12.

Consort Restaurant, Continental Hotel (d)
909 N. Michigan Ave.; telephone: 943–7200. Mon.–Fri., 12–3; daily, 6–1.

The Dining Room and The Terrace, Ritz-Carlton Hotel (d)
160 E. Pearson; telephone: 266–1000. Daily, 12–2:30, 6–11:30.

Greek Islands (w)
766 W. Jackson; telephone: 782–9855. Sun.–Thurs., 11–midnight; Fri.
and Sat., 11 AM–1 AM.

Maxim's de Paris, Astor Tower Hotel (n)
1300 N. Astor; telephone: 943–1136. Mon.–Thurs., 12–3, 6–12; Fri. and
Sat., 12–3, 6–1.

Sayat Nova (d)
157 E. Ohio; telephone: 644–9159. Mon.–Sat., 11:30 AM–12 AM; Sun.,
2–10.

Streeter's, Hyatt Regency Hotel (d)
151 E. Wacker Dr.; telephone: 565–1000. Restaurant named after Cap
Streeter, who, at the turn of the century, claimed squatter's rights to
his shanty town near this site. Daily, 6:30–2:30 PM.

Reasonably Priced Ethnic Restaurants

Dining tips for economy: eat main meals at noon; select specials from
menu; pick neighborhood restaurants.

Ann Sather's Swedish Diner (n)
925 W. Belmont; telephone: 348–2378. Daily, 11–8; Sun., 12–7.

The Bagel (n)
3000 W. Devon; telephone 764–3377. Tues.–Sun., 5:30 AM–10 PM.

The Berghof (d)
17 W. Adams; telephone: 427–3170. Mon.–Sat., 11–9:30.

Café Bohemia (d)
138 S. Clinton; telephone: 782–1826. Buffalo, moose, elk. Bargain at
lunch when they serve leftover game at reasonable prices. Mon.–Fri.,
11:30–midnight; Sat., 5–1.

Diana's Grocery and Restaurant (w)
130 S. Halsted; telephone: 263–1848. Good Greek food. Daily, 11 AM–
1 AM.

Gino's Upstairs Restaurant (d)
160 E. Superior; telephone: 943–1124. One of the best pizza places in town. Daily 11 AM–2 AM; Sun., 4 PM–2 AM.

Kasztelanka Café and Restaurant (n)
3129 N. Milwaukee; telephone: 588–6662. Sun.–Thurs., 11–10; Fri. and Sat., 11–11.

Louie's Cantonese Café (d)
937 N. Rush; telephone: 337–1248. Daily, 12–12.

Mini Max Tacos 'n Things (n)
1119 W. Webster; telephone: 348–3493. In rear of small grocery, great tacos. Daily, 11–11.

Sears Cafeteria (d)
233 S. Wacker; telephone: 558–8960. Imaginative use of space in feeding 3000 people. Notice Calder stabile. Mon.–Fri., 7 AM–3 PM.

Soul Queen Café (s)
2200 S. Michigan Ave.; telephone: 842–0292. Simple decor. Soul food has received raves. No liquor. Open 24 hours a day.

Zlata's Belgrade Restaurant (n)
1516 N. Milwaukee; telephone: 252–9514. Moussaka, kajmak, with or without slivowitz. Sun., Wed., Thurs., 5 PM–12 AM; Fri. and Sat., 5 PM–2 AM.

SHOPPING

General

Bonwit Teller (d)
875 N. Michigan; telephone: 751–1800.

Carson Pirie Scott and Co. (d)
1 S. State; telephone: 744–2000. Interesting promotions and foreign festivals.

Chernin Shoes (sw)
610 W. Roosevelt; telephone: 939–4080.

I. Magnin (d)
830 N. Michigan Ave.; telephone: 751–0500.

Independent Clothing Co. (s)
1313 S. Michigan Ave.; telephone: 427–2400. Great buys for men and women.

Lord and Taylor (d)
835 N. Michigan Ave.; telephone: 787–7400.

Marshall Field and Co. (d)
111 N. State; telephone: 781–1000. All-time favorite department store. Antique jewelry, fur, toys. Christmas windows and decorations, a delight.

Montgomery Ward and Co. (d)
140 S. State; telephone: 368–6117.

Saks Fifth Avenue (d)
669 N. Michigan Ave.; telephone: 944–6500.

Sears Roebuck (d)
403 S. State; telephone: 875–4900.

Water Tower Place (d)
845 N. Michigan Ave.; telephone: 440–3460. Shop day or night, Sundays or weekdays, big stores and small, new, great.

Wieboldts (d)
1 N. State; telephone: 782–1500. Reliable, moderate-priced department store with helpful salespeople.

Food Stores

Burhops Fish Market (d)
545 N. State; telephone: 644–7825. Best of everything that swims.

Conte de Savoia (w)
555 W. Roosevelt; telephone: 666–3471. Behind bank. Imported foods, fresh and canned, from India to Liverpool. Baskets and barrels. Pasta and cheeses.

House of Fine Chocolates (n)
3109 N. Broadway; telephone: 525–8338.

Hyde Park Co-op (s)
S. 56th St. and Lake Park Ave.; telephone: 667–1444. Cosmopolitan

to the core and catering to the tastes of Babel. Even a dietician who helps onlys, lonelies, and fatties to plan meals.

Kuhn's Delicatessen (n)
3053 N. Lincoln; telephone: 525–9019. Tempting treats from all over the Teutonic world.

Lutz Continental Pastries and Candy (n)
2458 W. Montrose; telephone: 478–7785. The very best in pastry.

Mikolajczyk Sausage Shop (nw)
1737 W. Division; telephone: 486–8870. Marvelous sausage. Carry-outs of all sorts of Polish delicacies.

Ricci and Co. (d)
162 W. Superior; 787–7660. Superior shelled nuts.

Stop and Shop (d)
16 W. Washington; telephone: 726–8500. Four generations have run this food store/bakery/catering house in the middle of downtown.

Toscana Bakery (n)
2130 N. Sheffield; telephone: 348–5576. Bakes the bread for all the good French restaurants of the city. Marvelous Christmas baked goods.

Treasure Island (n)
3460 N. Broadway; telephone: 327–3880. "It's the best grocery in the nation," says Julia Child.

Vienna Sausage Mfg. Co. (nw)
2501 N. Damen; telephone: 235–6652. Factory outlet; kosher store; restaurant for lunch; gives tours.

Specialty Shops

Anna Flower Shops, Inc. (d)
100 E. Walton Pl.; telephone: 943–1425. Beautiful and costly; sells everything from anemones to zinnias.

Crate and Barrel (d)
850 N. Michigan Ave.; telephone: 787–5900. At first used crates and barrels for displays. Glassware, cookware, great splashy fabric. A bulletin board announced ship unloadings at Navy Pier.

Eddie Bauer (d)
123 N. Wabash Ave.; telephone 263–6005. Best sports store in town.

Fishman's Fabrics (sw)
1101 S. DesPlaines; telephone: 922–7250. Yard goods from all corners of the globe. Leftover bolts from the couturier houses.

Jade House (d)
700 N. Michigan Ave.; telephone: 266–0911. Treasures from the Far East.

Kroch's and Brentano's, Inc. (d)
29 S. Wabash Ave.; telephone: 332–7500. Great bookstore; largest paperback selection in USA.

Navigation Equipment Co. (d)
228 W. Chicago; telephone: 944–3634. Maps, charts, instruments, books about the sea.

F.A.O. Schwartz (d)
835 N. Michigan Ave.; telephone: 787–8894. Toys galore.

Stanley Korshak (d)
912 N. Michigan Ave.; telephone: 337–7766. Elegant women's clothing.

C. D. Peacock Jewelers (d)
State and Monroe; telephone 630–5700. Superb jewelry since 1837.

Colby's Furniture (d)
129 E. Chestnut; telephone: 266–2222.

TOURS

Archicenter (d)
310 S. Michigan Ave.; telephone: 782–1776. Tues. and Thurs. at 10 (2-hour walking tour); Sat. at 2 (bus tour).

Chicago Board of Trade (d)
141 W. Jackson; telephone: 435–3626. Mon.–Fri., 9:30–3, visitor's gallery, 5th floor.

Chicago (East Side) Chamber of Commerce (s)
3654 E. 106th St.; telephone: 721–7948. Each August an all-day tour

Molten iron, part of the steel-making process at U.S. Steel
Corporation South Works. *U.S. Steel Corporation*

of lake and industrial plants. Experts discuss the role of industry in
Chicago.

Chicago "Culture Tour Bus" (d)
Bus south of Art Institute on Michigan Ave. and Adams; telephone:
836–7000. Sun. only, 11:30–4:30, leaves every half hour; 3 routes:
Lincoln Park area, west side, and south side.

Chicago Sun Times (d)
401 N. Wabash Ave.; telephone: 321–2032. Mon.–Fri., 9:30, 10:30;
reservations necessary.

Chicago Tribune (d)
441 N. Michigan Ave.; telephone: 222–3993. Mon.–Fri., 9:30, 11, 1:15,
2:45. Sat., 9:30, 12, 1:15; reservations necessary.

First National Bank (d)
Madison, Monroe, Dearborn, and Clark; telephone: 732–6067. Mon.–
Fri., 10 and 3; reservations for groups.

Glessner House and Prairie Avenue District (s)
1800 S. Prairie; telephone: 326–1393. Chicago's first Gold Coast. Tues.,
Thurs., Sat., 10–4; Sun., 1–5.

Historic Pullman Center (s)
614 E. 113th St.; telephone: 785–8181. Restoration and redevelopment
of old company town. Tours, May to Oct., First Sun. of month at 1:30.

Johnson Publishing Company (*Ebony* Magazine) (d)
820 S. Michigan Ave.; telephone: 322–9200. Mon.–Fri., 11, 1:30, and
3:30; reservations necessary (only six at a time).

Quaker Oats Test Kitchens (d)
Merchandise Mart Plaza, Wells Ave., just north of river; telephone:
222–6809. Mon.–Fri., 1:30 and 3:30.

U.S. Steel South Works (s)
3426 E. 89th St. at Lake and Calumet River; telephone: 933–2218.
Three-hour tour of mills, furnaces, water recycling system; film.
April–June; Sept.–Oct; group tours with your own bus; reservations
necessary.

VISTAS

Chapel in the Sky of the Methodist Temple (d)
77 W. Washington; telephone: 236–4548. Daily tour at 2; Sun. after
church services.

Burnham Park (d)
1300 S. Lake Shore Dr. and the Lake (between the Shedd Aquarium
and the Adler Planetarium). Great view of the city at sunset.

Michigan Avenue Bridge at the Chicago River (d)
400 N. Michigan.

Pinnacle Room of the Holiday Inn (d)
644 N. Lake Shore Dr.; telephone: 943–9200. Restaurant turns 360°
for a spectacular view of whole city. Mon.–Fri., 5:30–10:30; Sun.
brunch, 10:30–2:30.

Raleigh Room of the Drake Hotel (d)
100 E. Lake Shore Dr.; telephone: 787–2200. Ask for table at north
end for a view of the Lake. Daily, 5:30–10; Sun., 4–10.

Sears Tower Observatory (d)
103rd floor, 233 S. Wacker Dr.; telephone: 875–9696. Daily, 9 AM–
midnight.

Seventy One Club of the Executive House (d)
71 E. Wacker Dr.; telephone: 346–7100. Mon.–Thurs., 6–11; Fri., 6–1;
private club at other times.

Signature of the Holiday Inn, 15th floor of the Apparel Center (d)
350 N. Orleans; telephone: 836–5000. See seven bridges on south
branch of Chicago River, site of Wolf Point where fur traders once
gathered. Daily, 5:30–11; closed Sun.

Sky Observatory of the Hancock Building, 94th floor (d)
875 N. Michigan Ave.; telephone: 751–0900. Daily, 9 AM–midnight.

Stand on the Jackson Ave. Bridge (over I-94, the Dan Ryan
Expressway) (d)
700 W. Jackson. More traffic flows underneath here than at any other
spot in country.

Evanston

Population: 80,000   Area Code: 312   Zip Code: 60201
Chamber of Commerce: 807 Davis Street; telephone: 328–1500

Evanston has always been an area seeking a definition. Is it a big city? A suburb? A big city with the virtues of a suburb, or the reverse? The debate has continued and Evanston is now the sixth largest city in Illinois.

Many architects have lived in the community: Daniel Burnham, the Perkins family, William Holabird, and Walter B. Griffin (the designer of Canberra, Australia's capital). The town sparkles with wonderful old houses along Sheridan Road, a skyscraper in downtown Evanston done by the Mies group, sculpture by Richard Hunt, and a number of examples of Frank Lloyd Wright's Prairie school of architecture. The well-organized community has several guides to all this fine architecture available at the local Chamber of Commerce.

Evanston prides itself on a variety of things: the home of the Cradle (the famous adoption agency), the location of the first auto race, the birthplace of the ice cream sundae. An early stop on the Underground Railroad, Evanston had a black settler as early as 1850. Evanston also integrated its schools early (1966). It is a headquarters city, home base for Rotarians, pediatricians, law enforcers, casket manufacturers, and National Merit Scholars to name only a few. It is also a town full of nature lovers who cherish the beautiful elms and maples that arch the streets; the community puts out a special guide to its most famous trees. Evanston claims more churches than any other town its size in the country. Often called the Methodist Vatican, early Wesleyans gave land to other denominations as well. Today, there are sixty-six churches, four synagogues, and two seminaries.

Historically, the Lake has played an enormous role in Evanston's development, starting with Pere Marquette and his followers who launched ten canoes on the beach here in 1674. Many first families are descended from early Lake captains who came from the Eastern seaboard, and its maritime flavor has given Evanston the title "finest New England village in the Midwest."

When the first settler, Major Edward Mulford, arrived in 1836, this area of swamp and ridge, called Grosse Point, extended all the way south to Graceland Cemetery in Chicago. From 1857 and for forty years thereafter, Evanston was a Lake port with loading piers at Davis and Dempster streets and a sufficient number of boat accidents to prompt a group of Northwestern University students to form a water-rescue squadron. There is a commemorative plaque in Northwestern's Patten gym which tells the story of young Edward Spencer, a student who plunged into the freezing water repeatedly to save seventeen struggling survivors of a sinking ship. His last words before he died were, "Did I do my best?" Now there is a Coast Guard station nearby to handle such disasters, but the Grosse Point Lighthouse, built in 1873, remains, and in more recent acknowledgment of the Lake's importance, Northwestern has created a new peninsula campus jutting out into the water.

For many years it was impossible to separate Evanston from Northwestern, for the university was really the city's reason for being. In 1853, a remarkable man named John Evans came looking for land upon which to build a Methodist university. Evans, a professor of obstetrics at Rush Medical School, a supporter of Lincoln, and builder of railroads, became territorial governor of Colorado, founded Denver University, and won a Nobel Peace Prize. Northwestern was chartered in 1851, and opened in 1855 with five students (today it has 15,000). In 1863, when the town around the campus was incorporated, it was named for the amazing baby doctor.

One of the remarkable people on the early faculty was Frances E. Willard, dean of women, who dreamed that Northwestern might become "a Methodist Cambridge of the Prairie." Perhaps she was partially responsible for a covenant that went with the land and prohibited liquor sales (and Evanston has been dry until very recently). Frances Willard left in 1874 to organize the Women's Christian Temperance Union and the Prohibition Party, which has permanently given Evanston its reputation as the cradle of the Eighteenth Amendment to the Constitution. Today the Willard home is a museum and listed on the National Historic Registry.

Old College Hall, the first building, had a tower where early presidents lit a huge candle once a year, a symbolic "light of education." The University's fine Deering Library is a replica of King's College, Cambridge. Today the university has many fine departments, includ-

Aerial view of Northwestern University, Evanston, Illinois, with old Deering Library in foreground and new library behind.
Hedrich-Blessing

ing its technological school and dental schools, and, on its Chicago campus, first-rate law and medical schools.

Today the separation between town and gown has grown, for Evanston has become so large that it supports some manufacturing, a downtown shopping area of importance, numerous satellite shopping sections, and a sophisticated and heterogeneous population.

SOURCE OF INFORMATION

Most of Evanston's activities involve the university in one way or another.

Northwestern University, 1851
1800–2400 N. Sheridan Rd.; telephone: 492–7271. Points of interest: Dearborn Observatory, Lindheimer Astronomical Research Center, Technological Institute, Dyche Stadium, McGaw Memorial Hall, Byron S. Coon Sports Center, Deering Library. For schedules of daily events, contact the Norris Center information desk at 1999 Sheridan Rd.; telephone: 492–5400. Parking: 619 Emerson (sticker available at no cost). Total enrollment: 15,000 (all campuses).

ARCHITECTURE AND HISTORIC BUILDINGS

"Evanston Architecture, a Sampler of Self-Guided Tours"
Municipal Building, Planning Department, 2100 Ridge Ave.; telephone: 328–2100. Mon.–Fri., 9–5.

Grosse Point Lighthouse, 1873
2535 Sheridan Rd.; telephone: 864–5181. This lighthouse, still in use, can be climbed.

Art Centers

Evanston Art Center
2603 Sheridan Rd.; telephone: 475–5300. Monthly exhibits, art rentals, sales gallery, handcraft shop. Mon.–Fri., 10–5; Sat., 10–4; Sun. 2–5. Free admission.

Evanston Arts Council
927 Noyes; telephone: 328–2100 or 491–0266. Provides information on and coordination of cultural arts events. Administers Noyes Cultural Art Center.

Noyes Cultural Art Center
927 Noyes; telephone: 491–0266. Visitors welcome. Houses visual and performing art classes; provides studios for artists. Home of Piven Theater Workshop, and branch of Old Town School of Folk Music. Mon.–Sat., 9–10; Sun., 10–6

MUSEUMS

Charles G. Dawes Home, 1894
225 Greenwood; telephone: 475–3410. Costumes, period rooms, Evanston history displays. Also home of Evanston Historical Society. Daily, 1–5; closed Wed. & Sun. Free admission on Fri.

Dearborn Observatory
2131 Sheridan Rd.; telephone: 492–3173. Call in advance for tickets. View the heavens through Northwestern University's 18 1/2″ telescope. Public viewing: April–Oct., Fri., 9–10; 10–11.

Lindheimer Astronomical Research Center (Observatory)
2353 Sheridan Rd.; telephone: 492–3173 or 492–7651. April–Oct., Sat. afternoon 2–4.

Frances E. Willard House, 1865
1730 Chicago Ave.; telephone: 864–1396. Maintained by Women's Christian Temperance Union. Historical data relating to establishment of this organization. Registered National Historic Landmark. Mon.–Fri., 9–noon, 1–4:30. Free admission.

ORCHARDS AND GARDENS

Garrett Theological Chapel Garden
2121 Sheridan Rd. A lovely, recessed garden with stations of the cross.

International Friendship Garden (Rotary Club).
2024 McCormick Blvd. between Emerson St. and Green Bay Rd. Part of Ladd Memorial Arboretum and Ecology Center.

Merrick Rose Garden
Oak Ave. and Lake St. Formal gardens with more than 1000 rose bushes. Note Centennial Fountain, 1876.

Shakespeare Garden
Located between Northwestern's Technical Institute and Garrett-

Evangelical Theological Seminary on Sheridan Rd. Contains a bronze bas-relief of Shakespeare and features only plants mentioned in his plays and poems.

PARKS AND NATURE CENTERS

Ladd Memorial Arboretum and Ecology Center
2024 McCormick Blvd. between Emerson St. and Green Bay Rd.; telephone: 864–5181. Twenty-three acres, with bird sanctuary, bicycle path, environmental education; programs, lectures and exhibits overseen by a resident naturalist. Daily, 6 AM–midnight.

Lighthouse Nature Center and Wild Flower Garden
2535 Sheridan Rd.; telephone: 864–5181. Inside lighthouse are a terrarium and aquarium. April 30–Oct. 10, Sat. & Sun., 2–5.

RECREATION

For general information, contact the Evanston Recreation Department, 1802 Maple Ave.; telephone: 328–2100.

Birding

Lake Michigan Beaches
Northwestern University, 1800–2400 N. Sheridan Rd.

Bicycling

Bike-path maps are available at the Evanston Civic Center, 2100 Ridge; telephone: 328–2100.

Boating

To launch a boat, daily or seasonal "patches" must be purchased at Dempster St. boat office.

End of Dempster St. (carry-in boats)
Nonmotor boats only; must be under 14-foot.

End of Church St. (powerboats)
Larger boats.

Golf

Evanston Community Golf Course (18-hole)
1030 Central St.; telephone: 475–9173

Indoor Ice-Skating

Robert Crown Ice Center
1701 Main St.; telephone: 328–9400

Swimming

For general information on beaches, call 328–2100, ext. 227.

Beaches (going north)
End of South Blvd., end of Lee St., end of Central St., end of Greenwood St., end of Clark St., and Lighthouse Beach (2535 N. Sheridan Rd.)

Swimming on beaches allowed only with patch, which may be purchased seasonally or daily at the Dempster Street Beach office at the end of Dempster St.

Winter Sports

James Park
Oakton and Dodge; telephone: 328–2100. Ski slope, toboggan runs, ice rinks.

RESTAURANTS

Café Provencal
1625 Hinman; telephone: 475–2233. Mon.–Thurs., 6–9; Fri.–Sat., 6–10; closed Sun.

The Dominion Room
501 Davis St.; telephone: 328–5252. Fresh fish, fresh vegetables, own bakery. Mon.–Sat., 11:30–2, 5–8; Sun., 11:30–7:30; closed Tues.

Emma's Food Shop
1229 Emerson; telephone: 475–9361. Soul food. Daily, 6–6; closed Sun.

Fanny's
1601 Simpson; telephone: 475–8686. Italian food. Mon.–Sat., 5–10; Sun., noon–8.

Fritz That's It
1615 Chicago; telephone: 866–8506. Good salad bar. Sun.–Thurs., 11:30–midnight; Fri.–Sat., 11:30 AM–1 AM

The Keg
810 Grove; telephone: 866–7780. Mon.–Thurs., 5–10:30; Fri.–Sat., 5–11:30; Sun., 4:30–9:30.

Old Havana Café
505 Main; telephone: 491–0333. Cuban food. Daily, 5–10:30.

Peacock's Dairy Bar
624 1/2 Davis; telephone: 864–4904. Some claim the ice cream sundae was born here. Daily, 11 AM–midnight.

The Spot
827 Foster; telephone: 869–2800. Folk or bluegrass music every night after 9 PM. Favorite haunt of Northwestern students. Mon.–Thurs., 9 AM–1 AM; Fri.–Sat., 11 AM–2 AM; Sun., 10:30 AM–1 AM.

Third Rail
832 Foster; telephone: 869–5095. Under the Foster El; great favorite of commuters. Mon.–Thurs., 11:30–10; Fri.–Sat., 11:30 AM–midnight; Sun., 11–10.

Upstairs, Downstairs
845 Chicago Ave.; telephone: 328–4100. British and Indian food. Mon.–Thurs., 5:30–9; Fri.–Sat., 10:30.

Yesterdays
1850 Sherman; telephone: 864–8464. Sun.–Thurs., 11 AM–1 AM; Fri.–Sat., 11 AM–2 AM.

SCENIC DRIVE

Evanston to Lake Bluff
Take Sheridan Road in Evanston at Calvary Cemetery all the way to Lake Bluff. One of the great suburban stretches in the country with elegant homes in every style and marvelous landscaping. In any community, side streets are worth detouring.

SHOPPING (Three major areas)

Evanston has three major shopping areas: Central Street, bounded by Ridge on the east and Hartrey on west; Downtown, bounded by Grove on the south, Clark on the north, Chicago on the east, and Oak on the west; and The Main, restored area between the 800 and 900 block on Main and Chicago.

Botti Studios of Architectural Arts
919 Grove; telephone: 869–5933. Make stained-glass windows. Mon.–Fri., 8:30–5:30; Sat., 10–4.

Farmer's Market
Maple Ave., between Clark and University Pl. Home-grown fruits and vegetables from Illinois, Indiana, and Michigan. Mid-June to end of Oct., Sat., 8–3.

Maiers Bakery and Pastry Shoppe
706 Main; telephone: 475–6565. An old German family-run bakery specializing in tortes and fancy cookies. Daily, 6–6.

Ships Unlimited
72 Old Orchard Shopping Center, Skokie; telephone: 676–1420. This remarkable hobby shop used to be in Evanston. Sells kits that cost up to $1000; has a clinic for model builders with problems that meets once a month. Only one of its kind in Midwest. Mon.–Fri., 9:30–9; Sat., 9:30–5; Sun., 12–5.

Vogue Fabric Shop
718 Main; telephone: 864–9600. One of biggest fabric houses in world! Mon.–Thurs., 9–9; Tues., Wed., Fri., Sat., 9–5:30.

SPECIAL EVENTS

Custer's Last Stand Art Fair
Main St. at Custer; for information, contact Evanston Art Council: 328–2100. Third weekend in June, 10–dusk.

Fourth of July
Parade with floats; egg-throwing contest, sack races. Fireworks at Dyche Stadium, 1500 block of Central St.

Garden Fair
Raymond Park, Grove and Chicago. Contact Evanston Art Council, 328–2100. May.

THEATER

Northwestern University
For information on performances, call: 492–5400.

Noyes Cultural Art Center
For information on performances, call: 491–0266.

Piven Theater Workshop and North Light Repertory Company

TOUR

Northwestern University Campus Walking Tour
For information, call 492–7271 (one-hour advance appointment needed).

Wilmette

Population: 32,000   Area Code: 312   Zip Code: 60091
Chamber of Commerce: 1150 Wilmette Avenue; telephone: 251–3800

The first settlers of Wilmette were a French Canadian fur trader and his part-Indian wife, Antoine and Archange Ouillmette. Because they had pleasant, mutually trusting relations with the nearby Potawatomi Indians, they were able to help a number of besieged whites after the Fort Dearborn massacre. They also were instrumental in persuading the local Indians to sign the Treaty of 1829, by which they sold their vast acreage to the United States in exchange for reservation lands in Iowa. The grateful government gave 1208 acres to Archange and these became widely known as the Ouillmette Reservation. Unfortunately, new settlers moving into the area squatted and infringed on the reservation, and the many Ouillmette children gradually sold off most of the acreage. The elderly parents, now almost landless, eventually settled with friends the Potawatomi in Council Bluffs, Iowa.

German farmers came to Wilmette in the 1840s (thirty years before incorporation) and so did the speculators and realtors who, for the next fifty years, billed the village as the Elm Forest of the North. The arrival of the Chicago Milwaukee Railroad made commuting easier, and the burning of Chicago in 1871 added more citizens. They (and their present descendants) had parties on the beach and took long tandem-bike rides south to Evanston or north to Glencoe. Today, the Green Bay Trail runs along the abandoned right of way of the old North Shore electric train, and the hike-and-bike trail runs north from Wilmette to Lake-Cook Road in Braeside.

Wilmette has a beautiful harbor, a yacht club, and a Coast Guard station. Gillson Park on the Lake was begun in the Depression as a project of the WPA. At its dedication, members of the Illinois Symphony, which consisted of WPA musicians, played from the top of the park's water tower to an audience of 30,000.

The town's newest addition is an area along the Lake which for years was called No Man's Land. It was precisely that, unincorporated, with no police or fire service of its own. Other suburban beaches might be privately armed, but this complex of pink stucco shops with fancy Spanish names allowed all comers to sun, swim, drink, or dance for a price. Bad fires swept through it over the years. Today it is a posh shopping area opposite a very expensive stretch of shoreline apartment houses.

ARCHITECTURE AND HISTORIC SITES

* **Baha'i House of Worship,** 1953
Sheridan Rd. and Linden Ave.; telephone: 256–4400. Begun in 1920, this nine-sided structure, dedicated to the basic principles of the oneness of God, has been called the Religious League of Nations. May 15–Oct. 15, daily, 10–10; rest of year, daily, 10–5; Sun. lecture, 3 PM.

Aerial view of the Baha'i House of Worship, Wilmette, Illinois.

MUSEUM

Wilmette Historical Museum
565 Hunter Rd.; telephone: 256–5838. History of Wilmette. Costume room. Tues.–Thurs, 9:30–12.

MUSIC

Wallace Bowl
Gillson Park (Lake St. at the Lake); for schedule, telephone: 256–6100. Concerts; some theatrical productions. July and August, Thurs.–Sun, 7:30 PM.

PARK

Gillson Park
Lake St. at the Lake; telephone: 256–6100. This 59-acre park along the Lake is the largest on the North Shore thanks to the insistence and foresightedness of Louis Gillson, park district president in 1908. Gillson Park was created from landfill by digging Wilmette's harbor and canal.

RECREATION

For information on beaches, ice-skating, cross-country skiing, and tobogganing, contact the Wilmette Recreation Department, 1200 Wilmette Ave.; telephone: 256–6100. Mon.–Fri., 9–5.

Birding

Gillson Park
Lake St. at the Lake. Whole beach area especially good at migration times.

Boating

Sailboat Rental, Gillson Park
Lake St. at the Lake

Wilmette Harbor Association (Launch)
Wilmette Harbor Dr.; telephone: 251–4234. Sailboats and power boats launched.

Disc Golf (Frisbee-ing)

Gillson Park
Lake Street at Lake Michigan. Eighteen-hole course for frisbee fanciers.

Golf

Wilmette Golf Course (18-hole)
Lake and Harms; telephone: 256–6100.

Swimming

Gillson Park Beaches
Lake St. at the Lake. Fee for nonresidents, payable at beach house.

RESTAURANT

Walker Bros. Original Pancake House
153 Green Bay; telephone: 251–6000. Best pancakes imaginable; made from grade AA eggs, 93-score butter, whipping cream. Sun.–Thurs., 7 AM–10 PM; Fri., 7 AM–11 PM; Sat., 7 AM–midnight.

SHOPPING

The main shopping district is on Central St. and Wilmette bounded by Lake St. to the north, Greenleaf to the south, Park Ave. to the west, and Tenth St. to the east.

Plaza Del Lago (between Evanston and Kenilworth on Sheridan Rd.)
Fancy shopping center that grew up in no man's land.

SPECIAL EVENT

Wilmette Community Fair
Central and Wilmette; telephone: 256–6100. Third Sunday in September.

TOUR

Coast Guard Station
Wilmette Harbor; telephone: 251–0185. Rescue service from Navy Pier to Waukegan. Tours arranged in advance.

Kenilworth

Population: 3000   Area Code: 312   Zip Code: 60043
Village Hall: 419 Richmond; telephone: 251-1666

Long after Wilmette and Winnetka were incorporated, Kenilworth
was still a tangle of woods where wagons rumbled north, cows from
nearby towns pastured, and Northwestern University students took
their botany field trips. Then Joseph Sears took his family to Scotland
for a holiday and had his imagination stirred by Walter Scott's Kenilworth. Sears had been thinking of moving his family to the country
for a long time, and, with the trip as a spur to action, he purchased
200 acres of land east of the railroad tracks near Wilmette. He formed
the Kenilworth Company, hired Daniel Burnham and several other
architects, and by 1891 had built a little town of twelve homes (six of
which still stand). It was well planned, with all streets running
northeasterly so that every room in every house had sunshine during
part of the day. The streets were named after characters in Scott's
novel and were constructed of macadam, the first used in the Chicago
area. The whole project attracted enormous interest, and during the
Columbian Exposition visitors from all over the world came to look
at the town. Kenilworth was incorporated in 1896 when the birth of
two babies brought its population up to the necessary 300.

Sears was a generous sort; he donated land for churches, a beach,
and a golf course. His largesse was matched by that of the Mahoney
family who had owned a large farm in the area, which they ultimately
subdivided and gave to the new town. The village had its last land
purchase in 1960 when the Northwestern Railroad right of way was
bought and a new park laid out near the railroad station.

Today, Kenilworth is less than a mile square, but its size is more
than compensated for by its civic pride. Particularly cherished by the
residents are the beautiful old elm trees.

The Church of the Holy Comforter, begun in 1899, has a fine
cloister, and it is here that the children's poet Eugene Field and his
wife are buried.

MUSEUM

Kenilworth Historical Society
415 Kenilworth Ave.; telephone: 251–2565. Mon., 1–3 PM.

RECREATION

Birding on the Beach
End of Kenilworth Ave. at the Lake

SHOPPING

Green Bay Rd. and Park Dr.

The Briar Patch
600 Green Bay Rd.; telephone: 256–5870. Topnotch handcrafted objects, from quilts to doll furniture. All made by handicapped people. (Operated by the Women's Board of the Easter Seal Society.) Mon.–Sat., 9–5.

The Federalist Antiques
523 Park Dr.; telephone: 256–1791. Tues.–Sat., 11–5.

SPECIAL EVENT

Kenilworth Union Church Annual Rummage Sale
211 Kenilworth Ave.; telephone: 251–4272. Free bus service from El to Church all day long. Marvelous collection from small items to fine treasures. First Thurs. in Oct., 7–5.

Winnetka

Population: 16,000   Area Code: 312   Zip Code: 60093
Chamber of Commerce: 841 Spruce Street; telephone: 446–4451

The watchword of Winnetka is *preservation,* and this applies to its trees, careful zoning, devotion to the GOP, and its excellent schools. Winnetka's early history was similar to the other suburbs: Indians in the background, a growth spurt after the Chicago fire, and a boom with the arrival of the Chicago Milwaukee Railroad. In the 1830s hundreds of New Englanders rumbled through in wagon trains, searching for better farmlands. Erastus Patterson was the first to arrive. Many of the next settlers came from the town of Trier in Germany; thus the township and Winnetka's famous high school were called New Trier.

In 1854, an influential new citizen, Charles Peck, Chicago leather merchant, contributed land for Winnetka's lovely common, and his wife gave the town its name. "Will it be called Pecktown?" someone asked her. "No, indeed. It will be *Winnetka,* Indian for 'beautiful land.' "

Winnetka was incorporated in 1869. Two years later Gilbert Hubbard began developing Hubbard Woods, the town's northernmost land. Today the drive along Sheridan Road proves that Hubbard Hills is still one of the loveliest stretches of the North Shore.

Winnetka has had more than its share of millionaires, though evidently not enough to support a helicopter service, which at one time scheduled seven landings daily in the suburb. But if helicopters weren't successful, the opening of a new road always was. When the last stretch of Sheridan Road, the main artery paralleling the Lake, was paved, a brigade of a hundred autos, led by Theodore Roosevelt, took a two-hour inspection drive north from the Art Institute of Chicago. The parade included a sixty-piece band, and was met by a crack drill team from Great Lakes Naval Station. Dignitaries shoveled the last pieces of dirt off the road with a silver-plated shovel, christened the street with champagne, and launched an 8-ton balloon. Although the bubbles were absent in 1951 when the Edens Expressway opened, it was an equally important occasion: a fast link to Chicago, and the opening of new development to the west of town. Today Winnetka has no place to go or grow, and though houses change hands, few new ones are built. Winnetka is justifiably proud of its schools. The system organized by Carleton Washburne in 1919 became famous for progressive education with emphasis on freedom, self-reliance, and individual growth. One of Winnetka's schools, Crow Island, has won numerous awards for excellent design. The Hadley Correspondence School for the Blind is also based in Winnetka. The founder, an ex-Chicago superintendent, lost his own eyesight, learned Braille, and started the renowned school.

Famous Winnetkans include Charlton Heston, Rock Hudson, and Ann Margret — all graduates of the same New Trier High School whose name is a reminder of the early German settlers.

PARK

Crow Island Park
Willow Rd., east of Hibbard Rd.; telephone: 441–6301. A wildflower, tree, and bird sanctuary. Spring, summer, fall.

RECREATION

Birding

Lake Michigan Beach
Tower Rd. at the Lake

Boating

Boat Launch
Tower Rd. and the Lake

Smelt Fishing

Tower Rd. and the Lake
License required.

Swimming

Lake Michigan beaches in Winnetka are at the end of Elder at the Lake and the end of Tower Rd. at the Lake. There is a charge for nonresidents.

RESTAURANT

The Sweet Shop
747 Elm St.; telephone: 446–1115. Toy train runs around the shop's ceiling every fifteen minutes. Marvelous for kids of all ages! Mon., 7–6; Tues.–Thurs., 7–10; Fri.–Sat., 8–11; Sun., 8–8.

SHOPPING

The major shopping districts are on Green Bay and Elm, bounded by Lincoln on the east and Chestnut on the west; and at Hubbard Woods (Linden St.) bounded by Scott.

It's a Small World
555 Lincoln Ave.; telephone: 446–8399. Miniatures for the collector. Mon.–Sat., 9–5.

Miss Clare, Inc.
552 Lincoln Ave.; telephone: 446–4777. Custom-made artificial flower arrangements. Mon.–Sat., 9:30–4:30 (closed Wed. and Sun.).

Caledonian, Inc.
562 Lincoln Ave.; telephone: 446–0912. Rooms and rooms of exquisite antiques from every period. Tues.–Sat., 9–5.

SPECIAL EVENTS

Christ Church Rummage Sale
700 Oak; for information, telephone: 446–4484. This annual rummage and antique sale has developed over fifty years into one of the best in the Midwest. First Thurs. in Oct., 7 AM–5 PM.

Winnetka Congregational Rummage Sale
725 Pine; for information, telephone: 446–4096. Marvelous antiques and rummage. Second Thurs. in May, 7 AM–5 PM.

Glencoe

Population: 11,000   Area Code: 312   Zip Code: 60022
Watts Center: 305 Randolph; telephone: 835-3030

Anson Taylor was an Indian trader who lived near Fort Dearborn and built the first bridge across the Chicago River. In 1830, he decided Chicago was too crowded (500 people), and rowed a boat north on the Lakefront in search of privacy. He found his spot 20 miles north where Harbor Street meets the Lake in present-day Glencoe. Then he returned to the city, packed his family and household possessions in a scow, and had a team of oxen pull all of them through shallow water along the shore. Land cost $1.25 an acre then and, in time, enough people followed Anson to form the settlement known as Taylorsport. His ultimate home was at 185 Green Bay Road, and, though the house is long gone, the evergreens he planted still grow on the grounds.

The true father of Glencoe, however, was neither Taylor nor the Mr. Coe whose glen gave the town its name. It was Alexander Hammond, a retired doctor who came from his farm in Rockford in search of an ideal spot along the Lake to form an ideal community. Finding Glencoe for sale, Hammond and ten friends bought it, setting aside a central square block (on Park Avenue) for a park. Each man built a home for himself and one to sell, and contributed money toward a school and a church. In the end the Utopia failed, and Hammond lost his whole investment. But the village, laid out to follow the curving lines of the local ravines, was incorporated in 1869. Its official seal has always been a replica of its namesake in the Scottish Highlands.

In the early days a good deal of timbering was done in the village to make charcoal and lumber for homes. By 1871, the thick woods had been so decimated that one early settler watched the Chicago fire burn from the top windows of his house.

Today Glencoe is, like the other Chicago suburbs, a posh bedroom community. Three quarters of its citizens are in business and the professions, and 90 percent of them own their own (expensive) homes.

Glencoe was the first town in the state to adopt the village manager system of government. In 1954, it was among the first in the country to combine its police and fire forces in a dually trained safety personnel system.

Glencoe currently has a large Jewish population as well as one of the oldest Negro settlements in the area. Archibald MacLeish, Pulitzer Prize–winning poet, Librarian of Congress, and son of one of the founders of the Carson Pirie Scott & Company department store, was born here.

ARCHITECTURE AND HISTORIC SITES

North Shore Congregation Israel, 1964
Minoru Yamasaki
1185 Sheridan Rd.; phone: 835–0724. This magnificent edifice serves a Reform Jewish congregation of 1800 families. Tours: daily, except Fri. and Sat., 10–1, 1–4; call in advance.

Pillared Southern Mansion, 1893
North side of Park Ave. and the Lake. Built originally as the State of Kentucky exhibit at the Columbian Exposition in Chicago. When the fair was over, the building was dismantled and shipped by boat to Glencoe, where it was reassembled at its present location.

PARKS AND NATURE CENTERS

Beach Front Park
Park Ave. and the Lake

Botanic Garden of Chicago Horticultural Society
Edens Expressway (I-94) between Dundee and Lake-Cook Rds.; telephone: 835–5440. 300 acres, including greenhouses, demonstration gardens, nature trails, education center, trees, and shrubs. June–Sept., Mon.–Sun., 9–4:30; rest of year, Mon.–Fri., 9–4:30. Tram tours, April–Oct.

Everly Wildflower Sanctuary
Jackson and Linden

Skokie Lagoons
Runs from north to south, west of the village; east of Edens Expressway, from Dundee to Willow Rd.; for information, call Cook County Forest Preserves: 446–5652. Built by the WPA. Picnicking, fishing, and boating permitted (bring your own).

RECREATION

Birding

Botanic Gardens
Edens Expressway, between Dundee and Lake-Cook Rds.

Glencoe Bird Sanctuary
Valley Rd and Park Ave.

Lake Michigan Beach
End of Park Ave. and the Lake

Skokie Lagoons
East of Edens Expressway between Dundee Rd. and Willow Rd.

Golf

Glencoe Golf Club (18-hole)
621 Westley Rd.; telephone: 835–0981.

Swimming

Lake Michigan Beach
End of Park or Hazel. Charge for nonresidents.

RESTAURANT

The Village Smithy
368 Park; telephone: 835–0220. Today's food served with yesterday's ambiance. Mon.–Fri. 11:30–2:30; Mon.–Thurs., 5:30–9; Fri.–Sat., 5–6:30–11.

SHOPPING

The major shopping district is on Vernon and Park Ave., bounded by Glencoe Rd. on the east.

Highland Park

Population: 32,000   Area Code: 312   Zip Code: 60035
Chamber of Commerce: 1811 St. Johns; telephone: 432–0284

Highland Park probably began about AD 500 with the Mound Builders, and certainly thrived as a Potawatomi campground. Today it
is a town of 34,000 people, who still occasionally dig up arrowheads
and pottery in their back yards and even debate about whether
the last three bent trees in town were once really Indian trail
markers.

In 1836, the federal government purchased land from the Indians,
and groups of Irish and Germans settled in the two small villages of
St. Johns and Port Clinton. Then the railroad poked through in 1855
and made a stop in what is now downtown Highland Park, causing
nearby St. Johns and Port Clinton to wane while Highland Park
waxed.

The early town had 1200 acres and 500 people; today it covers 12.5
square miles, and serves as the market hub for the whole suburban
area.

Highland Park was incorporated in 1869. The day before the event
there were eight saloons — the day after, none. Like the people of
Kenilworth whose devotion to their elm trees is intense, the early
Highland Parkers were distraught to find that the trees in their deep
ravines had been lumbered out, so they started a program of reforestation.

There was a time in the early days when four different railroads
came into town, and Highland Park and its various sections had
fourteen railroad depots. All that easy transportation drew people out
from the city, but it was not until after World War II that the sleepy
village became a bustling town and its population tripled.

The community has changed as well as grown, and although the
Lutheran and Catholic churches remain, today four synagogues cater
to a large Jewish population.

Ravinia, which is now a part of Highland Park, began in the 1890s
as a colony of summer artists who liked painting in the woods. One
resident was eager to convert the settlement into a Baptist village, a
suggestion that didn't take hold. Instead the beautiful little commu-

nity boomed in 1904 when the Ravinia amusement park opened. A few years later it was converted into a summer home for the Chicago Symphony Orchestra, playing under Walter Damrosch, and, in 1919, thanks to benefactors like Louis Eckstein, it became the setting for grand opera as well. Musical greats came from all over the world. Otto Kahn, impresario of the Metropolitan Opera of New York, once remarked, "Why is it my singers sing better here than they *can* sing?" The Depression closed the park in 1931, but a few years later when Mrs. Eckstein, then widowed, heard that Ringling Brothers was considering the property for winter quarters for the circus, she underwrote the park, which reopened as the Ravinia Festival. For over thirty years the Chicago Symphony has played here each summer, as have hundreds of visiting classical and jazz artists, making Ravinia the Tanglewood of the Midwest.

Highland Park has had numerous favorite sons: Elisha Gray who many believe invented the telephone before Alexander Bell; Kimball of piano fame; Stansfield Turner, present head of the CIA; and generals Mark Clark and Jonathan Wainwright (who were both probably army brats from Fort Sheridan).

ARCHITECTURE AND HISTORIC SITES

Analemmatic Sundial, 1976
Jerome V. Mann
Corner of St. Johns Ave. and Central Ave. Constructed for the Bicentennial. The Dial is a 26- × 15-foot granite slab; each hour is marked by a small tree. In order to ascertain time, people stand on the center line of the slab, opposite current date; the time is accurate within five minutes.

Elisha Gray's House, 1871
461 Hazel Ave.

Frank Lloyd Wright Houses, 1905, 1906, 1901
1923 Lake; 1689 Lake; 1445 Sheridan Rd.

Indian Trail Trees (only two left)
Exmoor Country Club, 700 Vine Ave. (near Golf Pro Shop); east side of Hazel St., north of Dole St. Long ago, Potawatomi Indians bent these trees to point out the trail to the beach where chipping stations were located.

Old Water Tower (landmark)
William Boyington
Central Ave. marks downtown section of Highland Park. One of few covered water towers in existence. Boyington also built the Morrison Hotel and the Chicago Water Tower.

ART CENTER

Suburban Fine Arts Center
472 Park Ave.; telephone: 432–1888. This center, founded in 1965, is designed to serve the artistic and cultural needs of the community, with art classes of all kinds held winter and summer. Gallery exhibits change monthly. Mon.–Fri., 9–5. Free admission.

MUSEUMS

Antique Auto Museum
3200 Skokie Valley Rd.; telephone: 433–4400. Full range of rare antiques and classic cars. Sun.–Thurs., 9–6; Fri.–Sat., 9–midnight.

Francis Stupey Log Cabin, 1850
1707 St. Johns Ave.; telephone: 432–7090. Cabin furnished in mid-1850s. Summers only, Sun., 2–4.

Highland Park Historical Society, Jean Butz James Museum
326 Central Ave.; telephone: 432–7090. Nineteenth-century furniture and toys. Daily, except Mon., 1–5; Sun., 2–4. Free admission.

Walter Durbahn Tool Museum
On grounds of James Museum. Fine collection of antique tools as well as those of a modern TV craftsman. Durbahn was head of vocational education at the local high school, whose students built many Highland Park homes in the 1930s, 40s, and 50s. Same hours as above. Free admission.

MUSIC

Ravinia Festival
Ravinia Park at Ravinia Rd.; telephone: 432–1236. Lovely woodland setting, 36 acres of land. Ravinia presents the finest in symphonic, concert, opera, recital, and chamber music programs, alternating with the best in jazz, blues, and folk concerts. Season closes with outstand-

ing theatrical fare in the Murray Theatre. Picnicking and fine restaurants on grounds. Art exhibit in the Casino Gallery. June–mid-September.

PARKS AND NATURE CENTERS

For information on all Highland Park parks, call: 831–3810.

Centennial Park
3500 Trailway Dr. Sixty-five acres; completely equipped for summer and winter sports.

Deer Creek Park
1377 Deer Creek Dr. 24 of the park's 71 acres are in their natural state.

Heller Nature Museum
Ridge and Half Day rds. 96 acres; this latest addition to Highland Park's nature centers is developing trails; will have museum and full-time naturalist eventually, but can be enjoyed now in present state.

Sunset Park
1801 Sunset Rd. 38 acres; fully equipped for sports; fitness trail; picnicking.

Birding

At Lake Michigan Beaches: end of Rosewood Dr. and the Lake; end of Ravinia Dr. and the Lake; end of Park Ave. and the Lake.

Boating

Boat Launch
Park Ave. and the Lake

Smelt Fishing

On Lake Michigan
Off Rosewood Dr., Ravinia Dr., and Park Ave. License required.

Golf

Sunset Valley Golf Course (18-hole)
1390 Sunset Rd.; telephone: 432–7140.

Swimming

Lake Michigan Beaches: Rosewood Beach, end of Roger Williams Ave.; Moraine Beach, end of Moraine St. Free admission.

SHOPPING

The central business district includes areas bounded by Laurel, Elm, Central, and Green Bay; Sheridan Rd. is its eastern boundary.

Crossroads
Clavey Rd., Lake-Cook Rd., and old Skokie Highway (#41).

Ravinia
Roger Williams Ave. and St. Johns Ave.

Aladdin's Lamp Antiques
1913 Sheridan Rd.; telephone: 432–0439. Seventeen rooms; antiques; general line. Tues.–Sat., 10–5.

The Squash Blossom
729 St. Johns Ave.; telephone: 432–3280. Good Indian crafts and jewelry; visiting Indian artists and craftsmen. Mon.–Sat., 10–4.

Highwood

Population: 5000   Area Code: 312   Zip Code: 60040
Chamber of Commerce: 32 Burtis Avenue; telephone: 432-3443

Buon giorno! Highwood is neither a suburb nor a city. It is an experience: a blend of charming gardens, soft Italian voices, bocce ball, and lots of good restaurants.

The Italians came here fairly late. The town census at the turn of the century showed three of them. Then in 1906 Joe Ori arrived from Modena. He wrote such glowing letters home that his friends followed him. They came to work as laborers at Fort Sheridan, on the railroads, and as gardeners for the affluent. Their children had some trouble with English at school, and there were clashes with the children of the patricians (Germans and Irish and Swedes) who two generations earlier had been immigrants themselves.

But Highwood was accustomed to dissension. Even its name had been a source of disagreement. The town began as St. John, became Port Clinton, then switched to Highwood. But in the 1880s when Fort Sheridan was established, the town fathers were so impressed with all the uniforms and fine cavalry officers that they called it Village of Fort Sheridan. So much friction developed between the fort and town, however, that in 1904 it became Highwood for good (a name with a literal meaning — it stood on the highest ground between Chicago and Milwaukee).

Francis Stupey, one of the pioneers, got in trouble right at the beginning. Quite unknowingly he built his cabin in the middle of an old Indian trail. And, as Indians walked by, they came right in the house, helped themselves to food, and terrified the Stupey family. There had been friction also about whether the town should develop as a Lake port or an overland route. That was settled when the train came through in the 1850s: Chicago to Highwood in an hour and a half. Previously, the trip had taken two days by wagon.

There had been dissension too about the town's image. The early planners had hoped to attract the wealthy. Instead, after the Civil War they got a host of immigrants whose languages and religions didn't mesh at all. Then there was dissension about Indian prisoners who had been captured in western battles and brought back to the fort. Though the kids loved it when the captives were allowed to wander about the streets in "garish paint and feathers," their elders were less pleased.

Finally, as the wet village among many drys, Highwood had constant battles with Fort Sheridan about liquor. There were times when the jails were so full of drunken soldiers, and the police so busy, that help was needed from neighboring Highland Park. In 1905, after four soldiers died in one month from the effects of drinking, a chemical report was ordered on the local whiskey. Reported components were sulphuric acid, ammonia, red pepper, whiskey essence, horse radish, and castor oil.

The first Italian mayor was elected in 1933. Today in addition to the Italian population, many Mexican-Americans have joined the gentlemen from Modena. They say *buenos días.*

RECREATION

Bocce, Italy's traditional bowling-style game, is played on clay courts in Highwood. For information on bocce, call: 432–9804

RESTAURANTS

Del Rio
228 Green Bay Rd.; telephone: 432–4608. Mon.–Thurs., 5–10; Fri. and Sat., 5–midnight; closed Sun.

My Favorite Inn
11 Highwood Ave.; telephone: 432–5121. Old, established, good Italian restaurant.

Scornavacco
550 Green Bay Rd.; telephone: 432–7651. Old, established Italian restaurant. Daily, 11–3, 4–midnight.

Shrimp Walk
405 Sheridan; telephone: 432–0500. It's what the name says! Tues.–Thurs., 5–10; Fri., 5–11; Sat., 4–midnight; Sun., 4–9.

Two Guys from Italy
50 Highwood Ave.; telephone: 432–2889. Mon.–Sat., 5–11; Sun., 4–11.

Fort Sheridan

Main Gate Entrance: U.S. 41 to Old Elm Rd., exit to Waukegan Ave. (extension of Sheridan Rd.); telephone: 926–2437

Fort Sheridan is situated on high bluffs overlooking the Lake, and nestles between Highwood on the south and Lake Forest to the north. It is always open to the public.

Often called the Army's biggest little Fort, it honors Philip Sheridan, a Civil War general who also played a big role in calming local disturbances during the Chicago fire. The fort came into existence in 1887 after a group of Chicago capitalists (all members of the Commercial Club of Chicago) petitioned the secretary of war for military help in controlling the labor unrest prevalent in Chicago during the mid-1880s. The gentlemen agreed to provide a tract of land for a fort, and a year later it became a reality.

Fort Sheridan has served as a military camp since the Spanish-American War. Today it is an administrative command and logistics support center for the army's Midwest activities. It employs 1400 civilians. There are periodic rumblings that it may close, followed by periodic petitions that it remain, especially on the part of neighboring Highwood whose economy flourishes because of its presence.

MUSEUMS

Fort Sheridan Museum
Ask directions at Main Gate. Contains Army memorabilia with emphasis on Fort Sheridan's history. Wed.–Sun., 10–3:30.

* Ft. Sheridan Tower, 1890
One of base's early buildings (modeled after Bell Tower in St. Mark's Square, Venice).

RECREATION

Birding on Lake Michigan Beach

TOURS

For information on group tours and a walking tour, call: 926–2437.

Tower, 1890, a landmark at Fort Sheridan, Illinois. *U.S. Army Public Affairs*

Lake Forest

Population: 16,500   Area Code: 312   Zip Code: 60045
City Hall: Deerpath Road; telephone: 234–2600

Lake Forest is probably the wealthiest suburb of them all. There is a story that in the 1850s many members of Chicago's Second Presbyterian Church found their new city a grand place to build fortunes and a wicked place to raise families. A group of ministers and laymen set off along a deer path, paralleling the Lake, to establish a college (Lake Forest) and a moral community to mesh with their New England standards. Forty miles north of the city they found their site. They hired Jed Hotchkiss, a young St. Louis architect, and paid him $1500 to design a town in a park fashion. Deerpath became its main street, the name of its fashionable inn, and for many years the name of a private railroad club car on the Northwestern line where Lake Foresters had their evening cocktails on the ride home.

From the beginning, Lake Forest was beautiful, but it was also a closed society with shades pulled, and with great wrought-iron fences hiding vast estates (many now subdivided) with fine gardens, statuary, and pools. There were houses by David Adler and Frank Lloyd Wright and a market square designed by Howard Van Doren Shaw. The local library won design prizes as did Lake Forest churches and schools. The small town has six private schools and two colleges.

The Lake Forest telephone book reads like a *Who's Who* of industry. Other notable citizens have been writer Dorothy Aldis, cartoonist John T. McCutcheon, and painter Franklin MacMahon.

ARCHITECTURE AND HISTORIC SITES

First Presbyterian Church of Lake Forest, 1887
Henry Ives Cobb
Sheridan and Deerpath Rds. Built with stones from burned ruins of Chicago's Second Presbyterian Church. Prime example of shingle style of architecture.

ART CENTER

Deer Path Gallery
253 Market Sq.; telephone: 234–3743. Sponsored by Deer Path Art
League; galleries exhibit local and other Midwest artists. Daily, 10–4;
closed Sun.

NATURE CENTER

Nature Preserve
Bounded by McCormick on the north, McKinley on the east, the
Lake on the west, Fort Sheridan on the south. Lovely area for birding
and picnicking.

RECREATION

Deerpath Municipal Golf Course (18-hole)
500 W. Deerpath Ave.; telephone: 234–1968.

RESTAURANTS

Deerpath Inn
255 E. Illinois; telephone: 234–2280. Old-world charm and good food.
Daily, 7–10, 11–2:30, 5–10; Fri., Sat., 5–11.

The Gallery
194 E. Westminster; telephone: 234–0770. Plants and classical music.
Lunch, weekdays, 11:30–3; dinner, Mon.–Thurs., 5:30–9, Sat.–Sun.,
5–8:30.

SHOPPING

Market Square
Shaw & Hotchkins
The main shopping area, and a building of architectural significance.

The Alaska Shop
777 N. Bank La.; telephone: 295–1910. Art gallery and gift shop,
specializing in Eskimo crafts. Mon.–Sat., 10–5.

Snowgate Antiques
654 N. Bank La.; telephone: 234–0655. Tues.–Sat., 10–5.

SPECIAL EVENTS

Annual Art Fair
253 Market Sq.; telephone: 234–3743. Excellent juried show. Labor Day weekend, Sun., Mon., 11–6.

First Presbyterian Church of Lake Forest Rummage Sale
700 N. Sheridan Rd.; telephone: 295–1214. Top-notch rummage. First Thurs. in May, 7–7.

Lake Forest Academy Antique Sale
1500 W. Kennedy Rd.; telephone: 234–3045. Most prestigious antique sale in area.

THEATER

Drake Theater of Barat College
700 E. Westleigh; telephone: 234–3000. Summer theater presents professional plays; rest of year, high-quality film forum and lectures.

Lake Bluff

Population: 5250   Area Code: 312   Zip Code: 60044
Village Hall: 40 E. Center Avenue; telephone: 234–0774

Lake Bluff, the last of the suburbs — and one of the swankiest — was once a stop on the Green Bay trail, used first by the Indians and then by the stagecoaches as they rumbled north. The early settlers were mainly Irish; in the 1840s, one of them ran a famous tavern for travelers. Thirty years later spirits were out as a group of Methodist ministers chose the area for their camp meeting ground. In due time they built a tabernacle large enough to hold 5000 followers, who were stirred by sermons and entertained by cultural events. In the early 1880s, Frances Willard began holding temperance meetings here and invited the foes of alcohol to organize. They did and the Prohibition Party got its start at the tabernacle in 1885. Although the structure stands no more, there is a small park in Lake Bluff whose benches are made of its wood.

In 1855, the Chicago to Milwaukee train (now the Northwestern) came through Lake Bluff, the only stop between Highland Park and Waukegan. This development gave impetus to a thriving summer resort. In the 1890s, when the town incorporated, many summer resorters built year-round homes. The Lake Bluff Meeting Association, led by Methodists, was formed. An artesian well was drilled and the overflow from it created a 10-acre lake, which in winter was used by the town as a source of ice. Artesian Park is in the center of Lake Bluff today, and it is surrounded by lovely homes, some of them the rebuilt summer cottages of an earlier era.

PARK

Artesian Park
Sheridan Rd. and West Sheridan Rd. Small town park (was a small lake in early days).

RECREATION

Golf

Lake Bluff Golf Course (18-hole)
Rockland Park; telephone: 234–6771.

Swimming

Lake Michigan Beaches
End of Scranton, Center, and Prospect at the Lake. Fee for nonresidents.

SHOPPING

The main shopping area is on East Scranton Ave. from Sheridan Rd.

Great Lakes Naval Training Center

Population: 30,000   Area Code: 312   Zip Code: 60088

Ever since 1911 when President Taft dedicated the Great Lakes Naval Training Center, it has been turning "landlubbers into seamen and seamen into sailors" — a total of 3 million over the years.

Great Lakes is the country's largest naval center, without a training boat on the premises. It spills over 1500 acres; trains 40 percent of the navy's recruits; has a population of 30,000, civilians included; and maintains a very large naval hospital. It is headquarters of the Ninth Naval District, under the command of a rear admiral.

If this prairie post seems an unlikely spot for a naval facility, it wasn't chosen lightly. The navy first arrived in the Midwest when American ships challenged the British fleet in the Great Lakes in the War of 1812. During the Spanish-American War it became obvious that a section of the country that was providing 43 percent of all naval recruits ought to have a regional facility to train them. Congressman George Foss, often spoken of as the father of Great Lakes, and a committee of Chicagoans looked at thirty-seven sites before they chose this area on the shores of Lake Michigan.

Suburbanites have varied memories of Great Lakes. Some remember ice-skating in the navy's indoor rink (now closed to the public). Others remember the period in 1942 when the first black middy reported for training (three years later each company had at least one black). A few who date back to World War I remember a lieutenant commander who not only trained 1500 musicians for 14 regimental bands but sometimes had them all play his own composition, "The Stars and Stripes Forever." The commander's name: John Philip Sousa. And many others remember the splendid weekly graduation reviews with navy bands, the Bluejacket choir, drum and bugle corps, and smart drill teams. They still go on every Friday from 1:30 to 3:00 (indoors in bad weather).

For more specific information, call: 688–5670 (to arrange tours for large groups, call on the Wednesday prior to the desired tour date).

North Chicago

Population: 47,000   Area Code: 312   Zip Code: 60064
City Hall: Argonne Drive and Lewis Avenue; telephone: 689–9000

This town, like its neighbor Waukegan, is highly industrial. First named Pettibone Creek, then South Waukegan, it became North Chicago in 1908. In 1937 there was a big strike in one of its plants, requiring the use of tear gas to rout the workers. The National Labor Relations Board ruled that the strikers must be rehired, but the ruling was reversed by the Supreme Court in 1939, the court holding that sit-down strikes were illegal.

North Chicago produces pharmaceuticals (at Abbott Laboratories), poultry supplies, and candy. Except for Foss Park, the town's Lakefront is largely commercial.

PARKS

Foss Park
Lake Michigan at the end of Second Ave.; telephone: 689–3824. The 33 wooded acres provide picnic areas, a swimming beach, playground, and park shelters.

Twin City Park
13th at Elizabeth. 16 acres of wooded and open space; playground; picnics; ice-skating.

RECREATION

Foss Park Golf Course (18-hole)
Argonne Dr. and Green Bay Rd.; telephone: 689–1633.

RESTAURANT

Adam's Rib
2505 Green Bay Rd.; telephone: 689–1999. Homemade soups and pies. Daily, 6 AM–10 PM.

TOUR

Abbott Laboratories
14th and Sheridan Rd.; telephone: 937–6100. Daily tours.

Waukegan

Population: 65,300   Area Code: 312   Zip Code: 53140
City Hall: 106 Utica; telephone: 689-7500

Abraham Lincoln slept here; Jack Benny grew up here; the movies were born here. Sounds glamorous, but Waukegan isn't. It is industrial to the core, with 140 plants — some of them as big as Johnson Motors, American Steel and Wire, and U.S. Gypsum. Ever since the St. Lawrence Seaway opened, the city's harbor has been one of Illinois's two ports of call on the Lake.

Like other Lakefront cities, Waukegan was a stopping place for early explorers and an Indian trading post.

Because of its five natural springs, it was hoped that Waukegan would become the Saratoga of the West. When that failed, the waters were used commercially for making soft drinks (notably Glen Rock) and British ale. The recipe for the ale was brought here by an Englishman named Besley, and his brewery used the crystal clear springs until Prohibition.

Another citizen, a doctor named Roberts, was one of the country's early oral surgeons, specializing in reconstructing jaws of people injured in horse accidents. He was an early conservationist and warned the community of the damage being done to their lungs by the soft coal burned in their factories, as well as the need to check the quality of the water discharged into the Lake by the factories.

Probably, they listened to the doctor more carefully than to Abraham Lincoln who, on April 12, 1860, delivered to Waukeganites his only incomplete speech. In the middle of his address, fire alarms went off, and the crowd grew so restless that the president finally told them all to leave "and help put it out." The dignitaries of the GOP insisted it was all Democratic dirty tricks.

Waukegan was the birthplace of the movies. Before World War I, two local men, George Spoor and Edward Amet, shot the *Battle of Santiago* in a specially constructed tank in Amet's backyard. Later they formed the Essanay Studio and moved to Chicago.

In reverse, the famous Chicago social worker Jane Addams, urged a wealthy friend, Mrs. Joseph Bowen, to purchase the Haines home, a pioneer homestead in Waukegan, for a summer camp and a social service center for the poor of Chicago. Today this waterfront land is Waukegan's Bowen Park. The Haines House is now the Waukegan Historical Center. The Center for the Performing Arts was named in honor of the city's most famous son, the man who never got older than thirty-nine and never forgot Waukegan: Jack Benny. However, Ray Bradbury, a science-fiction writer who was born in Waukegan, is currently the city's favorite son.

MUSEUMS

Jack Benny Center for the Performing Arts
Bowen Park, 1917 N. Sheridan Rd.; telephone: 244–1660. Open daily for lessons of all kinds; frequent performances and recitals.

Waukegan Historical Society
1917 N. Sheridan Rd.; telephone: 336–1859. Lovely old farmhouse built in 1853 and converted into local museum in 1960s. Its eight rooms are carefully decorated with representative period furnitures and includes a Lincoln room with the bed he slept in. Tues., 10–3.

MUSIC

Summer Band Concerts
North Beach Park, Sea Horse Dr. and the Lake; telephone: 689–7500. Tues., 7:30 PM.

PARKS

For general information on Waukegan's parks, call: 662–0186.

Belvidere Park
2000 Belvidere Rd. 34 acres; cross-country skiing in winter.

Bevier Park
2323 Yorkhouse Rd. 28 acres; full recreation.

* **Bowen Park**
1917 N. Sheridan Rd. 64 acres; gardens, hiking, full recreation.

RECREATION

Birding

Beach
North of Yacht Club to Sea Horse Rd., which leads to beach. May–June, terns; July–Sept., piping plovers and least bitterns.

Public Service Plant Pond
Good for waterfowl.

Boating

Port of Waukegan
101 Harbor Pl.; telephone: 662–5222.

Fishing

Waukegan Charter Boat Association
2024 Edgewood Rd.; telephone: 244–3474 (dial: BIG–FISH). April–October.

Government Pier
Waterfront. Excellent for landbound angler.

Golf

Bonnie Brook Golf Course (18-hole)
2800 N. Lewis; telephone: 336–7855.

Marina

Public Marina
Grand Ave. to the Lake; telephone: 623–6520.

Swimming

Lake Michigan Beach
Sea Horse Dr. Bath house; mile-long beach.

Yachting

Annual Race
Chicago to Waukegan and back (23 miles); for information, call: 623–4188. July.

RESTAURANT

Mathon's
6 Clayton St.; telephone: 662–3610. Old seafood restaurant that has stood the test of time. Mathon is famous for long-term weather predictions based on fishing conditions. Tues.–Thurs., 11–9:30; Fri.–Sat., 11–10:30; Sun., noon–8:30.

SHOPPING

Lakehurst Shopping Center
Waukegan Rd. (Rt. 43) and Belvidere Rd. (Rt. 120). 120 shops and services in an enclosed area.

Coho Fishing Shop
622 Grand Ave.; telephone: 623–4570.

SPECIAL EVENT

Waukegan Festival
North Beach Park, Sea Horse Drive and Lake Michigan; telephone: 689–7500. Waukegan's ethnicity celebrated. First weekend in August.

THEATER

Waukegan Community Players
Present five productions yearly.

Zion

Population: 25,000   Area Code: 312   Zip Code: 60099
Chamber of Commerce: 2780 Sheridan Road; telephone: 872–5405

Winthrop Harbor

Population: 5000   Area Code: 312   Zip Code: 60096

John Alexander Dowie was a Scotsman, a Christian evangelist, and he founded the International Divine Healing Association. He believed the world was flat and that "where God ruled, man prospered." After serving the cause of evangelism in Chicago, he decided to build a city where his Christian Catholic Church would dominate. He found his spot — 6300 acres midway between Chicago and Milwaukee — and he called it Zion. It is one of the very few wholly planned towns in the country. Some say it was designed after the British flag; others claim the crosses of St. George and St. Andrew served as inspiration. At any rate, it had wide boulevards and its focal point was a temple, placed strategically in a 200-acre park. Starting at Lake Michigan, all streets were given Biblical names: Bethany, Bethel, Bethesda, Bethlehem, until the town limits were reached.

In 1901, Dowie built Zion House, then called the Elijah Hospice, to house men who came ahead of their families to build their own homes. Next Dowie built his tabernacle, an edifice to seat 8000, many of whom commuted each Sunday from Chicago for services. Fire destroyed the church in 1937, but the outdoor amphitheater still remains, and each July and August the Passion play is performed here. (The original director frequently traveled to the Holy Land in search of proper sets and props.) Shiloh House, now the Zion Historical Society, was Dr. Dowie's own twenty-five-room mansion. He was a small man and his bookshelves were built with bases that pulled out and became step stools so he could reach his various religious tracts.

Before long 10,000 Dowie followers came to the area. Rules were strict: no liquor, tobacco, cards, pork, or travel on Sunday. A big cookie factory opened here and a lace factory, which required the importation of skilled workers from Nottingham, England. (Marshall Field & Company took over the factory in 1906 and ran it until 1952.) Within a few years of Dowie's death in 1907, the little theocratic community in Zion was bankrupt, and the property was sold to individuals.

Winthrop Harbor, 3 miles north, is a sister city of Zion. It is a pleasant village, once a large dairy farm; its well-landscaped homes are beautifully situated on ravines and streams. Nearby is the Zion Nuclear Plant, one of the biggest in the country.

ARCHITECTURE AND HISTORIC SITE

Sanctuary of the Christian Catholic Church, 1937
Center of Shiloh Park, Dowie Memorial Dr.; telephone: 746–1411. A unique example of precast gothic stained-glass windows, this 1300-seat church replaces the original tabernacle built by Dowie.

MUSEUMS

* **Shiloh House** (Zion Historical Society), 1903
1300 Shiloh Blvd.; telephone: 746–2427. Now the headquarters for the Zion Historical Society, Shiloh House was built for Dr. Dowie, originally costing $90,000. It has been restored, with many original items on display. June, July, August, Sat.–Sun., 2–5; at other times by appointment.

Zion Leisure Center
Shiloh Park, 2400 Dowie Memorial Dr.; telephone: 746–5500. Hub of Zion's cultural and recreational life.

PARKS

Chiwaukee Prairie (Winthrop Park)
Sheridan Road to 115th Street. Turn east until you come to the first road south (to your right). Go in on road a bit, paved road continues on winding to a marina. Don't continue, take unpaved road. The prairie is all through this area. Marvelous nature walk.

Illinois Beach State Park
On Wadsworth Rd., 2 miles east off I-131 between Waukegan and Zion; telephone: 662–4811. Nature Center open daily, 9–3. 7 miles of sandy shoreline and dunes along Lake Michigan. This 2124-acre park is divided into three areas: general recreation area in north portion;

Fishing for the big ones in Lake Michigan.

Not all the fish are big ones, especially in the harbors.

nature study area between Beach Rd. and Dead River; wildlife refuge area south of Dead River. The park has facilities for camping and swimming (four bath houses), a food concession, trails, fishing in small ponds, picnicking, bird watching, and a nature center with guided tours.

The only dunes on the Illinois shoreline are here. Since 1888 when Jens Jensen, the great landscape architect, took an interest in preserving its beauty, there had been talk of making it a park. Finally in 1948 the state began acquiring land. Dead River, a sluggish stream, is its stellar attraction. It serves as a reservoir for the park's upland marshes. Then, after heavy rains, it bursts over the sandbars at its mouth and flows into the Lake, draining the marshes and releasing the northern pike fish who breed in the wet meadows. It is a much studied area because of its 500 species of plants and the marvelous waterfowl that live here or use it as a seasonal flyway.

Shiloh Park
2400 Dowie Memorial Dr., telephone: 746–5500. Topnotch park complete with swans, bike trails, churches.

RECREATION

Golf

Shiloh Golf Course (9-hole)
2400 Dowie Memorial Dr., Zion; telephone: 746–5502.

Swimming

Lake Michigan Beach
Winthrop Harbor

RESTAURANTS

Holiday Inn Restaurant
Illinois Beach State Park; telephone: 249–2100. Lovely lake view. Daily, three meals.

Lakeview II
2021 Sheridan Rd., Zion; telephone: 746–3702. Half of this family-style restaurant lies in dry Zion Township; the other half lies in Benton Township. Consequently, restaurant has two dining rooms,

and in one you can have liquor with your meal. Daily, twenty-four hours.

SPECIAL EVENT

Jubilee Days
All-city participation produces parades, steer roast, queen coronation, carnival, fireworks. Labor Day weekend.

THEATER

Zion Passion Play
Amphitheater next to Christian Catholic Church Center of Shiloh Park; telephone: 746–2221. This world-renowned dramatization of the gospel and life of Jesus Christ is performed by a cast of 200 with settings as historically true as research can ensure. July–August, Friday evenings at 7 PM.

Wisconsin

FROM
KENOSHA
TO
MARINETTE

Rock Island
Washington Island
Gill's Rock
Ellison Bay •
Sister Bay
Fish Creek • Ephraim
Marinette • Bailey's Harbor
Peshtigo Egg Harbor
Jacksonport
Oconto •
Sturgeon Bay
• Brussels
Suamico • Algoma •
Green Bay Kewaunee •
Two Rivers •
Manitowoc •
W I S C O N S I N
Sheboygan •
Oostburg •
Cedar Grove •
L A K E
M I C H I G A N
Port Washington •
Milwaukee •
Racine •
Kenosha •

SANDERSON

Kenosha

Population: 86,175   Area Code: 414   Zip Code: 53141
Chamber of Commerce: 625 57th Street, Suite 710; telephone: 654–2165

Kenosha developed where Pike Creek enters Lake Michigan. Its harbor is graced on one side by Simmons Island Park, on the other by Lake Front Park. It is a city of well-kept homes, well-clipped parks (thirty-eight of them), and good recreational facilities (twenty-four inland lakes on Kenosha's outskirts). A ride down Third Avenue is a look at Kenosha's past and present: old mansions and new businesses blending in a pleasant, satisfying way.

The town really began in Hannibal, New York, in 1834 when a group of men held a public meeting to discuss the western land boom. They formed the Western Emigration Company and sold shares for $10 a person. The group wanted two things: a good lake port (and from what they'd heard, the western shore of Lake Michigan sounded best), and back country suitable for farming. They designated four men as scouts to represent the group. Those four walked to Chicago, eventually boating to Kenosha. The first to settle permanently (in 1835) was Charles W. Turner and he named the area Pike River. In 1840, when numerous New Yorkers followed him, the village was incorporated and its name changed to Southport, changing finally to Kenosha (the Indian word for pike). Those early years were hard, with Indian troubles, hunger, prairie fire, bitter winters, and endless disputes over claims. To make his point about ownership, one man transplanted a whole cornfield and fenced it in overnight, thus confounding his neighbors when they awakened in the morning.

From the beginning, the shallow harbor was a problem, partly because of rough seas and partly because passengers had to be transferred to smaller boats to reach shore. Help eventually came from Washington, but in the meantime an enterprising resident had built one of the first long piers out in the Lake. The first settlers were followed by German liberals, political refugees (Forty-eighters), who brought with them exciting ideas, formed discussion and lecture groups, and worked to make Kenosha a stop on the Underground Railroad. C. L. Sholes, the inventor of the typewriter, was one of

Aerial view of American Motors Corporation, Kenosha, Wisconsin.

them. As a state legislator in 1853 he helped pass Wisconsin's law banning capital punishment. Michael Frank was another. As mayor of Kenosha in 1850, he championed free public education; his work resulted in the first public school system outside New England.

After the Germans came waves of Lithuanians, Italians, Poles, Czechs, skilled workmen who helped Kenosha maintain its reputation as a peaceful labor market. A great strike in 1928 ended that, and Kenosha has been an open-shop town ever since.

Today the city has more than eighty industrial plants, among them Chicago Brass; the American Motor Company; Simmons Mattress; Jockey briefs for men; and the LeBlanc Company, which sends quality woodwind and brass instruments all over the world. The biggest of all the plants is American Motors, which puts the final touches on 1600 cars a day. Ocean Spray, the largest cranberry-processing plant in the world, is also Kenosha-based. The stubborn little berries cling so firmly to their vines in nearby marshes that fields must be flooded and the waters vibrated for the berries to pop up to the surface. Pickers then scoop them up and dump them in flat-bottomed boats for hauling to the packing house.

Kenosha is also headquarters for the Preservation and Encouragement of Barber Shop Quartet Singing in America, the largest singing society in the world (45,000 members). Home for them is Harmony Hall, the elaborate mansion of a former Nash Motors executive.

Famous Kenosha natives are Charles Nash, writer Irving Wallace, and actors Don Ameche and Orson Welles.

ARCHITECTURE AND HISTORIC SITES

Boys and Girls Library, 1904
5810 8th Ave.; telephone: 656–6052. This charming library, which was formerly a Unitarian Church, is sized for children of preschool age through eight years. Mon.–Fri., 8:30–5:30; Sat., 8:30–5.

* Gilbert M. Simmons Library, 1900
Daniel H. Burnham
59th Pl. and 8th Ave.; telephone: 656–6034. This library lies in the center of Library Park which is surrounded by lovely old historic homes (ask at Public Museum for self-guided tour of this area). Mon.–Fri., 8:30–9; Sat., 8:30–5.

MUSEUMS

Civil War Museum
Carthage College 2001 Alford Dr.; telephone: 552–8520. Civil War memorabilia includes guns, uniforms, documents, artwork, and currency. Mon.–Fri., 8–4.

Kemper Activities Center, 1874
6501 Third Ave.; telephone: 657–6005. This lovely 11.1-acre Lakefront site was built in 1874 as a private girls' school, and is now part of the Kenosha park system. Plays, film festivals, picnics, and even weddings in the beautiful chapel held here.

Kenosha County Historical and Art Museum
6300 Third Ave.; telephone: 654–5770. Restored mansion brings back the golden days of Kenosha. Tues. and Thurs., 2–4:30.

Kenosha Public Museum
5608 10th Ave.; telephone: 656–6026. The best part of this museum is the Lorado Taft dioramas of the studios of the world's great sculptors (ask for self-guided tour titled "A Walk Around the Park"). Mon.–Fri., 9–12, 1–5; Sat., 9–12; Sun., 1–4.

Veteran's Fountain, 1977
625 52nd St. Especially beautiful at night.

PARK AND NATURE CENTER

Bong Nature Trail and Recreation Area

7 miles SE of Burlington on Rt. W142; telephone: 763–7637. 4500 acres; the Nature Trail passes through several plant and animal communities including woodlands, grasslands, and marsh.

Lincoln Park Botanical Gardens

68th St. and 18th Ave. Formal flower garden.

RECREATION

Bicycling

Washington Park

1821 Washington Rd.; telephone: 656–6073. One of nation's finest natural bicycle racing tracks.

Birding

Harbor at 6th Ave.

Beach, pier, and channel at 50th and Lakefront. Good for waterbirds.

Boats

Harbor

Foot of 52nd St. at 6th Ave. This deep-water harbor will accommodate five major ocean liners.

Launching Facility (municipal)

Foot of 45th St.; telephone: 656–6151.

Charters

Captain Jim's

4807 7th Ave.; telephone: 652–6832.

Gary's Charter Service

8200 75th St.; telephone: 694–0400.

Lawrence F. Otto

2824 22nd Ave.; telephone: 652–9172.

Rudi's Charter Fishing

6014 Third Ave.; telephone: 654–0608.

Golf

Brighton Dale (27-hole)
Highways 75 and 142, Kansasville; telephone: 878–1440.

Petrifying Springs Park (18-hole)
761 Green Bay Rd.; telephone: 552–9052.

Washington Park (9-hole)
2205 Washington Blvd.; telephone: 656–6073.

Hunting

For exact seasonal dates and areas for deer, pheasant, rabbit, squirrel, and woodcock hunting, call: 763–7637. Hunting license required.

Bong Recreational Area
7 miles SE of Burlington on Rt. W142.

New Munster Hunting Grounds
8 miles S of Burlington near Rt. W50 and County K-D.

Marinas

Kenosha Yacht Club
5130 Fourth Ave.

Powerboat Marina (municipal)
South of end of 50th St. on Simmons Island; telephone: 656–6151.

Sailboat Marina (municipal)
North of end of 50th St. on Simmons Island.

Skiing

Wilmot Mountain
County C out of Kenosha to County W, .5 mile south; telephone: 862–2301. Thirty-one slopes and trails. Open daily during ski season, 10 AM–11 PM.

Swimming

Lake Michigan Beaches
3 miles of beaches.

Eichelman Park
3rd Ave. and 60th St.

Pennoyer Park
38th St. and Alfred Dr.

Simmons Island Park
5001 Simmons Island

Southport Park
End of 75th and 78th St.

Winter Sports

Brighton Dale Park
Highways 75 and 142; telephone: 878–1440. 362 acres.

Fox River Park
Junction County Rds. F and W; telephone: 889–4710. 148 acres.

Petrifying Spring Park
761 Green Bay Rd.; telephone: 552–9052. 350 acres.

Silver Lake Park
County F and Highway 50. 260 acres.

RESTAURANTS

Krok's Lake Shore
1300 Sheridan Rd.; telephone: 552–8311. Terrific steak sandwiches.
Tues.–Sat., 4:30 PM–10 PM; Sun., noon–10 PM

Oage Thomsen's
2227 60th St.; telephone: 657–9317. Tues.–Fri., 11:30–10 PM; Sat., 5
PM–midnight; Sun., noon–10 PM.

Ray Radigan's
South Sheridan Rd.; telephone: 694–0455. People come from Chicago
to eat here. Tues.–Sat., 11 AM–midnight; Sun., noon–midnight.

Southport Dining Room
Holiday Inn 5125 6th Ave.; telephone: 658–3281. Spectacular view of
harbor. Daily, 6 AM–10 PM.

SHOPPING

Farm Bell Antiques
10416 Green Bay Rd.; telephone: 694–2603 (call before coming). General line with specialty Danish Christmas plate.

Table-Top Antiques
822 Sheridan Rd.; telephone: 552–8242. General line; antique jewelry specialty. Mon.–Sat., 9–5.

SPECIAL EVENT

Cohorama
Coho fishing contest with prizes. Last week in June.

TOURS

American Motor Company
5626 25th Ave.; telephone: 658–7680. Advance reservations for groups of ten or more. No groups below fourth-grade level. No cameras. This is an assembly plant for AMC. Oct. 1–June 1, Mon.–Fri., 9:45 AM and 1:15 PM.

A Walk Around the Park
59th Pl. and 8th Ave.; for information call: 656–6026. Included in these old historic homes is the house of Reverend Deming which was used as part of the Underground Railroad for slaves during the Civil War.

S.P.E.B.S.Q.S.A., Harmony Hall
6315 Third Ave.; telephone: 654–9111. International headquarters for the Society for the Preservation and Encouragement of Barber Shop Quartet Singing in America! Lovely old mansion built by a Nash executive. Mon.–Fri., 8–5.

Racine

Population: 96,350   Area Code: 414   Zip Code: 53403
Chamber of Commerce: 731 Main Street; telephone 633–2451

Twelve miles north of Kenosha on a thumb of land jutting into the Lake is Wisconsin's second city, Racine. It rises where the Root River meets Lake Michigan, a clean industrialized city with an ethnic heritage almost as rich as Chicago's.

From the beginning, Racine (French for "roots") was cursed with a terrible harbor, laced with reefs and sandbars and a channel so snagged with growth that the explorers Marquette and Joliet found it impenetrable. Later arrivals had to be transferred to small boats (called lighters) to get ashore. The overland route along the Green Bay Trail was fine, however, and the mail was carried by a runner who each month covered the 480-mile Chicago-Green Bay round trip, with a stop at Racine. His sacks were loaded with letters and packages; his head filled with snatches of news and tidbits of gossip.

Settlers became interested in the area after the Blackhawk War and the settling of Indian treaties in 1833, at a time when Wisconsin fever was hitting many New Englanders and fortune seekers from western New York. The first permanent settler was Captain Gilbert Knapp (1834) whose statue overlooks Lake Michigan today. So many Danish people arrived that the settlement was called Kringleville, and so many Bohemians that it was also called Czech Bethlehem.

When Cornish miners in the western Rock River area began mining lead, the need for a harbor became imperative. In 1839 a survey was made, and when Congress refused to help Lake Michigan towns improve their facilities, go-getting Racinites taxed themselves at the rate of two days' work or the equivalent. By 1844 the steamer *Chesapeake* arrived in the newly dredged harbor, much to the delight of the community. By 1857 Racine's export business boomed with shipments of wheat, wagons, cigars, and soap. By the time the federal government pitched in to help build a breakwater, the railroads had arrived and the commercial importance of the Lake had lessened.

Wingspread, the building designed by Frank Lloyd Wright for the
Johnson family, is now being used as a conference center and
the headquarters for the Johnson Foundation.

Racine has always been a great labor town — almost 100-percent
unionized — and its skilled workers turn out farm implements, auto
parts, waxes, paints, and many other products. In 1887 the Horlick
Brothers gave America the first malted milk (the company is now out
of business). But no other concern has had quite the impact of S. C.
Johnson's Sons. The wax makers have waxed mightily in Racine, and
today there is a Johnson Foundation, headquartered in a handsome
complex called Wingspread; the Johnson Medical Research Center;
the Johnson Administration and Research Center (designed by Frank
Lloyd Wright); and Waxdale, the world's most efficient pressure
packaging plant. The Racine courthouse was designed by Holabird
and Root, with sculptural reliefs by Carl Milles.

Two reminders of Racine's past remain still: the oval Indian burial
mounds dating back to a time when the Woodland Indians roamed
the area, and the nearby ghost village of Pike River — settled in 1835,
but lost as early pioneers moved to the larger communities.

Racine had the first ordained woman minister in the country, the
Reverend Olympia Brown, a Universalist. It was also the home
of actor Fredric March, and General Billy Mitchell who got into
trouble for being an early and outspoken advocate of air power for
the United States.

ARCHITECTURE AND HISTORIC SITES

* DeKoven Foundation, 1852
600 21st St. Originally Episcopalian college.

* First Presbyterian Church, 1851
716 College Ave.

Harbor Lighthouse and U.S. Coast Guard Station
Mouth of Root River and the Lake

Hunt House, 1848
1274 Main St. Greek-revived "without the guiding hand of an architect."

* Knight House, 1842
1235 Main St.

* Kuehneman House, 1853
1135 S. Main St. Greek Revival.

Mound Cemetery
1147 W. Boulevard; telephone: 636–9188. Interesting old cemetery with Indian mound burial sites mixed with pioneer graves.

Wingspread Conference Center
Frank Lloyd Wright
4 miles east of Highway 32 on County G. Home of the Johnson Foundation: an instrument for creative programs that serve man. Former home of the Johnsons of Johnson Wax fame; these beautiful grounds can be entered but the conference center cannot be toured except by permission.

* Frank Lloyd Wright House, 1906
1319 Main St.

ART CENTER

Wustrum Museum and Art Center
2519 Northwestern Ave.; telephone: 636–9177. Active art center with fine small collection. Mon.–Thurs., 11–9; Fri.–Sun., 1–5.

MUSEUMS

1888 Schoolhouse

Five Mile Rd. at Highway 31. Constructed by the Bohemian community, this schoolhouse is a living museum for fourth grade students in the area. A schoolmarm, dressed in authentic 1880 period costume, teaches the three R's as they used to be taught. Visitors by appointment. For information, call Chamber of Commerce.

Classroom in session: September through November, March through June, and Monday through Friday.

* Racine County Historical Museum

701 S. Main St.; telephone: 637–8585. Contains cultural and natural history of Racine, plus 1500-volume genealogical library. Tues.–Sat., 9–5; Sun., 1–5. Free admission.

MUSIC

Alpine Valley Music Theater

Racine Waterfront. Weekends from middle of June to beginning of September; call Chamber of Commerce for schedule: 633–2451.

PARKS AMD NATURE CENTERS

Colonial Park

End of High St.

Quarry Lake Park

Highways 38 and MM. Swimming, fishing, picnicking, scuba diving (divers must be certified). Entrance fee daily from Memorial Day to Labor Day (except Thurs. and Fri.).

RECREATION

Biking

Trail Map

City Hall Annex, Department of Parks and Recreation, 800 Center St.; telephone: 636–9131.

Charters

For more information on charters, call Fishing Charters of Racine: 633–6113

Captain Ken Deakins
Rt. 4, Box 120, Elkhorn 53121; telephone: 642–3562.

Captain Dennis Maas
11945 S. Loomis Rd, Wind Lake 53185; telephone: 895–2916.

Captain James Mauer
2409 Green St.; telephone: 639–7676.

Captain Richard Mauer
1324 Center St.; telephone: 632–9380.

Dick Pugh
622 Four Mile Rd.; telephone: 639–3825.

Rick Olson
1703 Erie St.; telephone: 637–8009.

Bob Stone
1309 Cleveland Ave.

Angelo Trentadue
151 Ohio St.

Fishing

Pier Fishing
Large government pier on the Lake at end of State St.

Smelt Dipping
Lake Michigan at Wind Point off Highway 32 and end of County G

Cliffside Park
Highway 32 and Michiana Rd.

Golf

Ives Grove (18-hole)
14101 Washington Ave., Union Grove; telephone: 878–3714.

Johnson Park (18-hole)
6200 Northwestern Ave.; telephone: 634–9576.

Shoop Park (9-hole)
County Trunk G; telephone: 639–9994.

Washington Park (9-hole)
2801 12th St.; telephone: 634–9846.

Hunting

For exact seasonal dates and areas for deer, pheasant, rabbit, squirrel, woodcock, call: 763–7637. License required.

Honey Creek
2 miles north of Burlington on County W. 932 acres.

Tichigan
3 miles northwest of Waterford on Marsh Rd. 1220 acres.

Marinas

Palmer Johnson, Inc.
811 Ontario; telephone: 633–8883.

Pugh's Peerless Marina
1001 Michigan Blvd.; telephone: 632–8515.

Wharf
931 Erie; telephone: 634–9303.

Swimming

Lake Michigan Beaches
North Beach 1501 Michigan Blvd.

Zoo Beach
2131 N. Main St.

Zoo

Racine Zoo and Park
2131 N. Main St.; telephone: 636–9189. Lovely zoo on top of bluff overlooking Lake Michigan. Summer: April–Oct., daily, 10–6; weekends, 10–7. Winter: Daily, 10–5.

RESTAURANTS

Alfredo's
1234 Douglas Ave.; telephone: 634–0425. Steaks, seafood. Daily, 11 AM–1 AM.

Golden Lantern
5005 Washington Ave.; telephone: 637–8574. Friday night fish fry and

Sunday brunch especially good. Mon.–Thurs., 6:30 AM–10 PM; Fri.–Sat., 7:30 AM–midnight; Sun., 7:30 AM–9 PM

Guido's
405 Three Mile Rd.; telephone: 681–1550. Daily, 11:30 AM–11 PM.

The Hub
1346 Grand Ave.; telephone: 632–8096. Mon.–Fri., 11:30 AM–4 PM; Sat.–Sun., 4 PM–11 PM. Call ahead for reservations.

SPECIAL EVENTS

Monument Square Art Fair
Third weekend in June.

Starving Artist Art Fair
First Sunday in August. For details, call: 636–9177.

Winter Carnival
Johnson's Park, Northwestern Ave. and Newman Rd.; telephone: 636–9131.

Salmon-a-Rama
Third week in July. For details, call the Chamber of Commerce.

THEATER

Golden Rondelle Theater
Johnson Wax Company, 1525 Howe St.; telephone: 554–2154. Call for exact schedule. Free admission. Films shown on regular basis: *To Fly, American Years,* and *To Be Alive.*

Racine Theater Guild
2519 Northwestern Ave.; telephone: 633–4218. Performances from late September through early June; call for schedule.

TOURS

Johnson Wax Company
Frank Lloyd Wright Administration Building, 14th and Franklin Sts.; telephone: 554–2154. This forty-five-minute tour covers main architectural points of interest and gives a broad overview of the company. Tour schedule: June–Aug., Mon.–Fri., 9:15, 10:15, 11:15, 1:15, 2:15, 3:15; Sept.–May, Mon.–Fri., 10:15, 11:15, 1:15, 2:15.

Milwaukee

Population: 1,637,000   Area Code: 414   Zip Code: 53201
Greater Milwaukee Convention and Visitors Bureau: 756 N. Milwaukee Street;
*   telephone: 273–3950 or 828 N. Broadway; telephone: 273–3950 Fun Line*
*   (daily rundown on events and attractions): 799–1177*

The Indians gave Milwaukee its name ("meeting place of the rivers"), but the Germans gave the city its flavor. They arrived by boat early in the nineteenth century, and unpacked their culture along with their household goods, transplanting from their old country to this new place their love of good music and good brew and their ancient recipes for schnitzel and spaetzle. Today this heritage has been translated into a 13,000-acre system of parks, a fine symphony orchestra, an opera company, good restaurants, and world-renowned breweries.

However, Milwaukee is no longer exclusively a German town, for now Poles, Irish, blacks, Serbs, Italians, and Greeks have each carved a niche, as can be seen in the park statues dedicated to their national heroes, churches that reflect different architectural heritages, and ethnic restaurants where pastas vie with gyros and kolaches. But it is the Germans with their love of things *gemütlichkeit* who have made Milwaukee a hometown city. Often called the Munich of America and ranking eleventh in size among American cities, Milwaukee remains a town that you immediately sense would be a good place to live.

Actually the city started as three towns, bristling with rivalry and split by the Milwaukee River. In 1835, when the Milwaukee region was officially recognized at the Green Bay land office, three men formally came into possession of Milwaukee. Solomon Juneau, a French trader who had arrived in 1818, called his settlement Juneautown; it lay between the Milwaukee River and Lake Michigan. Byron Kilbourn, a New Englander, bought the section west of the river and named it Kilbourntown. George H. Walker, a Virginian, purchased a section to the south. Just one year later, in 1836, Milwaukee County was officially established and the three men's settlements grew spectacularly. While financial instability marked the next two years, caused in good part by the Panic of 1837, it didn't discourage the immigrants. So many arrived that the original inhabitants — the

Milwaukee skyline. *Milwaukee Association of Commerce*

Potawatomi Indians, remnants of the once mighty tribe — found themselves being forced out. In fact, the end of one era and the beginning of another was unofficially observed on a memorable day in 1838 when all domestic and commercial activity stopped and the entire Milwaukee settlement paused to watch the Potawatomi, loaded into wagon caravans, silently move off to a new home in Kansas.

Meanwhile, rivalry between Juneautown and Kilbourntown was so bitter that the two towns would not get together on the layout of their streets, and, when the need for a bridge arose, the streets that led up to the river were not directly across from each other. The result was a slanted bridge that is still standing as a reminder of the old rivalry (which long since has turned into peaceful coexistence).

The three original owners of Milwaukee left their mark. In Juneau Park there stands a statue of the old fur trader. Kilbourn is immortalized by the busy street that bears his name, and Walker's Point is still a vital part of today's Milwaukee.

That there was any time for feuding is remarkable in view of an epidemic of cholera in 1838, plague in the 1840s, and the sinking of the *Lady Elgin,* a ship that went down in 1860 with 300 passengers lost. But those early pioneers were a hardy lot, not only surviving these disasters but finding plenty of time to socialize. This was a time when

Milwaukee blossomed forth with scores of taverns and beer gardens where whole families came to exchange banter and to drink brew. Barstool highchairs were even provided for the babies. Beer was what the people drank, though a touch of class was evident in the fancy hands-off cabinets where liquor and wine were kept. Cuspidors were everywhere and signs often gave the message, "If you spit on the floor at home, spit here, because we want you to feel at home." At the same time, however, elegant ladies who did not frequent such establishments and who wished a higher tone for Milwaukee, carried little bells and rang them vigorously if they came upon tobacco-spitting men.

Beer and the barons who brewed it have made a big difference in the city's history (three of the country's biggest breweries are still headquartered there and can be toured). But in only one year did the breweries lead Milwaukee's industrial list. It just isn't true that beer alone made Milwaukee famous!

Today Milwaukee is a truly diverse industrial and commercial community, often called "the machine shop of the world," for 40 percent of its work force is employed on assembly lines. In its 2400 factories, Milwaukee turns out such products as sausages, electronics, leather, and fine graphics. Milwaukee steam shovels helped dredge the Panama Canal, the city's turbine engines were used in harnessing Niagara Falls, and its gears have operated rolling mills all the way to Japan.

Of course, Lake Michigan plays a vital part in the distribution of these manufactured goods, with a natural harbor that is often compared to the Bay of Naples, providing a ready outlet to the world's markets. Milwaukee's colorful harbor is also busy with ferry boats that ply the water lanes to Michigan, and with recreational boats of all kinds. Six major parks along the Lakefront and a string of fine beaches provide good picnic spots and playgrounds, and the three-and-one-half-mile shorefront Lincoln Memorial Drive allows visitors to enjoy a view of the Lake throughout the year. America's Munich not only boasts the big Lake, but there are 160 smaller lakes within an hour's drive north, south, or west of the city.

The Milwaukee park system has facilities for golf, tennis, and a dozen other sports, and includes the Mitchell Park Conservatory, the city's excellent zoo, and plenty of open lands for picnickers who want to have their first-rate beer and sausage under first-rate groves of trees.

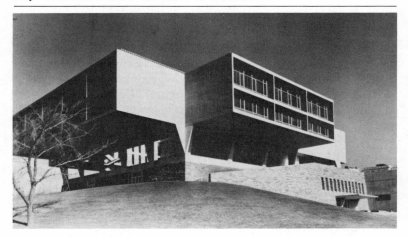

The Milwaukee Art Center and War Memorial, designed by architect Eero Saarinen. *Milwaukee Association of Commerce*

The city has a Performing Arts Center, a magnificent Museum of Natural History, the Milwaukee Art Center, and eleven institutions of higher learning. It is said that one out of every four Milwaukeans is in school either as a teacher or a student.

People have been among the city's proudest products, particularly the enlightened intellectual Forty-eighters who left Germany in the mid-nineteenth century, fleeing political revolutions, and bringing with them new educational and social ideas that contributed enormously to the city's cultural and political life. Carl Schurz, later secretary of the interior, was one of their leaders, as was Eric Seidel, the first socialist mayor of any American city (Seidel's secretary was a young man named Carl Sandburg). Other famous Milwaukeans have included General Douglas MacArthur; James Peck of Bad Boy fame; movie stars Spencer Tracy and Pat O'Brien; and Golda Meir.

The standards for civic excellence set by the Forty-eighters have influenced Milwaukee for generations, placing it high on the list of American cities in crime control, safety standards, and fire prevention. One year it was asked to withdraw from the nation's public health contest in order to give other cities a crack at the top prize!

Milwaukee has neither the excitement, the architecture, nor the variety of Chicago, its far bigger cousin just 80 miles to the south. But the nice thing about the city is that it doesn't much care. Milwaukee

St. Joan of Arc Chapel at Marquette University, Milwaukee.
Marquette University

seems to like its slower pace and its reputation as a safe and pleasant place to visit and an even better place to live.

ARCHITECTURE AND HISTORIC SITES

Annunciation Greek Orthodox Church, 1959
Frank Lloyd Wright
9400 W. Congress St., Wauwatosa; telephone: 461–9400. Frank Lloyd Wright reflecting St. Sophia. Mon.–Fri., 10–3; Sat., 2–4; guided tours by appointment.

* St. Josaphat, 1897–1901
2333 S. 6th St. Church (which is a basilica) and art museum of Polish history, built by common people from stones transported from Chicago's old Federal Building. Only Polish Basilica in North America.

St. Joan of Arc Chapel
Marquette University Campus, 601 N. 14th St. Fifteenth-century church from Rhone Valley brought to U.S. and ultimately donated to Marquette University. Exquisite tiny Gothic chapel with stone St. Joan kissed. Fine tapestries. Mass three times daily. Daily, 10–4.

* City Hall, 1895
200 E. Wells St. Flemish Renaissance building in tradition of great

public buildings of Europe. Tower bell with inscription: "When I sound the hour of the day/From this grand and lofty steeple/ Deem it a reminder, pray/ To be honest with the people."

Helfaer Community Service Building
1360 N. Prospect Ave. Jewish Federation building with Chagall tapestry in tribute to Golda Meir in the atrium garden. Weekdays, 8 AM–10:30 PM.

* Milwaukee Public Library, 1895
814 W. Wisconsin Ave.; telephone: 278–3000. Local history room contains material on the Great Lakes and fine ship model collection. Goethe House is in library. German-American collection and cultural affairs. Mon.–Thurs., 8:30 AM–9 PM; Fri., Sat., 8:30–5; Sun., 1–5.

* Turner Hall, 1882
1034 N. 4th St.; telephone: 273–5590. Headquarters for German turnverein movement.

Kilbournton House, 1844
Capitol Dr. and Highway 141. Original house occupied by pioneer Kilbourn. Summer: Tues., Thurs., Sat., 9–5; Sun., 1–5. Free admission.

* Frederick Pabst Mansion, 1890
2000 W. Wisconsin Ave.; telephone: 931–0808. Tues., Thurs., Sat., 10–3; Sun., 1–3.

ART CENTERS

Milwaukee Art Center and War Memorial
Eero Saarinen
750 N. Lincoln Memorial Dr. Tues.–Sun., 10–5; Thurs., noon–9; closed Mon.

* Villa Terrace Decorative Arts Museum
David Adler
2220 N. Terrace; telephone: 273–7290. Collection covers the period from 1620 to 1820. Sept.–June, weekends, 1–5; June–Sept., Wed.–Sun., 1–5. Admission free.

MUSEUMS

* **Charles Allis Art Library,** 1909
1630 E. Royall Pl.; telephone: 278–3010. Tues.–Sun., 1–5; Wed.,
6:30–9. Free admission.

EAA Air Museum
11311 W. Forest Home Ave. (10 miles SW on County 00, 1 1/4 mile S
of junction SR 24 and 100, Franklin, Wisconsin); telephone: 425–4860.
For the airplane buff. Mon.–Sat., 8:30–5; Sun., 11–5; closed Easter,
Thanksgiving, and Christmas.

Greene Memorial Museum
University of Wisconsin (Milwaukee) 3367 N. Downer Ave.; telephone: 963–4561 (call first). Mineral and fossil exhibits.

Milwaukee Public Museum
800 W. Wells St.; telephone: 278–2713. A fabulous natural history
museum. Daily, 9–5.

National Bowling Hall of Fame and Museum
5301 S. 76th St.; telephone: 421–6400, ext. 316. Ten strikes if you're a
bowler. Mon.–Fri., 9–4.

Brooks Stevens Automotive Museum
10325 N. Port Washington Rd., Mequon. An exceptional collection of
antique cars, including Excalibers. Spring and summer: daily, 10–5;
fall and winter: weekends only, 10–5.

MUSIC

Blatz Temple of Music
Washington Park, 4420 W. Vliet St.

Humboldt Park
3000 S. Howell Ave. Free outdoor concerts are held on summer
evenings at both Blatz Temple and Humboldt Park, but tickets for
seats must be reserved, call: 482–4270. You can bring picnics and sit
on grass. Light opera, classics, and popular musicals. Weekends, July
and first weekend in August.

The Milwaukee County Zoo covers more than 180 acres. *Milwaukee Association of Commerce*

Mitchell Park's three beehive-shaped domes. *Wisconsin Division of Tourism*

PARKS

Milwaukee is studded with small parks. For recreational information, call: 278–4366; the county park number is 278–4343.

Milwaukee County Zoo

10001 W. Bluemound Rd. (6 miles west on U.S. 18, between U.S. 45 and W-100); telephone: 771–3040. May–Labor Day, weekdays 9–5; Sun. and holidays, 9–6. After Labor Day, daily, 9:30–4:30.

Mitchell Park

524 S. Layton Blvd.; telephone: 278–4383. Milwaukee's spectacular conservatory, housed in three beehive-shaped domes. Plant collections are divided into tropical dome, arid dome, and show dome with changing flower shows. Park also contains every sort of recreational facility: tennis, skating, fishing, picnicking. Tues.–Sun., 9–9; Mon., 9–5.

Schlitz Audubon Center

1111 E. Brown Deer Rd. (U.S. 43, 10 miles north to W-100; at Brown Deer, exit and go east for 1 mile); telephone: 352–2880. 185 acres with endless trails, all sorts of eco-systems, and down to Lake Michigan's shores. Interpretive center. Also, hiking, cross-country skiing, and picnicking. Tues.–Sun., 9–5; closed Mon. and holidays.

Whitnall Park

5879 S. 92nd St., Hale's Corner; telephone: 425–8550 or 425–1130. Boerner Botanical Gardens: gorgeous outdoor gardens. Todd-Wehr Nature Center: 200 acres of prairie, savannah, woodlands, and wetlands. 20-acre lake; 4 miles of self-guided tours; outdoor amphitheater. Whitnall also offers every type of outdoor recreation with heavy emphasis on skating and cross-country skiing. Year round, 8 AM–10 PM.

RECREATION

Biking

Division of County Park

901 N. 9th; telephone: 278–4345. Trail maps for 76 miles of paths.

Charters

Lucky Boy Fishing
5600 W. Burnham; telephone: 545–9476.

Arjay Charter Service
8007 W. Meinecke Ave.; telephone: 453–3082.

Associated Fishing Charters of Milwaukee, Inc.
300 N. Plankinton Ave.; telephone: 263–2646. Association of seven different fishing boats.

Admiral's Wharf
236 S. Water; telephone: 276–0793.

D.J. Lake Michigan Fishing Charters
10722 S. 60 Franklin; telephone: 421–6581.

Joker's Wild Charter Service
8921 S. Chicago Rd.; telephone: 762–2770.

Ken's Fishing Charter Service
2859 S. 66th St.; telephone: 321–8552.

Kingfish Sport Charters, Ltd.
322 N. 62nd St.; telephone: 476–2590.

Wally's Charter Service
3310 N. 82nd St.; telephone: 871–7097.

Excursion Boats

The Iroquois
Milwaukee River dock at Clybourn St. Bridge; telephone: 354–5050. Trip takes about two hours. View Milwaukee's Lakefront, harbor, lighthouse, breakwater, and foreign ships in port. Travel under seven interesting river bridges. June–Labor Day; daily summer cruises, Mon.–Fri., 1 and 3 PM.

Golf

Brown Deer (18-hole)
7835 N. Green Bay Rd.; telephone: 352–8080.

Currie (18-hole)
3535 N. Mayfair Rd.; telephone: 453–7030.

Dretzka (18-hole)
12020 W. Bradley Rd.; telephone: 354–7300.

Grant (18-hole)
200 Hawthorne Ave.; telephone: 763–4646.

Greenfield (18-hole)
2028 S. 124th St.; telephone: 453–2340.

Lincoln (9-hole)
1000 W. Hampton; telephone: 962–2400.

Oakwood (18-hole)
3600 W. Oakwood Rd.; telephone: 281–6700.

Whitnall (18-hole)
5879 S. 92nd; telephone: 425–2183.

Horse Trails

Brown Deer Park
7600 N-3100 W.; telephone: 352–8080.

Ice-Skating

State Fair Park Olympic Ice Rink
Gate 6, 84th & Kearney; telephone: 476–3030. Only Olympic skating rink in U.S. U.S. Olympic team trains here. Hours vary.

Wilson Park Recreation Center
4001 S. 20th St., Milwaukee; telephone: 281–4610. Daily, 1–5, year round.

Marina

McKinley Marina
1750 N. Lincoln Memorial Dr.; telephone: 273–5224. 500 slips. Public boat launch.

Spectator Sports

BASEBALL

Brewers (American League)
County Stadium, East-West Freeway and Stadium Freeway; telephone: 933–1818.

BASKETBALL

Bucks (NBA team)
MECCA, 500 W. Kilbourn Ave.; telephone: 272–6030.

Marquette Warriors
MECCA, 500 W. Kilbourn Ave.; telephone: 224–7127.

Green Bay Packers (NFL football)
County Stadium, East-West Freeway and Stadium Freeway; telephone: 327–2717.

HOCKEY

Admirals
MECCA, 500 W. Kilbourn Ave.; telephone: 278–7711.

POLO

Polo Club (US Polo Association)
Uhlein Field, N. 70th and W. Good Hope Rd.; telephone: 224–5606.
June, July, August, on Sundays at 3 PM.

Swimming

Bay View Beach
3200 S. and 3200 E.

Big Bay Beach
5100 N. and 1700 E.

Bradford Beach
2400 N. and 2800 E.

Doctors Beach
8400 N. and 1900 E.

Grant Beach
6300 S. and 4000 E.

McKinley Beach
2000 N. and 2000 E.

South Shore Beach
2600 S. and 2400 E.

RESTAURANTS

Bavarian Wurst Haus
8310 W. Appleton Ave., Highway 41 N.; telephone: 464–0060. Daily, 11–11; Sun., 3–10.

Boder's On-the-River
11919 N. River Rd., Mequon; telephone: 242–9952. Fourth-generation country restaurant. Lunch and dinner; closed Mon.

Boulevard Inn
4300 W. Lloyd St.; telephone: 445–4221. Daily, 11:30–9; Sat., 11:30–10.

Grenadier's
747 N. Broadway; telephone: 276–0747. Elegant. Daily, 5:30–10:30; closed Sun.

Jacques (atop the Marine Plaza)
111 E. Wisconsin Ave.; telephone: 271–6356. Splendid Lake view. Luncheon, dinner; closed Sun. Free parking after 5:30.

Jean-Paul Restaurant
811 E. Wisconsin; telephone: 271–5400. Good French cuisine. Mon.–Thurs., 5–10; Fri., 5–11; Sat., 5–12.

John Ernst Café
600 E. Ogden Ave.; telephone: 273–5918. Oldest in Milwaukee. Excellent German fare. (Sing-alongs on Wed., Fri., and Sat. evenings.) Daily, luncheon and dinner; closed Mon. Free parking.

Karl Ratzsch's
320 E. Mason; telephone: 276–2720. Dinner music by a Viennese string trio. Daily, 11:30 AM–10:00.

Kosta's White Manor Inn
1234 E. Juneau; telephone: 274–4029. Daily, 11–11. Ample parking.

Mader's (downtown)
1041 N. 3rd St.; telephone: 271–3377. German; valuable collection of rare steins. Daily, 11:30–9. Ample free parking.

Old Town Serbian Gourmet House
522 W. Lincoln; telephone: 672–0206. Serbian restaurant with live tamburitza music Fridays and Saturdays. Lunch, 11:30–2:30; Tues.–Fri., dinner 5–11; closed Mon.

Oliver's Chalet (disco dancing)
728 N. Milwaukee St.; telephone: 278–8866. Wide variety of sandwiches. Dancing under an exciting lighting and sound system. Lunches; disco 9–2 AM (3:30 Sat.)

Pandl's Original Whitefish Bay Inn
1319 E. Henry Clay; telephone: 964–3800. Delicious and moderate-priced. Mon.–Sat., 11:30–2:30; Mon.–Thurs., 5–9; Fri.–Sat., 5–11.

Pieces of Eight
550 N. Harbor Dr.; telephone: 271–0597. Daily, 11:30; Sun. brunch, 11–3; dinner from 5. Ample parking.

Watts Tea Shop
761 N. Jefferson; telephone: 276–6352. Mon.–Sat., 11–3.

SCENIC VIEWS AND DRIVES

Lake Shore Drive
Along Lake Michigan from South Milwaukee into the northern suburbs. Drive includes Juneau Park with pioneer Juneau's log cabin, former Coast Guard station, War Memorial Center; good view of ducks and migrating birds in season, the Port of Milwaukee with ships of the world, yacht basin, swimming beaches, and eventually the elegant suburbs on the north shore of the Lake.

Walker's Point Area
Area around Walker Square, near 6th and National. For tours, call: 645–9222. This near south side area dates back to 1870s and is being restored. The huge clock on Allen Bradley Building dominates the

area and is a beacon for Lake ships. Interesting small homes of working-class people of the nineteenth century.

Water Tower Area
At Lakefront at North Ave. Contrasting area of upper-crust Milwaukee families of last century whose focal point was the 170-foot water tower.

SHOPPING

Florentine Antiques
18715 W. Greenfield Ave. New Berlin, Wisconsin; telephone: 782–5080. English, elegant, expensive, and discriminating. Sat., Sun., 11–5; weekdays, by appointment only.

Mindy's Antiques
W-220 (N. 5651-Townline Rd.) Sussex, Wisconsin; telephone: 246–3183. New England and Pennsylvania Dutch. Very good and very expensive. Daily, 9–5; closed Sun.

Peter Bentz
771 N. Jefferson; telephone: 271–8866. Excellent broad range from eighteenth century to Chinese. Tues.–Sat., 11–5.

Mid-America Antique Center
341 N. Milwaukee St. Seventy-five dealers on three floors. American primitives to art deco. Caveat: know your stuff before you bargain. Daily, 10–5; Sun., 1–4.

Stonewood Village
17700 W. Capital Dr., Brookfield. Interesting shops, boutiques, studios, and restaurant in a recreated New England village. Daily, 10–5:30; Sun., 1–4:30.

Cedar Creek Settlement
Cedarburg (15 miles northwest of Milwaukee). Built to resemble Cedarburg in 1892; browse through shops, art studios, clothing stores, crafts stores, and the Stone Mill Winery. Mon.–Sat., 10–5; Sun., 12–5.

Stonecroft
Highway C, Grafton. European-style merchants', artists', and craftsmens' village. Ice cream parlor and pub provide delicious food. Summer festivals and entertainment. Tues.–Sat., 10–5; Sun., 1–5.

SPECIAL EVENTS

Holiday Folk Fair
MECCA, 500 W. Kilbourn; for information, call: 933–0521. Great ethnic affair. Second or third weekend in November.

Lakefront Festival of Arts
750 N. Lincoln Memorial Dr.; for information, call: 271–7434. Giant fair of all the arts. Early summer.

Oktoberfest
Old Heidelburg Park, 700 W. Lexington Ave.; for information, call Visitors Bureau: 963–6971. Sausage, song, and everything in German tradition. Last three weekends of September, as in Munich.

Summerfest
Lakefront festival grounds; for information, call: 273–2680. Billed as largest, longest outdoor music festival in world. Early July.

Wisconsin State Fair
State Fair Park, East-West Freeway and W. Allis; for information, call: 257–8800. First or second week of August

THEATERS AND CIVIC CENTERS

MECCA (Milwaukee Exposition and Convention Center and Arena)
500 W. Kilbourn Ave.; telephone: 271–2750.

Melody Top
7201 W. Good Hope Rd.; telephone: 445–3777. Summer theater with leading Hollywood names.

* Pabst Theater
144 E. Wells; telephone: 271–3773. Nineteenth-century theater hosts dramatic and musical productions, dance performances, children's plays. Tours available (call first).

Performing Arts Center
929 N. Water; telephone: 273–7206. Home of Milwaukee's well-regarded choral, ballet, symphony, and theater groups.

TOURS

Miller Brewing Company
4000 W. State St.; telephone: 931–2000. The best beer tour in the biggest beer city. Slide show and a visit to Caves Museum (before refrigeration, beer was stored in caves). Ample free samples. Daily (except Sun.), on the hour; call in advance for group tours.

Pabst Brewery
917 Juneau; telephone: 347–7300. Beautiful copper kettles and fine hospitality in the Sternwirt Room. Daily (except Sat.), on the hour; call in advance for group tours.

Joseph Schlitz Brewery
234 W. Galena St.; telephone: 224–5262. The story of beer made clear here — from hops to Brown Bottle Hospitality Center. There are enough Schlitz stores on premises to serve three glasses to every adult in U.S. Small sample for you. Daily, on the hour; call in advance for group tours.

Usinger's Sausage Shop, 1880
1030 N. 3rd St.; telephone: 276–9100. Before touring a brewery, stop here and choose from dozens of varieties to go with your beer. Daily, 9–5; closed Sun.

Port Washington

Population: 10,000   Area Code: 414   Zip Code: 53074
Chamber of Commerce: 105 N. Franklin Street; telephone: 284–0900

Port Washington, though only 25 miles from Milwaukee, is not a bedroom community. Over the years it has kept its small-town flavor, partly because it is a fishing town and partly because it has maintained its identity as one of two major settlements of Luxemburgers in the U.S. The center of their life, St. Mary's Church, is now 125 years old.

Port Washington is called the City of Seven Hills. Its earliest settlers (starting with Worcester Harrison in 1835) were interested in establishing a harbor and a commercial fishing business. The latter flourished; the former floundered. The Smith Brothers Company has been catching and wholesaling and retailing fish since 1848, and they still run the popular Fish Shanty Restaurant. Though there are other commercial fishermen as well, and sport fishing has become big business, Port Washington's harbor is considered the worst on the lake. Some say that before each big storm, fishermen have to rush out to move their boats to safer open water. Despite the fact that the harbor has not been much improved in two rebuildings, oil tankers and coal and ore boats still manage to enter to service the city and the Wisconsin Electric Company, which supplies current to all of southern Wisconsin. Port Washington's factories and smoking chimneys seemed so typical of industrialized America that in 1888 they were photographed and used on post cards for distribution in Germany as illustrations of the fine Wisconsin employment market.

Port Washington was incorporated in 1848, the year Wisconsin became a state. It has suffered through two great fires, flood, tornado, and major unrest during the Civil War. In the early 1860s when the governor asked all able-bodied men to serve in the Union Army, some (Europeans who had come here to escape conscription) responded by destroying the draft rolls, throwing the commissioner down the court house steps, and capturing the local cannon.

Before the turn of the century it was more common to hear German than English at public gatherings. It was also common for excursion boats from Milwaukee to steam down for a Sunday

Port Washington Harbor. *Smith Brothers Fisheries*

afternoon in Columbia Park, complete with beer, song, and dance.

Today Port Washington is concerned with its heritage and is re-storing some of its old mansions and its historic district. The biggest private industry now is Simplicity Garden Equipment, a company started by a local boy in his family's garage.

ARCHITECTURE AND HISTORIC SITES

Eghart House, 1872

316 W. Grand Ave.; telephone: 284–4918. This marvelous restored house is an authentic representation of its era. May–Nov. 1, Sun., 1–5 PM; by appointment, year round.

Kiekhaefer Barn, 1897

1/4 mile east of U.S. 141 on County M, Mequon, WI. Now on grounds of Our Lady of the Lake Convent, this octagonal barn is typical of several barns in the area.

* Ozaukee County Courthouse, 1902

109 W. Main St. Richardsonian-style Romanesque building.

Ozaukee County Pioneer Village

Wisconsin 57 and 84 (Fredonia); telephone: 692–9910. June–Oct., Wed., Sun., noon–5 PM.

* Pebble-Dodge House, 1848

146 Wisconsin Ave. A gatehouse for the power plant, this house was built from pebbles picked up from Lake Michigan's shores.

* St. Mary's Catholic Church, 1882

N. Johnson and Van Buren. This French-Gothic church serves as a landmark to Lake Michigan sailors because of its prominent hill site.

St. Mary's Cemetery, 1854

N. Webster and Dodge St. This beautiful old cemetery was originally established to bury the many victims of a cholera plague.

Union Cemetery, 1855

Park and Chestnut St. This interesting old cemetery marks the resting place for the anchor from the steamship *Toledo,* wrecked in 1856, and contains the remains of the bodies from the steamer, *Niagara.*

U.S. Lighthouse, 1860

311 E. Johnson. Originally the light was on the roof. Now this old building is a residence for the Coast Guard.

MUSEUM

Sunken Treasures Maritime Museum

At Harbor off S. Wisconsin St.; telephone: 284–5614. Histories, artifacts, and sunken treasures recovered by skin divers. May–Oct., daily, 10–8.

PARKS

Harrington Beach State Park

7 miles north of Port Washington on Highway 32; at Cedar Beach Rd. in village of Belgium turn east to Lake Michigan; telephone: 285–3015. This lovely 636-acre shoreline park has facilities for picnicking, fishing, swimming, hiking. Open year round, 8 AM–11 PM.

Lower Lake Park and Upper Lake Park

Lake Dr. Two separate city park areas with picnicking. Upper Lake Park is on the north bluff and the panoramic view of town, harbor, and lake is spectacular.

RECREATION

Boats

Port Washington Harbor
End of Grand Ave. at Lake Michigan. Facilities for pleasure boats.

Charters

In addition to the charters listed below, there is good fishing from harbor and pier for landlubbers.

Triton Captain Craig Smith
Telephone: 284–0433 (business); 284–2196 (residence).

Fishing Pox Captain Gus Rankey
Telephone: 377–8824.

Fox Bros. Captains Dan and Mike Fox
Telephone: 258–0657.

Captain Terry Thierbach
Telephone: 284–3695.

Captain Ralph Zachow
Telephone: 284–3589.

Golf

Hawthorne Hills (18-hole)
County I, Fredonia; telephone: 692–2151.

Meekwon Park (18-hole)
6333 W. Bonniwell Rd., Mequon; telephone: 242–1310.

RESTAURANTS

Port Hotel Restaurant, 1902
101 E. Main; telephone: 284–9473. Famous for roast beef and steaks. Daily, 5–10:30; Sun.–Fri., 11:30 AM–2 PM.

Smith Bros. Fish Shanty, Est. 1848
100 N. Franklin; telephone: 284–5592. Wonderful fish dinners. Daily, 11:30–9; summer hours longer.

SHOPPING

Ewig Bros. Fish House
128 S. Wisconsin; telephone: 284–5855. Fresh fish, smoked fish, delicatessen. Daily, 8–7.

Smith Bros. Fish Shanty
100 N. Franklin; telephone: 284–5592. Fresh fish, smoked fish, delicatessen. Daily, 8:30–7; longer summer hours.

Smith Bros. Fisheries
109 E. Grand Ave.; telephone: 284–5578. Retail store in wholesale fish house. Daily, 8–6.

Horicon Marsh

State Headquarters: Headquarter Hill, N. Palmatory Street, Horicon; tele-phone: 414–485–4435
Federal Headquarters: Rt. 2 Mayville; telephone: 387–2658

A trip to Horicon, though way off the Lake's shore, is a must for anyone with extra time. The period from late August through December provides one of nature's four-star revues as hundreds of thousands of Canada geese wing into the Horicon Marsh (part of the Mississippi flyway) on the way from Hudson Bay to their wintering grounds at the confluence of the Ohio, Missouri, and Mississippi rivers.

The Marsh is 45 miles west of Port Washington on Wisconsin Rt. 33. It is jointly owned: the federal government owns 20,796 acres to the north (Horicon National Wildlife Refuge) and the state of Wisconsin 10,857 acres to the south (Horicon Marsh Wildlife Area). The total area, marsh and uplands, is a birder's paradise with some 240 species of birds, including egret, blue heron, all manner of duck, and the remarkable great gray visitors from the far north. There are also white-tailed deer, muskrats, fox, and numerous other small game.

Hunting and fishing are permitted in season (the former is scientifically planned to keep any species from overpopulating). There are canoe trails, hiking trails, many marked snowmobile trails, and a boat tour that bills itself as the Little Everglades of the North, and does indeed cut through the vast wetlands. It is also possible to drive the whole circumference of the Marsh . . . on what is happily billed as the Wild Goose Parkway.

TOUR

Blue Heron Tours
101 Main St.; telephone: 485–2667. Memorial Day–October, tour begins at 2 PM. Call ahead for reservations.

Canada geese congregate at the Horicon Marsh during fall migration. *Edgar G. Mueller*

Only days old fawn lies in a secluded spot in a Wisconsin nature preserve. *Edgar G. Mueller*

Cedar Grove

Population: 1400   Area Code: 414   Zip Code: 53013

Oostburg

Population: 1400   Area Code: 414   Zip Code: 53070

A few miles south of Sheboygan, just off Rt. I-43, lie Cedar Grove (on W-32) and Oostburg (County AA just east of W-32), two small communities that still retain their Dutch flavor though they were first settled by Hollanders in the 1840s. A roadside sign describes the tragedy of the steamboat *Phoenix,* sunk in 1847, when 127 immigrating Hollanders lost their lives. (See Sheboygan — a Dutch bible rescued from the shipwreck is on display in the Sheboygan County Museum.) It's worthwhile to get off the expressway to visit these towns, to see the lovely old churches, the big windmill and museum in Cedar Grove, and to sample the *oliebollen* (fried dumplings) or *vetbollen* (coffee cake) in a local restaurant. The annual Dutch Festival in July, sponsored by both communities, is a colorful tribute to the area's ethnic origins.

MUSEUM

Het Museum
118 S. Main. Sponsored by the Holland Guild Gezelschap, this restored blacksmith shop contains local items and artifacts dating back to 1853. July 1–Labor Day, Wed. & Fri., 6:30–8:30 PM.

RESTAURANT

DeSmidt's Good and Plenty
115 S. Main; telephone: 668-8915. The Dutch menu provides many good foods. Mon.–Sat., 8 AM–10:30 PM.

SPECIAL EVENT

Dutch Festival
Cedar Grove's Main St. Begins on Thursday night of the last weekend

in July with street scrubbing and ends on Sunday with a joint community worship service. Parades, bands, folk dancing, drill teams, and lots of Dutch food.

Oostburg and Cedar Grove, Wisconsin, celebrate their Dutch ancestry in their annual Holland Festival. *Division of Wisconsin Tourism*

Sheboygan

Population: 49,250   Area Code: 414   Zip Code: 53081
Chamber of Commerce: 531 N. 8th Street, P.O. Box 687; telephone: 457-9491

The Chippewa named Sheboygan (which means "sound of wind and rumbling") for the rushing rapids of the Sheboygan River. Since then it has been called the city of cheese, chairs, children, and churches, and it is also the place where the Kohler Company's indoor plumbing put a welcome end to the outhouse. Today Sheboygan is a shopping hub for more than 175,000 residents of nearby communities.

Missionaries and fur traders came here but the first settler was William Farnsworth who helped plat the place in 1836, buying half the plat himself, and setting aside land for hog pasture that later became the public square.

The Mouth, as Sheboygan was called, boomed when the wagons came rumbling through on the way to the Northwest, and stopped to load up on salt and codfish, peppermint candy, and whisky. Some of the people stayed, of course, and by 1845 one enterprising resident had a fleet of boats traveling the Lake, using Sheboygan as home harbor. Daily steamships checked in from Chicago and Buffalo . . . until the weather closed in. In 1847 a young woman wrote her grandfather, "The boats have stopped running for about a week past, and we are of course, like all the lake towns in this newly-settled country, somewhat isolated from the rest of the world." But religious and political strife in Germany (and then in Holland) brought large numbers of Europeans to Sheboygan. Promoters' leaflets handed out in the old country had told of good farmland and opportunity. And so they came, some of them the intellectual Forty-eighters fired by their devotion to political freedom, importing their singing societies, their debate clubs, and their athletic groups (there were even wooden exercise horses in the public square for a time). They built neat houses and gardens, and they gave Sheboygan the home-loving feeling it still has. Some settled on farms, raising first wheat, then peas, and eventually dairy herds. They built plank roads into the interior and, with federal money, improved their harbor. Today the harbor is partly commercial, partly for pleasure boats.

Waelderhaus in Kohler, Wisconsin. *Kohler Foundation, Inc.*

While the area still had forests and lumbering, woodwork and furniture factories were vital industries. Millions of chairs were built in Sheboygan. It also produced shoes and brooms, limestone, gloves, and pianos, and by 1875 there were forty-five cheese factories. But as the timber ran out, forty factories closed. Fortunately, by then there were two major employers, the J. J. Vollrath Company, founded in 1850, and the Kohler Company, 1873. The latter was to become synonymous with Sheboygan. During its first ten years the company manufactured farm instruments, but in time the emphasis shifted to the modern bathroom, from the one-piece lavatory (1908) to the apron tub, and on and on to a great empire. In time, John Kohler moved his company 4 miles out of town, believing that his workers deserved "roses as well as wages." A planned town (named Kohler of course) was laid out by the great designer Frederick Law Olnstead (who had also created New York's Central Park). Ever since those days there have been Kohlers in public life, serving as Sheboygan mayors, as Wisconsin governors, and as general benefactors. They restored the Old Wade House (an early and fine stagecoach stop), and in 1954 gave the people Old Wade House State Park. They donated an art center, the country's largest outdoor ethnic museum, the beautiful John Michael Kohler–Terry Andrae State Park on Lake Michigan, and the Waelderhaus, a magnificent museum built in the style of ancient homes in the Austrian province from which the original Kohler came.

ARCHITECTURE AND HISTORIC SITES

A walking tour taken from the pamphlet "Heritage Walk in Old Sheboygan" is available at the Chamber of Commerce.

* Zaegel Building, 1886
632 N. 8th St. Late-Victorian retail store.

* Jung Carriage Works, 1877
829 Pennsylvania Ave. Pretentious Richardsonian Romanesque built to house Jacob Jung's flourishing carriage and wagon trade.

Third Ward Schoolhouse, 1876
Typical two-room primary schoolhouse. Notice stand of silver maple trees, said to be as old as building.

The Fishing Shanties
North River Bank. Evidence of an important early Sheboygan industry.

1840 Settlement
North 7th Street and Jefferson Ave. The original remaining buildings are at 523 S. 7th St., 707 Jefferson Ave., 719 Jefferson Ave., 721 Jefferson Ave., and 519 S. 7th St.

* Friendship House, 1880
721 Ontario Ave. Well-preserved Italian villa residence. Note "Tuscan" cupola.

Grace Episcopal Church, 1871
N. 7th St. and Ontario Ave. Cream-colored bricks locally made. Victorian Gothic.

First Baptist Church, 1845
521 Ontario Ave. New England–type church patterned after Greek temple.

Henry Jung Home, 1901
530 Ontario Ave. Happy combination of several styles: Victorian Gothic, Palladian, Neo-Classic, Victorian, and Baroque!

Blackstock House, 1864
507 Washington Ct. Imposing example of the Victorian Italianate style translated into wood.

Peter Reiss Home, 1906
1227 N. 7th St. Very grand old home that was often the scene of early Sheboygan's grand social events. Romanesque and Gothic.

Zion Church, 1888
North 6th and Erie Ave. Fine example of Gothic style; windows are thought to be among finest in city.

CEMETERY

Sheboygan Indian Mound Park
From Bus 141S, turn east on County EE; at South 12th St., turn south to Panther Ave. (east of Hoffmann's at Riverdale Park entrance) and travel east on Panther Ave. to South 9th St.
Fifteen-acre park contains eighteen rare early Wisconsin Woodland Indian mounds dating AD 500–1000. One of these mounds, shaped like animals, displays an exposed burial with artifacts. Daily, 7 AM–9 PM.

MUSEUMS AND ART CENTERS

John Michael Kohler Arts Center
608 New York Ave.; telephone: 458–6144. Built by John Michael Kohler in 1882, this Italian villa–style home was deeded by the Kohler family in 1966 to be used as a community arts center. Mon., 7–9 PM; Tues.–Fri., noon–5; Sat.–Sun., 1–5. Closed Jan. and holidays.

* Sheboygan County Museum
3110 Erie Ave.; telephone: 458–1103. Built in the early 1850s by a German architect for Judge David Taylor, this old brick house served as a dairy farm; county jail; German prisoner-of-war detention center during World War II; and finally, in 1954, became a museum. (If the guards permit, you can see prisoners' graffiti in the tower.) April–Sept., Tues.–Sat., 10–5; Sun., 1–5 PM.

Waelderhaus
Highway 23 West from Lake Michigan to High St. in village of Kohler, turn left on High St. and follow to end; telephone: 458–1972. Lovely, authentic hand-carved reproduction of an Austrian "house in the woods." Tours daily, 2, 3, 4 PM, except holidays.

Wade House and the Jung Carriage Museum, 1850
Route 23 and Kettle Moraine Dr.; telephone: 526–3551. Built as a stagecoach inn along the old Sheboygan–Fond du Lac plank road, this and its companion Butternut House have been painstakingly restored. The Carriage Museum, a short ride in a horse-drawn bus from Wade House, features one of the U.S.'s finest carriage collections. May–Oct., daily, 9–5.

ORCHARD

Waldo Orchards
Rt. 1 (Highway 28 southwest of Sheboygan), Waldo; telephone: 528–8336. Apples! Apples! Apples! Thirty varieties grown on 75 acres of trees. Cold storage room makes apples available all year round. Pick your own in season. Open daily.

PARKS

City

Fountain Park
N. 8th St., between Erie and Ontario. Sheboygan's public square, land for this park was set aside in 1836. If you can stand the taste, the famous mineral water is still available.

Shooting Park
6th at Wilson. This 25-acre park overlooks Lake Michigan.

Quarry Park
Bus 141 at Pigeon River. Woodsy with good swimming and picnicking facilities; 45 acres.

Vollrath Park
North Third at Park Ave. Natural bowl for sports; playground and picnicking; 14 acres.

Snowmobiler sets off near Sheboygan, Wisconsin.

Terry Andrae State Park, Sheboygan, Wisconsin. *Wisconsin Natural Resources Department*

County

Broughton Sheboygan County Marsh Park
Highway 67 and County FF; telephone: 876–2535. A 6,900-acre park with fifty campsites, a marina, wildlife refuge, hiking and snowmobiling trails, hunting, fishing.

State

John Michael Kohler–Terry Andrae State Parks
2 miles south of Sheboygan off U.S. 141 at County V on Lake Michigan; telephone: 452–3457. Magnificent stretch (1,000 acres) of shoreline park includes 105 campsites, beaches, hiking and cross-country ski trails, bridle trails, and nature tours and lectures in Sanderling Nature Center in summer.

Kettle Moraine State Forest Northern Unit
Highway 23 west out of Sheboygan to Greenbush; telephone: 626–2116. This geologically significant region comprises deep lowlands and kettle lakes with 32 miles of hiking trails, 23 miles of snowmobile trails, 12 miles of bridle trails, plus facilities for picnicking, hunting, fishing, camping, bicycling, and general sightseeing; 12,500 acres.

RECREATION

Boating

C. Reiss Coal Company Marina
1011 S. 8th St.; telephone: 457–4411.

Riverside Marina
525 S. Commerce St.; telephone: 457–2241.

Sheboygan Yacht Club
214 Pennsylvania Ave.; telephone: 458–6601.

The Wharf
733 S. Franklin; telephone: 458–0051.

Fishing Charters

Captain Merle Johnson
Telephone: 233–1522.

Captain Bruce Klein
Telephone: 284–0224.

Captain Dennis Rakow
Telephone: 452–0860.

Captain Chuck Reilly
Telephone: 787–3665.

Captain Ken Stegemeyer
Telephone: 452–9748.

Captain Ed Vasselos
Telephone: 458–4208.

Fishing on Lake Michigan

Fishing spots are listed in geographical order, north to south.

Mouth of Black River
End of Black River Rd. at Lake.

Edgewater Plant
End of Washington Ave. at Lake.

Jetties off North Side Beach

South Pier at Sheboygan Harbor
Fisherman's Rd. at Lake.

North Pier at Sheboygan Harbor
End of Ontario at Lake.

Jetties at Water Plant
End of Broughton Dr. at Lake.

Mouth of Pigeon River
End of County L-S at Lake.

Golf

Riverdale Country Club (18-hole)
5008 S. 12th St.; telephone: 458–2561.

Town and Country (18-hole)
6521 County Trunk J; telephone: 458–8724.

Music

Band Concerts
Fountain Park Band Shell, N. 8th St., between Erie and Ontario. June, July, August, Wed., 7:30 PM.

Swimming

King Park (south side).
End of Washington Ave. at Lake.

Base at North Pier
End of Ontario at Lake.

RESTAURANTS

Baxters Beef and Pizza
821 N. 8th St.; telephone: 457–2496. Daily, 11 AM–2 AM.

Geno's Top of the First
607 N. 8th St.; telephone: 457–9050. Sheboygan's skyscraper restaurant with good view of Lake Michigan and the city. Mon.–Fri., 11 AM–2 PM, 5–9:30 PM; Sat., 5–10 PM.

Hoffbrau Cocktail Lounge and Supper Club
1132 N. 8th St.; telephone: 458–4153. Tues.–Sun., 11:30 AM–2 PM; Tues.–Thurs., 5:30–10 PM; Fri.–Sat., 5:30–11 PM; Sun., 4:30–10 PM.

Hoffman's at Riverdale
5008 S. 12th St.; telephone: 458–2128. Country club setting. Mon.–Sat., 5–11 PM; Sun., noon–10 PM.

Zieggy's Tavern
933 Indiana Ave.; telephone: 457–9758. Super sandwiches. Tues.–Sat., 11:30 AM–11 PM; Sun., 10 AM–6 PM.

SHOPPING

James Darkow Antiques
110 E. Mill, Plymouth; telephone: 892–2786. General line. Sun.–Mon., 12–4; Wed.–Sat., 9–5.

Two in the Attic Antiques
RR 3–141 S.; telephone: 452–5424. Browsing in a farm setting! Mon.–Sat., 10–6; Sun., noon–6.

Plaza 8
North 8th St. between St. Clair and Center. Beautiful renovated open-air complex includes forty stores, three theaters, an art center, library, and eleven restaurants.

Plymouth Cheese Counter
Highway 57 and County PP; telephone: 892–8781. Mon.–Fri., 8–6; Sat., 9–6; Sun., 10–6.

Schwarz Retail Fish Company Market
828 S. Franklin; telephone: 452–0576. Fresh Lake fish from one of Lake Michigan's largest fish houses. Mon.–Thurs., 8–6; Fri., 8–8; Sat., 9–4:30.

The Wharf
733 S. Franklin; telephone: 458–0051. Have your own fish cleaned or smoked or buy your own. Mon.–Fri., 7–6; Sat., 9–5; Sun., 9–3.

SPECIAL EVENTS
For specific information, call the Chamber of Commerce.

Polar Bear Club
Lake Michigan swim. January 1, New Year's Day.

Dog Show
Sheboygan Municipal Service Building. Seventeenth Sunday of the year.

John Michael Kohler Art Center Art Fair
Third weekend in July.

Lightning Sail Races
Off Sheboygan Yacht Club. Wednesday evenings in the summer.

Coho Derby
Second Friday, Saturday and Sunday in August. Prizes awarded.

Sheboygan County Fair
County Fairgrounds, Plymouth. 4-H contestants exhibit projects, grandstand shows. Labor Day Weekend.

Road America Sports Car Races
Elkhart Lake on W67. Billed as 4 miles of the greatest natural road-racing track in the world. One weekend in June, July, and August.

TOURS

Gibbsville Cheese Company
West on County oo off W 32, Sheboygan Falls; telephone: 564–3242. Family-run for over fifty years, this cheese factory specializes in cheddar and colby cheeses. Retail store on premises. April through October. By appointment.

Kohler Company
I-43 west on Highway 23; telephone: 457–4441. Hour-and-a-half tour includes every aspect of plumbing production from foundry work to the enamel producing. No cameras. Mon.–Fri., 9 AM and 1 PM (only children over fourteen). Reservations suggested.

Lake-to-Lake Dairy
1606 Erie Ave.; telephone: 457–5566. Modern dairy, including cottage cheese and cream products. Tours by appointment.

Manitowoc

Population: 35,000   Area Code: 414   Zip Code: 54220

Two Rivers

Population: 15,000   Area Code: 414   Zip Code: 54241
Manitowoc–Two Rivers Chamber of Commerce: 1515 Memorial Drive, Box 603
  Manitowoc, WI 54220; telephone: 684–5575

Manitowoc (which means "home of the good spirit") and Two Rivers have much in common: wonderful locations on the Lake, lovely parks cut by glaciers into kettle moraines, good harbors and navigable rivers that made it possible for pioneers to boat into the interior. And both have seen terrible shipwrecks off their shores.

Manitowoc is the larger of the two. In 1847 the *Citizen,* first wooden sailing ship built on Lake Michigan, was launched. The clipper ships followed; the town has been called the Clipper City, and has a reputation as a shipbuilding town. Manitowoc was home base for the Goodrich Steamship Company, which built the *City of Ludington;* the *City of Grand Rapids;* and the *Christopher Columbus,* a gleaming white boat with pink stacks, which ferried 2 million people along the Chicago Lakefront during the World's Columbian Exposition. (One of the best Goodrich skippers was Fredrick B. Pabst, who later became a blue-ribbon brewer in Milwaukee.) During World War I, Manitowoc built thirty ocean-going freighters, and a war later, submarines, LCTs and tankers. Although today the only shipbuilder is Burger Boats, which makes custom yachts, the life of the Lake lives on in Manitowoc's first-rate maritime museum aboard the U.S.S. *Cobia,* which is anchored downtown, and in the fact that many retired seamen make Manitowoc home port.

In the early days Manitowoc had bear roaming the countryside, and the Ringling Brothers Circus purchased its first bears from this area.

Today Manitowoc has 125 industries, which produce toys, evaporated milk, lift cranes, and canned vegetables. The two cities are

U.S.S. *Redfin* on its maiden voyage. Lake Michigan was the practice area for the submarines built in Manitowoc during World War II. *Manitowoc Maritime Museum*

among the country's largest producers of aluminum cookware. South of town is a shop that has restored Duesenbergs for such celebrities as Gary Cooper and William Randolph Hearst. Probably the most startling thing to hit Manitowoc was a fragment of the Russian Sputnik IV, which two policemen found embedded in a local sidewalk one morning. NASA verified it, and the government sent most of it back to Russia, but a replica stands today in the Rahr Civic Center in downtown Manitowoc. Thorstein Veblen, the economist, was the city's most famous native.

If Manitowoc built the boats, Two Rivers (named for the Neshote and Mishicot rivers) caught the fish, and the town still has one of the major commercial fleets on the Lake. French Canadians, many of whose descendants still live in the area, started it all in their Mackinaw boats. By the 1870s a local fishery was handling 400,000 pounds of whitefish a year. When the whitefish began to disappear, the men turned to trout and sturgeon, including what is reported to be the largest sturgeon ever caught, weighing 160 pounds and measuring over 6 feet. When the lamprey eel appeared, the trout dwindled too, leaving mostly alewives (used for animal food) and smelt. Since the mid-60s the introduction of chinook, coho, and steelhead has turned things around. Today Two Rivers is an ideal fishing ground because its sand point (the largest on Lake Michigan's shores), stretches 9 miles out into the water. The current fleet moors half a mile from the harbor at 17th Street.

Two Rivers has a Catholic Church at one end, staring at a Lutheran Church at the other. Perhaps both of them stare even more sternly at the Big Point Beach Nuclear Plant operating just north of the city.

The lovely old Two Rivers lighthouse, built in 1883, is now part of the Rogers Street Project, a restored fishing village with a museum.

Two Rivers claims (as does Evanston, Illinois) that it was the birthplace of the ice cream sundae. In 1881, George Hallauer asked the local soda fountain proprietor to top his ice cream with the chocolate sauce ordinarily used for sodas. He did, charged a nickel, and began to sell the concoction only on Sundays. One weekday a little girl ordered the ice cream with sauce, pleading "Pretend it's Sunday." Later the bell-shaped dishes became known as "sundae dishes," and the treat appeared in soda fountains all over the world.

ARCHITECTURE AND HISTORIC SITES

A marvelous county historical map entitled "Foot Paths of Our Heritage" is available at the court house, 1010 S. 8th. ($1.00).

Coast Guard Station
13 East St., Two Rivers. This station, with two boats assigned to it, is one of the largest on the lake.

First German Lutheran Church, 1872
S. 8th Street and Marshall, Manitowoc. A simple brick house of worship.

North Pier and Lighthouse
North Lake St., Manitowoc. The North Pier, half a mile long, protects the Manitowoc harbor. Great spot for fishing and ferry watching.

Rogers Street Fishing Village and Museum
Two Rivers. The two-block area along the East Twin River has always been a gathering place for Two Rivers' fishermen. It includes an 1883 lighthouse, museum building, and fishing equipment. Daily, 10–4.

St. Boniface Catholic Church, 1888
S. 10th Street and Marshall, Manitowoc. Appreciative of its past, St. Boniface being the oldest Catholic church in town, the congregation has kept this Victorian Gothic as it was built.

Spindler House, 1895

N. 6th and Park, Manitowoc. Built by a family in the construction business, the four-story house reflects what was considered the best in its time.

MUSEUMS

Historical Village

5 miles west of Manitowoc on County JJ. This restored village depicts Manitowoc County as it was at the turn of the century. Donations welcome.

Manitowoc Maritime Museum

809 S. 8th St., Manitowoc; telephone: 684–8381. Great museum telling the story of the Great Lakes through the media of well-displayed exhibits, models, and photographs. One section devoted to submarines built in Manitowoc during World War II. June 1–Labor Day, daily, 9–5; rest of year, Mon.–Fri., 11–4; Sat.–Sun., 10–5.

Rahr-West Civic Center and Public Museum

610 N. 8th St., Manitowoc; telephone: 684–4181. Housed in an 1891 Victorian mansion are Indian and early settler artifacts alongside modern art and a Chinese Ivory collection, but all tastefully displayed. Well worth seeing. Don't miss the Sputnik IV fragment. Tues.–Fri., 9–4:30; Sat.–Sun., 1–4; closed holidays.

Submariner's Memorial U.S.S. *Cobia*

9th and Quay St., Manitowoc; telephone: 684–8381. Tour this World War II submarine. June 1–Labor Day, daily, 9–5; rest of year, Sat.–Sun., noon–5.

PARKS

City

Lincoln Park and Municipal Zoo

122 N. 8th St., Manitowoc.

Manitou Park

On Michigan Ave., 1 mile west of 18th St., Manitowoc. Small park for picnicking; boating on river.

Neshota Park

Pierce and 22nd, Two Rivers. Beaches and picnicking.

Silver Creek Park
1/2 mile south of Viebahn St. on County LS. Beautiful park for all seasons along Lake Michigan.

Two Creeks Park
Two Creeks Rd. and Lake Michigan (8 miles north of Two Rivers). Lovely setting on Lake Michigan.

Two Creeks Sunken Forest
In town of Two Creeks on M42, north of Two Rivers. Recently discovered glacial forest and petrified wood. Park being developed.

County

Maribel Caves County Park
18 miles north of Manitowoc on U.S. 141. Limestone formations and native fauna will delight nature lovers and hikers. April through Oct.

Richard Drumm Memorial Forest
W 147, 1/4 mile east U.S. 141 (18 miles north of Manitowoc). Owned by the Izaak Walton League; 36 acres feature a unique forested area. Hiking paths follow river.

Woodland Dunes Nature Center
Highway 42 to Woodland Dr. to Goodwin Rd. An oasis of marshland, swamps, sandy fields and meadows, and wooded ridges between Manitowoc and Two Rivers. Wildlife research area and wildflower sanctuary.

State

Point Beach State Forest and Rawley Point Lighthouse
6 miles northeast of Two Rivers on W42 to County VV. Turn right on VV into park; telephone: 794–7480. This 2,770-acre state forest lies next to Lake Michigan and provides swimming, fishing, hiking, 149 campsites, and winter sports. Rawley Point Lighthouse, 1853, which is in Point Beach State Forest and is operated by U.S. Coast Guard has one of the most powerful beacons on Lake Michigan. With advance reservations, visitors may scale lighthouse.

RECREATION

Boating

Hika Park
County LS (Cleveland) at Lake

Manitowoc Harbor Municipal Boat Ramp
N. Lake St. at Lakefront

Manitou Park
On Michigan Ave., 1 mile west of 18th St.

Two Rivers Harbor
Mouth of river at Lakefront

Charters

You can also fish on piers and in harbor areas in Manitowoc and Two Rivers (see Parks for additional sites).

Two Rivers-Manitowoc Charter Fishing Association
P.O. Box 82 Two Rivers; telephone: 793–3474.

Sauve's Charter Service
Cool City Marina, 1902 Washington St., Two Rivers; telephone: 793–3344.

Captain Glenn Schultz
2023 E. River St.; telephone: 388–4010.

Terry's Charter Service
1160 Stead Dr., Menasha,; telephone: 725–6952.

Trophy Charter Service
1341 Kellner St., Manitowoc, telephone: 682–4041.

Two Rivers Charter Service
1618 29th St.; telephone: 794–1215.

Golf

Fairview Golf Course (9-hole)
Route 2, Two Rivers; telephone: 794–8726.

Fox Hills Country Club (27-hole)
Route 1, Mishicot; telephone: 755–2376.

Meadow Links (18-hole)
1540 Johnson Dr., Manitowoc; telephone: 682–6842.

Skiing

There are five sites in the county for downhill skiing. For details, contact the Chamber of Commerce.

Snowmobiling

68 miles of public snowmobile tracts in county. For details, contact the Chamber of Commerce.

Swimming

Lake Michigan Beaches
1900 S. 9th St., Manitowoc. See Parks for other swimming sites.

RESTAURANTS

Carlton Supper Club
1515 Memorial Dr., Two Rivers; telephone: 793–1314. Lovely view of Lake Michigan. Daily, 6:30 AM–10 PM.

Fox Hills Resort
Route 1, Mishicot; telephone: 755–2376. Good variety. Daily, 7 AM–10 PM.

Martine's
214 N. 8th St., Manitowoc; telephone: 684–7179. Good Italian food. Mon.–Fri., 11:30 AM–2 PM, 5–11; Sat.–Sun., 5–11.

Stephen's Charcoal House
U.S. 151 near Silver Lake Park, Manitowoc; telephone: 682–4636. Steaks are the specialty. Tues.–Thurs., 5–10 PM; Fri.–Sat., 5–11 PM; Sun., 11–2, 4–8.

SHOPPING

Mid-Cities Mall Shopping Center
Between Manitowoc and Two Rivers along W42. Twenty-five stores

and services, featuring a summertime farm market on Saturdays and flea market on third Saturday of each summer month.

SPECIAL EVENTS

Call the Chamber of Commerce for details.

Whitewater Canoe Races
4-mile race on Manitowoc River. First weekend in April.

Manitowoc County Art Show
May.

Snow Festival Days in Two Rivers
Parade and holiday built around last year's saved snow. First weekend in July.

Submariner's Festival and Memorial Services
In honor of men who go down in ships. August (week long).

Manitowoc County Fair
Third week in August.

TOUR

Point Beach Nuclear Plant Information Center
13 miles north of Two Rivers off M42; telephone: 755–4334. Explanation of how nuclear energy is generated. Daily, 8:30 AM–5 PM; closed Thanksgiving, Christmas, New Year's Day, and Easter.

TRANSPORTATION

Boat Terminal on U.S. 10 and Lakefront
Ferries sail across the Lake from Manitowoc to Ludington and Frankfort. Accommodations for passengers, cars, and trailers. Check at terminal for schedule.

The world's tallest grandfather clock overlooks the harbor area in Kewaunee, Wisconsin.

Kewaunee

Population: 3,000   Area Code: 414   Zip Code: 54216
Chamber of Commerce: Union State Bank Building; telephone: 388-4822

The big event in Kewaunee each day is the arrival, in all seasons, of the car and railroad ferry from Frankfort, Michigan, across the Lake. Kewaunee (Indian for "prairie hen") is a tiny town of 1000 people. Long ago, it had big dreams of rivaling Chicago as a port. It has a fine natural harbor, and a channel that is navigable for 7 miles. What's more, there were once rumors of gold in the red clay hills in back of town. So the fortune hunters and speculators charged into Kewaunee, and even swamp lots sold for $1000 each. But all that receded into history, the railroad came to Chicago, and the rivalry ended early.

Kewaunee had a trickle of earlier visitors, starting in the seventeenth century with the explorer Nicolet. Immigrants came in about 1836, and when they didn't find gold they settled for lumber. The most elegant of them all was John Volk who arrived in 1843 dressed in a frock coat and high silk hat. He bought a mill site and began cutting thousands of acres of timber on land that belonged to the government and not to him. When officials pointed that out, he left town, but by then the wood was gone too.

For years Kewaunee specialized in building school and church furniture, and some of its artisans traveled the country carving woodwork and church decorations. Samples still can be seen in some local buildings. The Kewaunee Engineering Company built boats for a number of years, including the famous U.S.S. *Pueblo* that was captured in 1968 by the Koreans as a spy vessel.

Today this little town has fine fishing and a harbor that remains open throughout the year, thanks to the steel-hulled car ferries that can push through the worst ice floes of winter.

ARCHITECTURE AND HISTORIC SITES

Law Office
408 Milwaukee St. This turn-of-the century building is typical of old Kewaunee.

MUSEUM

Kewaunee County Museum, 1876
Court House Square; telephone: 388–2244. Sheriff's residence and old county jail contain rare books and pioneer and Indian memorabilia. Memorial Day–Labor Day, Thurs.–Sun. and holidays, 12:30–4.

PARKS

Bremer County Park and Zoo
Junction County C and County F (about 2 miles west of Kewaunee). Picturesque 40-acre park, good for hiking, picnicking, birding.

Pioneer Park
End of Kilbourn at Lake. Beach, picnicking.

Selner Park
End of Main at Lake. Beach, picnicking.

RECREATION

Boating

There are public launch sites in the harbor area.

Charters

There is fishing at the Lake off piers at harbor and lighthouse and Coast Guard station. Smelt during season near Kewaunee Generating Plant and north of Kewaunee. For fishing on inland lakes, get county map from the Chamber of Commerce.

Angler Charter Service Don Young
Rt. 3, Box 53 A; telephone: 388–4151.

Kewaunee Charter Association
823 Ellis; telephone: 388–4010.

Dick Knudson
Box 266; telephone: 388–4010.

Stan Kubec
RR 1; telephone: 388–3732.

Golf

Alaska Golf Course (9-hole)
Route 3; telephone: 388–3940.

Northbrook Country Club (18-hole)
Route 1, Luxemburg; telephone: 845–2383.

Hunting

There are two public hunting areas: approximately 4 miles west of Kewaunee on County C; and approximately 4 miles northwest of Kewaunee on County E.

RESTAURANTS

The Grove
Rt. 3; telephone: 388–3751. Daily, 11:30–11; closed Tues.

Happy's
Highways 42 and 29; telephone: 388–2812. Try the ribs! Tues.–Thurs., 11:30 AM–1:30 PM, 5–10; Fri.–Sat., 5–11; Sun., 11–1:30, 4:30–10.

Northbrook Country Club
Rt. 1, Luxemburg; telephone: 845–2306. Rustic dining room overlooking an 18-hole golf course. Daily, 5–10.

SHOPPING

Chantilly House, 1874
521 Milwaukee St.; telephone: 388–4371. Gingerbread house converted to gift shop; overlooks Lake Michigan. Jan.–March, weekends, 9–4; Apr.–Dec., Mon.–Sat., 9–5; Sun., noon–4.

Svoboda Industries
303 Park St.; telephone: 388–2691. Clocks of all sizes to buy and kits for sale to make your own. Thirty-five-foot-high grandfather clock on shop's exterior *works!* Mon.–Sat., 9–5; Sun., 10–4.

SPECIAL EVENT

Annual Kewaunee Trout Festival
Prizes, food, entertainment, trout boil. Second weekend in July.

FERRY

Green Bay and Western Railroad Co. Car Ferry
Highway 29 and Lakefront; telephone: 388–3575. Overnight car ferries to Frankfort and Ludington, Michigan.

Algoma

Population: 4000   Area Code: 414   Zip Code: 54201
Chamber of Commerce: 512 Lake Street; telephone: 487–2041

In the old days, on the Lord's Day, Algomans piled into boats after church and went 3 miles upstream to Dewey Springs. The fishing was superlative, so there was always a trout boil, plenty of beer, and a big brass band. The trout boils still go on today, and the fishing is said to be better than ever. Now the town is hip deep in tourists and charter fishing.

Algoma (which means "park of flowers") is 25 miles east of Green Bay, a place of rolling hills, forests, lovely farms, and grasslands. Algoma grew where the Ahnapee River enters the Lake, and its fish, forests, and farmlands attracted Germans, Belgians, Bohemians, and Scandinavians.

Joseph McCormick from Manitowoc was the first traveler to come here in 1834, and he was so enthusiastic that seventeen years later some of his friends brought their families to settle. Their boat capsized entering the harbor and, though the people were saved, all their worldly goods were lost. Perhaps the first real settler was Abraham Hall, a New Yorker who opened a store and, along with a native named Indian Joe, kept an eye on the community. Joe, being something of an expert with medicinal herbs, also served as amateur pediatrician for the local children. No one remembers what his remedy was on the day three Indian children were found splashing in maple syrup stored in a hollowed log.

The settlement was incorporated as Wolf River in 1866, then became Ahnapee, and finally, in 1897, Algoma. In those days there were twelve commercial fishermen who worked year round in stubby-shaped boats with steel keels that could cut through the ice at the river's mouth. The commercial fishing is almost over, but some of those boats have been rebuilt as charters. The area still has a nautical flavor, with old shanties, sheds, nets, and two concrete piers that serve as protective breakwaters. For many years Algoma had a lacework factory and a pea cannery. One early traveler wrote, "The peas are prepared with a speed most astonishing. Within 30 minutes from the time the vines are cut, the peas are canned and on their way to the warehouse, thus retaining their original freshness." Today the town has nine plants. Five of them manufacture wood products: various plywoods, doors, toilet seats, and wood dowels. Hammocks and farm equipment are also made here, and the Wisconsin Label Corporation, newest industry in town, produces tapes and labels.

ARCHITECTURE AND HISTORIC SITE

Fish Shanties

Along banks at mouth of Ahnapee River. A nostalgic atmosphere recalling the good old days when Algoma was a big commercial fishing town. Also, notice the bright red lighthouse in Lake Michigan!

MUSEUMS

Mrs. Gray's Doll Museum

80 Church St., Harbor Village. The museum has over 3000 dolls on display. Memorial Day–Oct. 31, daily, 9:30 AM–4 PM.

Living Lakes Expo

80 Church St., Harbor Village; telephone: 487–3443. The Great Lakes story told through "the magic of technodynamatronics"; translation: talking sea creatures. Daily, 9–4.

PARKS

LaSalle County Park

County U off County S (8 miles north of Algoma). Swimming beach, picnicking in lovely sylvan wilderness.

Peterson City Park

End of 4th St., Algoma. Picnic, playground.

RECREATION

Bicycling, Hiking, Snowmobiling

Ahnapee State Park Trail

Algoma: County M from town (signs from Highway 42); Sturgeon Bay: County S (parking lot on north end). Lovely 15.3-mile trail (part of an Ice-Age trail) on old railroad grade.

Boating

The Point
End of Steele St. Launching ramp.

Olson Coho Park
Highway 42 and Lake St. Launching ramp.

Algoma Marina
End of Church St.

Fishing

Fishing map available at Chamber of Commerce.

Lake Michigan
Pier and dock area.

Algoma Street
County U.

Three Mile Creek
Rt. 42 (3 miles south of Algoma).

Charters

Captain Jerry Guth
Telephone: 487–4591.

Captain Merlin Hill
Telephone: 487–2726.

Captain Bob Kirk
Telephone: 487–5374.

Captain Gale Mielke
Telephone: 487–3722.

Captain "Toots" Wenniger
Telephone: 487–2343.

Swimming

Lake Michigan Beaches
Good swimming along most of Algoma beaches.

RESTAURANTS

Captain's Table
133 N. Water St.; telephone: 487–5304. Lots of fish. Daily, 6 AM–9 PM;
Fri.–Sat., 6 AM–10 PM.

Fireside Inn
527 4th St.; telephone: 487–2793. Homemade pie. Daily, 5:30 AM–9
PM; Fri.–Sat., 5:30 AM–10 PM.

Hotel Stebbins Dining Room
201 Steele St.; telephone: 487–5521. Try Friday night's smorgasbord.
Daily, 11:30 AM–9 PM.

SHOPPING

Gaslight Antiques
1000 Tremont St.; telephone: 487–5705. Good selection of antiques in
one of Algoma's charming old homes; shown by appointment.

Harbor Village
80 Church St. The hub of Algoma's shopping community.

Toots Fish Market
80 Church St., Harbor Village; telephone: 487–2343. Fresh and
smoked fish from Lake Michigan. July–Labor Day, daily, 9–5; rest of
year: Tues.–Fri., 10–5, Sat., 9–12.

SPECIAL EVENTS

The Antique and Contemporary Doll Show
Third weekend in July.

Trout and Coho Festival
Labor Day Weekend. Cash prizes.

TOURS

Renard Dairy and Cheese Factory
5 1/2 miles north of Algoma on County S; telephone: 487–2825. If you
arrive in the morning, you can see how cheese is made in the heart
of Wisconsin's dairy land. Tours: Mon.–Sat., 8 AM–11 AM; store hours:
Mon.–Sat., 7:30 AM–5 PM.

Von Stiehl Winery and Gift Haus

115 Navarino St.; telephone: 487–5208. Housed in an old brewery that dates back to the 1880s; this tour offers the pleasure of samples in addition to watching the wine-making process. Tours and store: May–Oct., daily, 9–5.

TRANSPORTATION

Algoma Railroad

Caboose Depot on Highway 42; telephone: 487–2293. A two-hour, 28-mile railroad trip from Algoma west to Casco Junction, through deep forest. Mid–June to mid–October, daily trips at 11 AM and 2 PM. Spring and fall, weekends only, 2 PM.

Sturgeon Bay

Population: 7,800   Area Code: 414   Zip Code: 54235
Door County Chamber of Commerce: Highways 42 and 57, Box 219; telephone:
743–4456

Sturgeon Bay has had a star-studded list of historical visitors: Marquette, Robert de LaSalle, Father Allouez, and pioneer Increase Claflin.

Lumbering began early, but during the panic of 1857, hungry workers raided the mill stores, and Chicago creditors moved in to strip them of their property, leaving many impoverished.

The government owned a quarry in the area, but when that failed, 1200 acres of this Sturgeon Bay Reservation were given to the state, later becoming Door County's Potawatomi Park. After the Chicago fire there was a lumbering boom, which lasted only as long as the rebuilding. Then Leatham and Smith, largest of all the mills, turned to building ships. To this day Sturgeon Bay is the top shipbuilding area on the Lake, with three giant yards and a great harbor.

Biggest of the shipbuilders today is the Bay Company, which during World War II employed 6700 people and produced more than 90 vessels for wartime use. Now this company is building huge 1000-foot Great Lakes freighters at a cost of about $30 million each. Another company, Peterson, turns out special boats such as the world's largest fishing vessel and Alcoa's Sea Probe. Palmer Johnson, third of the trio, designs and builds custom yachts for racing. Many of those who work in the boat yards now learn their skills at the local Northwestern Wisconsin Technical Institute.

In 1881, after much lobbying by pioneer Joseph Harris, the Sturgeon Bay and Lake Michigan Canal was finally built, creating a channel between the Lake and Green Bay. This has had major significance for shipping, just as the new bridge has had for auto traffic. (At the old bridge, there is a bait shop where you can bring your catch to be cleaned for free.)

In addition to its marine industries, Sturgeon Bay manufactures shoes, motors, plastics, electronic organs, and commercial kitchen equipment.

Aerial view showing the work area of the massive Bay Shipbuilding Corporation, Sturgeon Bay, Wisconsin.

ARCHITECTURE AND HISTORIC SITES

U.S. Coast Guard Station Lighthouse, 1882
Lake Forest Rd. and Canal Rd. (eastern foot of canal). Sat.–Sun., 1–4 PM.

Old Rugged Cross Friends Church, 1880
216 Maple. The hymn "Old Rugged Cross" was composed here in 1921 by Reverend George Bennard.

Sherwood Point Lighthouse
County Trunk M at Islewild (Potawatomi State Park). Navigational aid to ships.

ART CENTER

Miller Art Museum
4th and Nebraska Ave.; telephone: 743–6578. Local and area artists. Six shows of Door County artists annually. Mon., Wed., & Fri., 10–12, 1–5, and 7–9; Sat., 10–12.

MUSEUMS

Door County Historical Museum
18 N. 4th Ave.; telephone: 743–5809. Indian artifacts, nautical display. May 15–Oct. 15, Tues.–Sat., 10–12 and 1–5.

Maritime Museum
3rd Ave. and Georgia St.; telephone: 743–5809. Once a steamship office, now contains books on Great Lakes and antique instruments and anchors. Best place to look at Bay Ship Company ships. May 31–Sept. 15, daily 10–5.

ORCHARDS AND GARDENS

University of Wisconsin Experimental Fruit & Potato Research Center
North on Rt. 42; telephone: 743–5406. Self-tours with maps.

PARKS AND NATURE CENTERS

Ahnapee State Park Trail
County Road 3 (see Algoma). National recreational trail from Algoma to Sturgeon Bay. Mapped Ice-Age trail.

The Farm
4 miles north on Rt. 57; telephone: 743–6666. Pioneer farmstead and nature center.

Gardner Wildlife Refuge Area
Off County C on Gravel Pit Road, 6 miles NE of Brussels. 992 acres; hunting in season; lowlands; cross-country skiing.

Potawatomi State Park
West of Sturgeon Bay on Sawyer Harbor, Rt. 42 and C; telephone: 743–5123. 1100-acre park, originally government quarry in 1832. Trails, picnic, cross-country skiing, tobogganing, camping. Great view from tower.

Whitefish Dunes State Park
Highway 57 north from Sturgeon Bay to village of Valmy; 3 miles east of Valmy on Clarks Lake Rd.; telephone: 823–2400. Newly developed 750-acre park with good swimming beaches, hiking, nature setting.

RECREATION

Boats

City Dock
West end of Highway 42 and bridge. Launch.

Pagel's — Riley's Point Marina
County C, North Stevenson Pier Rd.; telephone: 824–5130. Launch and boat rental.

Sawyer Harbor
Protected harbor between bay and mouth of canal on Lake Michigan.

Sturgeon Bay Yacht Club
Nautical Dr.; telephone: 743–9924.

Trade Winds Charter Yachts, Ltd.
42 Kentucky (east side); telephone: 743–9997. Bare boat charters and other yachts.

Charters

There is also good fishing along the canal, city dock (west end of Business Highway 42 and 57 bridge), breakwater. Green Bay freezes over and ice fishing is great.

R. F. Balsom Guides Unlimited
Rt. 7, 3022 Canal Rd.; telephone: 743–2163.

Captain Rod Baudhuin
Telephone: 743–5555.

Captain Stanley Fuller
621 Nautical Dr.; telephone: 743–9687.

Glidden Lodge
Rt. 3; telephone: 743–4944.

Captain Norman Knutson
106 Kendale; telephone: 743–2518.

Golf

Pepperdine Golf and Country Club (18-hole)
North of city on Dunn Rd.; telephone: 743–7246.

Lost Creek Golf Course
County C, right onto M; telephone: 743–6880.

Scuba Diving

Rusche Diving Service
3893 Cherry Rd.; telephone: 843–5427. Instruction, equipment, and diving for wrecks.

Swimming

Otumba Beach
Juniper St. on west side of bay.

Portage Park
East of Sturgeon Bay to Lake Michigan, Lake Forest Dr. to Coast Guard Station.

Sand Bay Beach
County C from Sturgeon Bay; right on Sand Bay Beach Rd. to shore.

Sunset Beach
Northeast from downtown Sturgeon Bay, beaches off 3rd Ave.

RESTAURANTS

Bay Shore Inn
N. Bay Shore Rd.; telephone: 743–4551. Homemade breads and pies. June 12–Labor Day, Fri., 6:15 PM; Labor Day–Oct. 15, Sat., 6:15 PM. Reservations required.

Leathem Smith Lodge
1640 Memorial Dr.; telephone: 743–5555. Four dining rooms open to public. Leatham Smith was the Henry Kaiser of the Great Lakes. President and manager of Smith Shipbuilding Company, he was drowned in the bay in 1946.

The Nautical Inn
234 Kentucky St.; telephone: 743–2344. Lunch and dinner; fish boils; between 5:30 and 8:00 PM; closed Sunday.

SHOPPING

Country Door Interiors
6th and Jefferson; telephone: 743–6734. Remodeled 100-year-old church. Fine antiques, furniture.

Mac's Sport Shop
40 S. Madison; telephone: 743–3350. Favorite of summer fishing crowd.

Marine Equipment and Service Corp.
455 N. 3rd; telephone: 743–6166. Nautical artifacts — ship wrecks, bells, portholes, lights, name plates.

Jonlee Peterson "Corner House Shops"
Kentucky and 2nd Ave.; telephone: 743–3557. Excellent. The proprietor is the daughter-in-law of a shipbuilder.

Gerhard C. F. Miller Gallery
3 miles north on Bay Shore Rd.; telephone: 743–6365. Drawings and watercolors. June–August, Wed. and Sat., 2–5.

Produce and Craft Market
Market Square, 4th and Michigan. Mid-July–mid-October, Sat., 9–4.

Wisconsin Farm Market
Rt. 6, County Highway S; telephone: 743–5834.

Woodcarver's Gallery
505 Oregon St.; telephone: 743–5976. Best known for fishermen caricatures and wildlife figures. Daily, 10–5; Sun., 1–5 PM.

SPECIAL EVENT

Door County Fair
Fairgrounds at 14th Ave. Tractor pull, horse races, stock cars. Mid-August.

TOURS

Coast Guard Cutter *Acacia*
City Dock, Highways 42 and 57 at bridge. Interesting tour of ice-breaker cutter. June–Aug., Sat. & Sun., 9:30–11:30 and 1–4.

Door County Winery Company
Highway 42 at Carlsville (7 miles north of Sturgeon Bay); telephone: 743–7431. Tours and tasting. Door County's apple, cherry, and plum wines. May–Nov., daily, 9–5; July 1–Labor Day, 9–7.

The Good Ship Lollipop
West end of Highway Bridge; telephone: 743–4377. June 5–Sept. 5, daily, 9–5. Narrated one-hour tour at 1, 2, and 3 PM.

House and Garden Historical Tour
Chamber of Commerce; telephone: 743–4465. Countywide tour. Last Tuesday in July

Richard's Aviation
At Cherryland Airport on #C, south of Sturgeon Bay; telephone: 743–7820. Scenic tours of peninsula. Daily; call for reservations.

Door County

Population: 22,500
Door County Chamber of Commerce: Highways 42 and 57, Box 219; telephone:
743-4456

This lovely peninsula is variously called the spout of the Wisconsin
teakettle, the thumb, and the Cape Cod of the Midwest. It has three
state parks, and twenty-one swimming beaches scattered along 250
miles of shoreline with Lake Michigan on the east and Green Bay on
the west. Its population explodes between cherry blossom time in the
spring and foliage time in autumn.

Door's 477 square miles are a montage of woods, splendid water
views, ridges, bluffs, and caves. An early fur trader called it "a delicious kingdom," a description still endorsed by all the people who
have chosen it as a place to build fine houses, anchor fine yachts, and
enjoy summer holidays. It is the boating capital of the Great Lakes
and a fisherman's dream, with its offshore waters and numerous inland lakes rich with salmon, trout, perch, bass, and walleye.

Quaint little towns along the shore often remind visitors of Norwegian fjord villages, and many of the pioneer families were attracted to
the county because it was so like their Scandinavian homeland. Galas
and summer events take place in town after town throughout the
summer, so there is usually an art fair (the area abounds in artists and
craftsmen), a golf tournament, or a boat race taking place somewhere.
(Check with Door County Chamber of Commerce for specifics as well
as information about new bicycle, hiking, and snowmobile trails.)

This is glacial country, with a thin layer of topsoil and great boul-
ders, reminding one that right below the surface is limestone, which
usually must be dynamited to plant cherry and apple orchards. From
1910 to 1960 this was a cherry heaven despite the hostile soil. "Red
gold" they called it. But in recent years the orchards have been
thinning out as the land has become a developer's delight, bringing
more and more tourists each year. Over the years tourism has become
the prime business, surpassing all prior businesses: fur, fishing, timber,
potatoes, peas, dairy herds, apples, and cherries.

There were many Indians on the peninsula before the white men

Boating and swimming in Door County. *Door County Chamber of Commerce*

came, but most of them had fled across the Mississippi by the 1830s, as the Irish, Germans, Scandinavians, Icelanders, and a large cult of religious Norwegians called Moravians arrived. By the end of the century the Door had developed quite a limestone industry, and for a time great slabs were quarried to build the breakwater in Michigan City and the Illinois Central breakwater in Chicago, as well as the main Chicago post office.

The peninsula is a great outdoor museum for wildflowers, with some thirty-five varieties of orchids, twenty-five of fern, rare dwarf iris, bird's eye primrose, and many other exotic species. It is also one of the four top diving areas in the country. Between Gill's Rock, at the end of the peninsula, and Plum Island lies a treacherous passage, 3 miles wide and 12 miles long, called the Portes des Mortes ("door of death") from which the peninsula gets its name. Uncertain currents and winds have wrecked hundreds of boats. Since the water is salt free, many of the sunken wrecks are still well preserved, with shifting sands covering and uncovering them from season to season. Divers come from far away, as do underwater photographers and spear fishing enthusiasts. Caveat: don't attempt the diving without proper training.

One cannot write about Door County without mentioning its omnipresent, always pleasant fish boils — a modern adaptation of an old Scandinavian custom. Trout or whitefish are boiled in washtubs with onion and potatoes. When the chowder is just done, oil is thrown in the pot, creating a great bubbling and a whirl of fire. The oil is what makes the fish boils on the west side of the Lake differ from the equally popular ritual on its eastern shores.

Jacksonport

Once an Indian village called Mechingan, Jacksonport became a wood refueling port for Great Lakes ships during the Civil War, and then a fishing village. Today it is a quiet town which, like Marinette and Petoskey on the Lake's eastern shore, claims to be the midpoint between the North Pole and the equator. It has a lovely old Catholic church and cemetery, and a Maifest each May Day, which dates back to its early settlement by Germans.

Whitefish Dunes State Park near Jacksonport. *Door County Chamber of Commerce*

PARK

Cave Point County Park
Highway 57 north, turn right on Clark Lake Rd. Largest active sea cave on Lake Michigan. Good picnicking, scuba diving.

SPECIAL EVENT

Maifest
Horse show, horse pull, parades. Memorial Day.

SWIMMING

Sevastopol Township Park
Sand Dunes Beach, end of County T at Lake Michigan.

Town Beach
Lake Michigan.

Bailey's Harbor

Captain Justice Bailey sailed into Bailey's Harbor during a terrible lake storm, staying just long enough to give the oldest Door peninsula village his name. The town was actually settled by a Swede named Andrew Seaquist. It is an area of first growth birch, maple, cedar, and pine, and has the best harbor on the peninsula. Off shore, one can see nearby Cana Island.

ARCHITECTURE AND HISTORIC SITES

Cana Island Lighthouse, 1851
Northeast of Bailey's Harbor. Automated — not open to public.

Chapel Bjorklunden
South of Bailey's Harbor, Chapel La. Duplicate of a Norwegian *stavkirke*. June 15–Sept., Wed., Sat., Sun., 1–3:30.

MUSEUM

Music Box Museum
Highway 57, 3 miles south of town; telephone: 839–2448. Antique music-making machines. July and Aug., daily, 10–4.

PARKS

* **Mud Lake Wildlife Area**
County Q, 6 miles northeast of town. Public hunting grounds.

* **Ridges Sanctuary**
Yacht Club Rd.; telephone: 839–2802. Visitors must register at center. Marvelous wildflowers indigenous to Wisconsin; Ice-Age flora. Twenty-five species of orchids, sixteen wooded sandcrests marking ancient Lake shorelines. May 30–Sept. 1, daily, 9–5; Sunday, 1–5.

RECREATION

Boating

Anclam Town Park
The Village. Launch.

Cana Island Lighthouse off Bailey's Harbor. *Door County Chamber of Commerce*

Bailey's Harbor Yacht Club
Ridges Road, Harbor Dr.; telephone: 839–2336. Slip rental.

Nelson Shopping Center
The Village; telephone: 839–2326. Dock, boat rental.

Swimming

Bailey's Harbor public beach
Center of town.

RESTAURANTS

Bailey's Harbor Yacht Club
Box 164, Ridges Rd., 2 miles east of town; telephone: 839–2336. Wonderful lake and yacht views. Swimming. May–late Oct., fine Sunday brunch, 9:30–2.

Gordon Lodge
North on County Q; telephone: 839–2331. Expensive and elegant. Late May–mid-October, three meals daily; reservations advised.

SHOPPING

Red Geranium
Main St. Paintings, graphics, ceramics. May 26–Labor Day. 10 AM–6 PM.

Swanson's Yum Yum Tree
Main St.; telephone: 839–2622. Homemade candy and ice cream. Can watch it being prepared.

Sister Bay

This little town on the Green Bay side of the peninsula was founded by a Scandinavian named Ingebret Torgerson, and named for the nearby Sister Islands. The islands are breeding grounds for gulls and tern, and birds banded here have turned up as far away as Panama and Martinique. Now a resort area, Sister Bay earlier had both lumbering and shipping industries. It looks newer than nearby towns because it was rebuilt after a severe fire in 1912.

ORCHARDS AND GARDENS

Koepsels
3 miles south of Highway 57, between Bailey's Harbor and Sister Bay; telephone: 854–2433. Fruit, vegetables, cheese, homemade pies.

Larson's Orchards
Highway 42, 3 miles north of village; telephone: 854–4242. Door's largest apple and cherry orchard. Pick your own. Watch packing and pressing operations. Call for dates. Aug.–Nov., daily, 8–6.

RECREATION

Boating

Anchor Marine
Highway 42, north of village; telephone: 854–2124. Docking and repairs.

Door County Sailing
Telephone: 854–2124. Rental, cruises.

Sister Bay Village Dock
Telephone: 854–4457. Launch.

Fishing

Lots of fishing on Lake Michigan shore.

Golf

Bay Ridge Golf Course (9-hole)
Highway 42, south of Bay Ridge; telephone: 854–4085.

Riding

Carole's Corral
Highway 57, 1/4 mile south of village (Vacationland Farm); telephone: 854–2525. Daily, summers.

Swimming

Sister Beach
Green Bay, in village

RESTAURANTS

Bakery and Coffee Shop
Main St.; telephone: 854–4660. Mon.–Sat., 8:30–5; Sun., 8:30–3.

Hotel Du Nord
Main St.; telephone: 854–4221. Breakfast, May 15–Oct. 15, 8–10 AM; lunch, late June–Oct. 15, 1:30–2 PM; dinner, May–Jan. 2, 5:30–8:30 PM; Sunday brunch, 9–1 PM.

Al Johnson's Swedish Restaurant
Bay Shore Dr.; telephone: 854–2626. Features Swedish food. Goats graze on roof. Daily, 6 AM–8 PM.

Woerfel's Restaurant and Delicatessen
Highway 42, in village; telephone: 854–4514. Deli items, fish specials to go or eat there. Food fresh, prices reasonable. Open daily.

SHOPPING

The Gages, Inc.
Bay Shore Dr.; telephone: 854–2359. Rooms and rooms of outstanding displays; elegant shopping.

Ingwersen Studio/Gallery
Old Stage Rd., 1 1/2 miles east of town; telephone: 854–4072. In season, Wed. & Sat. 2–5; or by appointment.

SPECIAL EVENT

Fall Festival
Main St., village; telephone: 854–2812. Biggest fall colorama, parade, dance, helicopter rides, food. Second weekend in October.

Ellison Bay

John Ellison (Johan Eliason) founded this hilly town, once a fishing village, now a center for cherry and apple orchards. It is probably best known as the site of the Clearing, the artists' colony established by the great landscape architect and conservationist, Jens Jensen. Jensen began work as a day laborer for the Chicago Park District, helping to design Illinois Beach Park and Chicago's Garfield Conservatory and forest preserves. His Clearing is a glorious 128 acres of cliffs, rugged shoreline, and woods. It has been run by the Wisconsin Farm Bureau since 1953 and has a rich curriculum of continuing education that attracts poets, artists, and nature lovers.

ARCHITECTURE AND HISTORIC SITE

* The Clearing
Garret Bay Rd., north of village; telephone: 854–4088. Home of great landscape artist. Now center for painting, nature study, humanities. May–Oct. Sunday, open to visitors, 1–4 PM.

PARK

Newport State Park
Rt. 42 (till it heads north) and pick up County Rd. to Lake; telephone:

854–2500. Camping, swimming, skiing, sand dunes, hiking trails. One of the loveliest and quietest of state parks in Door County.

RECREATION

Boating

Ellison Bay Municipal Dock and Ramp
Highway 42 in center of village.

Fishing

Green Bay
Ellison Bay Women's Club Park, Highway 42, south end of village.

Lake Michigan
Europe Bay Rd. at Lake.

Mink River
Rowley's Bay at County ZZ; Mink River flows into here, and at Mink River Fishing Camp.

Swimming

Ellison Bay Women's Club Park
Highway 42, south end of village on Green Bay.

Europe Bay Town Park
Europe Bay Rd. and Lake Michigan.

Newport State Park
End of Rt. 42 on Lake Michigan.

RESTAURANTS

Viking Restaurant
Rt. 42, in village; telephone: 854–2998. Claims to be the first in Door County to serve fish boils; still featured most nights. Daily, all year, all meals.

Wagon Trail
End of County Z; telephone: 854–4272. Home cooking. No liquor, no air conditioning. Open daily.

SHOPPING

Collector's Corner Gallery
Highway 42, north end of village. Enamel on copper, silver and gold. May 15–Feb. 15, daily, 10 AM–5 PM.

The Galleries
Highway 42. Midwest artists and craftsmen. In season, daily, 10:30–5.

The Passport
Highway 42, south end of village; telephone: 854–4550. Excellent selection of gifts from around the world. April 1–Dec. 31, daily, 9–5.

Pioneer Store, 1900
Rt. 42 and village center; telephone: 854–2805. Even today a general store in the pot-bellied tradition.

Tria Gallery
Highway 42, 3 miles north of village; telephone: 854–2298. Painting, sculpture, graphics. July–Sept., daily, 10:30–6; Oct., Fri.–Sun., 11–5.

SPECIAL EVENT

Old Ellison Bay Days
Parade, fish boils, bazaars. Third week in June.

Gill's Rock

This fishing village on 170-foot bluffs at the tip of the peninsula was founded by Elias Gill in the 1830s. The ferry leaves from here for Washington Island, and customers leave from the fish stores with all manner of bass and trout and the newest delicacy, whitefish livers. One of the legendary people of the peninsula was Allen Bradley. He was said to have hands like shovels, a chest four-feet around, and a beard so long that men could swing on it. He lived like an Indian and in Paul Bunyan style could cut seven cords of maple a day. Gill's Rock is the take-off point for scuba diving. To give some idea of the treasure trove off its shores: on one stormy 1880 day, thirty sailing ships entering the harbor (the Portes des Mortes) were smashed against Gill's Rock.

PARKS AND NATURE CENTERS

Door Bluff Headlands Park

4 1/2 miles northwest of village. Lovely. Little visited. Trails along bluff. This is Death's Door, the most dangerous passage on Lake. Two hundred known wrecks off these shores.

* Portes des Mortes Archaelogical Site

North Port, end of Rt. 42 and Lake. Excavation of Indian cultures. Good fishing off pier.

RECREATION

Boating

Weborg Boat Ramp

1/4 mile south of ferry dock.

Charters

Captain Jeff Bremer

Telephone: 854–2606.

Captain Paul Voight

Telephone: 854–4614.

Diving

"On the Rocks" Lodge and Shop

Rt. 1, Box 164, zip code 54210; telephone: 854–2808. A lodge for the diving crowd. Instructions, excursions, underseas photography. Divers who are not guests obtain permission at dive shop.

RESTAURANT

Shoreline Motel

Highway 42. July & August, Mon., Thurs., Fri., & Sat. nights; June, Sept., and Oct., Sat. nights.

SHOPPING

Weborg Fish Company

1/2 mile south of Ferry Docks; telephone: 854–2860. Specialty: whitefish livers. Great view of ferry activity. Seasonal.

TRANSPORTATION

Washington Island Ferry Line, Inc.
Gill's Rock phone: 854–2595; Washington Island phone: 847–2546.
Service between Gill's Rock and Washington Island. Take a ride over
the famous Portes des Mortes with its sunken ship graveyard.

Washington Island

Three centuries ago Robert de LaSalle traded with the Indians of this
island, and the furs he collected were carried by canoe to Montreal,
a long tedious process which convinced LaSalle of the need for faster
transportation. So at Niagara he built the *Griffin,* the first sailing
vessel on the Lake. LaSalle sailed to Washington Island in 1679,
loaded his ship with furs, and ordered his men on to Montreal with
the cargo, promising to wait for them at the mouth of the St. Joseph
River at the southern end of the Lake. What happened to the *Griffin*
has been a mystery ever since, but undoubtedly it was Lake Michigan's first — and most famous — shipwreck.

Washington Island has been a fishing and wood-cutting town;
today it abounds in deer, pheasant, grouse, and has three fine harbors
— though, despite all the water surrounding the island, every drop of
drinking water comes from wells. This island has its own islands:
Plum, Pilot, Detroit, Hog, and Fish, none of which is available to the
public. Island natives are enthusiastic wildflower collectors. They
have snowmobiling treks that wind up with great pig roasts, and in
the summer there is the usual fish boil, although this one is a fly-in,
involving more than 200 planes.

Perhaps the best description of Washington Island's pleasures and
excitements came from a local man. "Well," he said, "ain't much.
Maybe this is the place to tell you that we have got a lot of pleasures
of a kind here. We like the sun coming up, and watching it go down
on the water; we notice all the birds, and we watch the changes of
seasons."

ART CENTER

Washington Island Center for Creative Arts and Nature Study
Main and Jackson Harbor Road. July–Labor Day, daily, 10:30–4:30

ARCHITECTURE AND HISTORIC SITE

Bethel Church, 1865
Jackson Harbor Rd.

FARM

Havegard Garden Farm
Range Line Rd. Model farm, crops, vineyard, orchard, herbs, natural grains flour milling. June 15–mid-Oct.; daily, 10–5; closed Sun.

MUSEUM

Jacobsen Museum
Little Lake Rd., northwest corner of island. Island relics, Indian artifacts. June 15–Sept. 15, 10–4:30.

Washington Island Fishing Village
Jackson Harbor Rd. Fishing, Great Lakes boating in old fishing sheds.

PARK

Jackson Harbor Natural Area and Park
Jackson Harbor, 8 miles from Lake. Beach, fishing, docks, harbor, nature area, twelve ridges. Hikes scheduled at Nature Center.

RECREATION

Boating

Public ramp
Jackson Harbor.

Public ramp
Detroit Harbor.

Lobdell's Point
Detroit Harbor; telephone: 847–2533.

Hank's Island Marine
Detroit Harbor; telephone: 847–2533. Boat rentals.

Charters

Jack Hagen
Telephone: 847–2076.

Krueger's Kap's Marina
Telephone: 847–2640.

Golf

Maple Grove Golf Course (9-hole)
Main Rd.; telephone: 847–2017.

Riding

Fieldwood Farm
W. Harbor Rd.; telephone: 847–2490. Icelandic horses. Late June–
Sept.

Swimming

Sand Dunes Park Beach
East of Detroit Harbor on South Shore Dr.

East Side Beach
East Side County Park, middle section of island.

Schoolhouse Beach
Washington Harbor.

RESTAURANT

Findlay Holiday Inn
Detroit Harbor, across from post office; telephone: 847–2526. Break-
fast, lunch, dinner. Decorated with Norwegian rosemaling. July and
August.

SPECIAL EVENTS

Scandinavian Festival
Smorgasbord, dance. First week in August.

Island Fair
Parade, games, exhibits. Third week in August.

Ice Fishing Festivals
February.

TOUR

Cherry Train
Detroit Harbor. Narrated island tour. Late June–Labor Day, September weekends.

TRANSPORTATION

Karfi Ferry Service
At Jackson Harbor. Ferry service from Washington Island to Rock Island State Park. Ten-minute ride.

Rock Island

No cars at all! This 999-acre island is a state park, uninhabited except by hikers brought in by ferry and people who moor their boats along the shore. The 1837 lighthouse is still in operation, and both the Manor House and boat house, built by an Icelandic immigrant Chester Thordarson, still stand. The Ottawa Indians once lived here; they had fine gardens and ancient burying grounds. The most unusual visitor may have been David Kennison, the last survivor of the Boston Tea Party and veteran of the War of 1812, who was brought here by his son when he was 110 years old. After his son's death, he returned to Chicago where, finding it impossible to live on his $8-per-month pension, he displayed himself in a museum as an ancient relic. Kennison is buried in Lincoln Park in Chicago.

ARCHITECTURE AND HISTORIC SITES

Archeological sites of ancient Indian camps and villages

Manor House of Thordarson Estates, 1920

Potawatomi Lighthouse, 1837
North end of Rock Island. Automated.

PARK

Rock Island State Park
Washington Island, 54248; telephone: 847–2235. Entire island is state park. Backpacking; forty campsites. Great swimming. May 1–Dec. 1 (can be reached by boat or snowmobile in winter).

Ephraim

Ephraim is called the Summer Capitol of Door County. It is a charming village, with a church steeple at each end of town, and in between a crescent-shaped harbor. It was settled by Moravians from Norway, and their no-liquor stricture still holds. The immigrant cult (which practiced Christian Communism) was led by A. M. Iverson. When the Moravians were in dire straits in Milwaukee in the early 1850s, a rich idealist named Nils Otto Tank came to their aid and bought land in Green Bay (where the Tank House still stands, the oldest in Wisconsin). When a feud developed, one branch, under Iverson, moved up to Ephraim, where the Iverson church and home remain. Ephraim is now the heart of the holiday area. It still has an ancient Norwegian midsummer celebration in mid-June, the Fyr Bal Fest. The festivities include the usual mammoth fish boil, the crowning of a Viking king and queen, and a ring of bonfires that glow along the shores of Eagle Harbor.

ARCHITECTURE AND HISTORIC SITES

Anderson Dock & Store, 1858
Rt. 42, north side of village. Restored store-museum. Lots of boat graffiti.

The Thomas Goodletson House, 1857
One of first permanent houses on peninsula. Authentically restored and furnished. Open late June for season; free admission.

* Eagle Bluff Lighthouse, 1868
Peninsula State Park (between Ephraim and Fish Creek). Summers, daily, 10–6.

Iverson Parsonage, 1853
Moravia St. Not open to the public.

Moravian Church, 1858
Moravia St. Sunday services. Reverend Iverson's church.

Pioneer Schoolhouse, 1869
Moravia St. Summers, Mon.–Sat., 10–12; 1–5.

A famous Door County fish boil. *Door County Chamber of Commerce*

Totem: Ephraim Pole Cemetery
Near Peninsula State Park, SE of golf course. Burial ground of Potawatomi chief.

RECREATION

Boating

Anderson Dock
Telephone: 854–4676.

Ephraim Village Boat Ramp
Rt. 42 at village center at bay.

South Shore Pier
Telephone: 854–4324. Boat rentals.

Fishing

Shoreline
Tremendous marina.

Golf

Bay Ridge Golf Course (9-hole)
Between Ephraim and Sister Bay; telephone: 854–4085.

Peninsula State Park (18-hole)
Between Ephraim and Fish Creek; telephone: 854–9921. Bay view.

Swimming

Eagle Harbor Beach
In center of Green Bay.

RESTAURANTS

Brookside Tea Garden
Brookside Lane off Highway 42; telephone: 854–2235. Moderate priced. Lunch, dinner; Sunday smorgasbord.

Wilson's Restaurant
Highway 42 in town; telephone: 854–2041. Breakfast all day; soda fountain; short orders. A gathering place. Seasonal, 8 AM–11 PM.

SHOPPING

Bellaire Gallery Antiques
Highway 42, south end of town; telephone: 854–4362. Best in Door County. China, glass, French crystal, kraut cutters, Chippendale, Oriental rugs. Daily, 10–6.

Bungener's Antiques
Telephone: 854–4159. Excellent. Everything from jewelry to furniture, paintings to silver.

Statham Enamels
Highway Q. In season, daily, 10–5.

SPECIAL EVENT

Fyr Bal
Coronation chief arrives by boat to celebrate Scandinavian arrival of summer. Parades; fish boils. Mid-June.

Fish Creek

Asa Thorpe built a cabin and a pier here early in the nineteenth century, and the cabin remains in the town square. Eventually a group of vacationers from St. Louis established this high-bluffed town as a resort area. There is some farming and fishing nearby. Off the mainland is Chambers Island, whose lighthouse is on the National Registry. Pirate, Horseshoe, Jack, Adventure, Eagle, and Little Strawberry islands lie off shore, though none are accessible except by private boat.

ARCHITECTURE AND HISTORIC SITES

Church of Atonement, 1878
Main St., three blocks west of Rt. 42. Former fisherman's house with added Gothic steeple.

* **Eagle Lighthouse,** 1868
Peninsula State Park. Summer, daily, 10–6; admission.

Log Cabin of Founder, Asa Thorpe, 1853
Founder's Square at village center.

Proud Mary Hotel, 1889
Main St., second block west of Rt. 42. Restored turn-of-the-century hotel.

MUSIC

Heritage Ensemble in Amphitheater
Folklore plays, folk song, musicals. June 30–Sept. 3, nightly, 8 PM; closed Sun.

Peninsula Musical Festival
Gibraltar High School; telephone: 854–4060. Concert series: guests soloists; professional musicians. Started with Frederick Stock in 1939. Check for dance activities, too. First week in August.

PARK

Peninsula State Park
Rt. 42, between Ephraim and Fish Creek; telephone: 868–3258. Lovely 3760-acre park. Hiking, swimming, golf, boat launches, winter

sports, camping (465 campsites). Mid-June–Labor Day, twenty-four hours; remainder of year, 8–4:30.

RECREATION

Bicycling

Omnibus Outfitters
Highway 42, south of Fish Creek; telephone: 868–3013. Bicycle rentals and most other sports equipment. In season, daily, 10–6.

Boating

Alibi Dock
Cedar St.; telephone: 868–3300.

Fish Creek Dock
Maple St.; telephone: 839–2418. Boat rentals from both.

Charter

Captain Steve Ellmann
Telephone: 868–3478.

RESTAURANTS

Kortes English Inn
Highway 42 north; telephone: 868–3076. Lunches and dinner. Summer–October.

White Gull Inn
Main St.; telephone: 868–3517. Fish boils. May–October, daily, three meals.

SHOPPING

The Potter's Wheel
Rt. 42, 1 mile north of village; telephone: 868–3371. Artist Abraham Cohn turns the wheel. Summer only, daily, 10–5; closed Tues. and weekends.

SPECIAL EVENTS

Firemen's Festival
Parade, water fights, corn roast, bratwurst. Late August.

Door County Antique Show
Early August.

THEATER

Peninsula Players
Rt. 42, 3 miles south of town, telephone: 868–3287. Oldest professional resident summer stock company in Midwest; produce Broadway and Off-Broadway plays. June–Sept.: weekdays, 8:30; Sun. 7:30. Write for schedule.

Egg Harbor

Egg Harbor is the southernmost of the Green Bay resort towns. LaSalle and his men almost starved here in 1680, chewing their moccasins for sustenance until they were rescued by Indians. There are several versions of how the Harbor got its Egg, the most colorful relating to a June morning when a group of Green Bay yachtsmen in high spirits began pelting hard-boiled eggs from boat to boat. At any rate, Egg Harbor is a well-established, well-heeled community with a fine deep harbor.

ARCHITECTURE AND HISTORIC SITE

Cupola House, 1871
Rt. 42, north of town. House of Levi Thorpe, one of town founders.

MUSIC

Birch Creek Farm Performing Arts
3 miles east on County Road E; telephone: 868–3763. Eight concerts; workshops; jazz and chamber music. July.

RECREATION

Boating

Egg Harbor Village Dock
Telephone: 868–3056.

Stone Dock
Telephone: 868–3417.

Golf

Alpine Lodge (27-hole)
County G, south of village; telephone: 868–3000.

Swimming

Frank E. Murphy County Park
Egg Harbor Village Beach.

RESTAURANT

Alpine Lodge
County G, 1/2 mile southwest of village; telephone: 868–3000. Family
style. Summers only, breakfast, lunch, dinner.

SCENIC DRIVE

Egg Harbor to Sturgeon Bay, County Road B
This picturesque road from Egg Harbor follows the Green Bay shoreline through the tiny village of Little Harbor into Sturgeon Bay.
Fabulous water views varied with colorful cottages and elegant homes
set in woodsy settings make this twisting road an interesting drive.

TOUR

Door Peninsula Winery
Highway 42, 8 miles south of town; telephone: 743–7431. May–Dec.
31, daily, 9–5.

Brussels

One hundred and twenty-five years ago ten farming families from
Brabant, Belgium, came to the peninsula to settle. They had been told
that French was spoken in the area and that life would be good.
French wasn't spoken, and life, for a while, consisted of drafty log
cabins, beds of branches, and chairs of split logs. There was also
cholera, loneliness, and the difficulty of clearing the land. In time,
however, things got better and the immigrant community grew. The
Belgians raised tobacco for their pipes, hops for their beer, and food
for their five hearty meals a day. They baked enormous yeast pies in
outdoor ovens of white limestone, a few of which still stand. They

brought so much linen that wash day occurred twice a year when the ladies went to a creek to scrub, and used the grassy banks for drying.

The fire of 1871 hit this area with a vengeance, and Tornado Memorial Park, a lovely area of pine groves, is now a memorial to the many lives lost in that fire. On the road between Brussels and Namur, some of the post-fire red brick or stone houses remain today, with half-round windows set under the gables. A few white roadside shrines also still stand.

Nowadays in Brussels livestock is raised, wool shorn, and butter and cheese manufactured. Like the Dutch in Holland, the Belgian-American community here has a Bon Voisin Club, and close cultural links to — and interchanges with — the old country. At the end of the summer there is a Kermiss Festival — a day of thanksgiving with mass, feasts, and dancing. And each year on Assumption Day many people make pilgrimages here because a native girl, Adele Brice, saw visions of the Queen of Heaven and earned a reputation as a healer.

Green Bay

Population: 92,000   Area Code: 414   Zip Code: 54303
Chamber of Commerce: 400 S. Washington; telephone: 437–8704
Visitor and Convention Bureau: Packer Hall of Fame, 1910 S. Oneida; 494–9507

Green Bay was discovered by explorers in search of China. In 1634, Jean Nicolet, draped in a gorgeous Oriental robe, stepped out of his canoe and fired two pistol shots in the air. Having set forth to discover "the western sea," Nicolet was prepared to serve as emissary to Peking. Instead a band of startled Indians was there to greet him and to treat him to a mighty feast that included 300 beaver. All this a few miles north of today's city and only fourteen years after the Pilgrims landed at Plymouth.

Ideally situated, Green Bay grew at the confluence of the Fox River and an arm of the Lake that the French called La Baye Verte because of its green water. Up this waterway three decades later came Father Claude Allouez to found missions, and Nicholas Perrot to represent the French crown in its fur dealings with the Indians. When the brilliant Perrot was recalled to France, his gentle policies were abandoned and the military era began. Several forts were built. One, at La Baye, was ruled by the French till 1761 when they lost it to England. The British, in turn, lost it to the Americans in 1816. The town that grew on the site of the fort was incorporated as Green Bay in 1895.

The early fort stabilized the area and attracted settlers. Charles de Langlade was one. He came down from Mackinac, established a trading post, fought in ninety-nine battles, and earned the title Father of Wisconsin. John Jacob Astor was another. He monopolized the fur trade after the war of 1812, and platted a section of Green Bay. Perhaps the most colorful early settler was Eleazar Williams, half Indian, from western New York. As a boy he was told he resembled the French royal family, the Bourbons, and he took the description to heart. Proclaiming himself the lost Dauphin of France, he led the Oneida Indians to the Green Bay area in an attempt to unite the six Indian Nations into an empire with himself at the helm. He was denied in France, ridiculed in Green Bay, and now "sleeps with the untitled."

After the fur trade began to wane, French Canadian settlers built their "ribbon farms," wide as a city lot, but stretching deep as a man could plow. With the defeat of Indian Chief Black Hawk in the 1830s, Germans and Belgians and Scandinavians poured in to farm, lumber, and some of them to mine for lead in the Galena Territory to the west. This westward motion deprived Green Bay of many settlers and was a factor in the selection of Madison as the capitol when Wisconsin achieved statehood in 1848.

Early Green Bay was an active lumber center, a port, a railroad hub, and a thriving dairy community. When the lumbermen were finished, the stump land they left was worthless and eventually reverted to the county to be sold for a dime an acre.

After the Civil War, ice became as expensive as fuel and was almost as badly needed by the growing breweries, packinghouses, and railroads. At one time Green Bay supplied five Chicago ice houses, manufacturing 300,000 tons of ice a year. Competition for workers became so intense that one company lured men with a brass band on its steam launch.

Today, highly industrialized Green Bay is an important distribution center and port of call on the St. Lawrence Seaway, with 270 boats coming and going between April and December to serve an eleven-state area to the west. Once the shingle-making capital of the country, it is now tissue-town for the world with sixteen paper mills stretching south along the river.

Green Bay also produces brick, tile, awnings, and wood and foundry products. It is a city of bridges, sprawling over 80 square miles, with a highly industrialized waterfront. An island for recreational purposes is being developed in the bay. Green Bay has some landmark houses, including the Tank home, oldest in Wisconsin, which once was a center for a Utopian community of Moravians (see Sturgeon Bay and Ephraim).

Although there have been several distinguished local sons, none compare with the generations of Green Bay Packers, who since 1919 have brought glory to this oldest of American football cities. Many years ago, a sportswriter said of the city, "Nearly 50,000 wild-eyed maniacs make up its population, and they know more about football than any other 50,000 people on earth." Today, although Green Bay has almost doubled in size, the mania remains. As a matter of fact,

A sell-out crowd at Lambeau Field, home of the Green Bay Packers.

the only time a season ticket to the games comes on the market is when the last member of a clan of Packer backers dies.

ARCHITECTURE AND HISTORIC SITES

Hazelwood, 1837–39
1008 S. Monroe St.; telephone: 497–3767 (Neville Museum phone). River house of prominent lawyer. Grandest house in territory. First draft of Wisconsin Constitution made here. Year round, daily, 10–5; closed Mon.

Heritage Hill
2632 S. Webster; telephone: 497–4368. Historic river restoration includes Tank cottage (1776), early law office, Fort Howard Museum, Cotton House. Spans 40 acres; lots of history. Tractor-pulled wagon drives visitor around. Summers 9–5.

Eleazar Williams's House (Fox River Cabin, 1820s)
Lost Dauphin Dr., DePere. Pretender to throne of Louis XVI of France. Was ambitious Mohawk Indian who spied for Americans in 1812. Came to Green Bay with false dreams of empire.

MUSEUMS

Green Bay Packer Hall of Fame
Lambeau Field, Rt. 41 and Lombardi Ave.; telephone: 499–4281. The Hall of Fame contains everything from the Packers' helmets to their jock straps. A football fan's paradise. Daily, 10–5. Watch practice: Daily, July 15–Labor Day.

National Railroad Museum
2285 S. Broadway; telephone: 435–5875. Fifty-five engines, famous trains, even a boxcar for pickles. May 1–Oct. 1, daily, 10–5.

Neville Museum
129 S. Jefferson; telephone: 497–3767. Art, history and changing exhibits. Ostensorium, censorium, first French religious object ever used in the U.S. Daily, 9–5; Sun., 2–5; free admission.

PARKS AND NATURE CENTERS

Bay Beach Wildlife Sanctuary
Sanctuary Road off East Shore Dr.; telephone: 497–3677. Summer, weekdays, noon–9; weekends, 10–9.

Pamperin County Park
2879 Memorial Dr. (at northwest edge of city, village of Howard); telephone: 497–3292 (Brown County Park Commission).

RECREATION

Amusement Park

Bay Beach Amusement Park
Sanctuary Road off East Shore Dr. Inexpensive. Kids will love it. May–Labor Day.

Golf

Woodside Golf Club (18-hole)
530 Erie Rd.; telephone: 468–5729.

Village Green (18-hole)
302 Riverdale Dr.; telephone: 434–3939.

RESTAURANTS

Carlton East
2607 N. Nicolet Dr.; telephone: 468–1086. View of bay. Steak and potatoes. Daily, 5–11 PM.

Eve's Supper Club
2020 Riverside Club; telephone: 435–1571. Steaks and prime ribs. Mon.–Fri., 11 AM–1 AM; Sat., 4:30–1 AM.

Kroll's Restaurant
1990 S. Ridge; telephone: 497–1111.

River's Bend Supper
792 Riverview Dr.; telephone: 434–1383. Mon.–Fri., lunch, 11:30–2; dinner, 5–10; Saturdays, 5–11.

Union Hotel
200 N. Broadway, DePere; telephone: 336–6131. Closed all of July and on Friday evenings.

SHOPPING

Stone Lion Complex
1523 Main; telephone: 432–4221. Tour of four buildings, all redecorated 1880 vintage homes. Ice cream, candy, and cards, Ego Gift Shop, Copper Kettle.

THEATER AND CIVIC CENTER

Brown County Veterans Memorial Arena
1901 S. Oneida; telephone: 494–3401. Shows, sports events, concerts, trade shows. Open year round.

TOURS

American Can Company
Day and Quincy sts., at river; telephone: 432–7721. Paper products–converting operation. Daily, 10 AM; minimum age, fourteen; write ahead for reservations.

Green Bay Packaging, Inc.
1107 N. Quincy, at river; telephone: 465–5000. See full production,

from pulp to roll of corrugated liner. Daily, 9–3 (four-hour tour); minimum age, sixteen; reservations.

Procter and Gamble Paper Products Company
800 University; telephone: 468–2241. June–Aug., Mon.–Fri., 10 AM and 1:30 PM, one-week notice rest of year; minimum age, twelve; telephone reservations necessary.

Ice fishermen beside their creative huts in Green Bay, Wisconsin.

Suamico

Population: 3500   Area Code: 414   Zip Code: 54173

The 1941 WPA Guidebook listed Suamico as a recreational center with a population of 206 and a general store that sold hunting and fishing equipment. Today the population is 3500, the general store is still there, and a fine 1500-acre recreational park is just 3 miles out of town. Although the majority of its citizens work and shop in nearby Green Bay, there is a hard-core of old timers still around. They recall their childhoods when they used to discover Indian burial mounds along the river banks and, digging down, always found arrow heads and other artifacts. (Archeologists take note: there's never been any serious digging done in this area.)

With its outlet to Green Bay, the mouth of the Suamico River was a natural site for a village in the 1840s. Suamico (Indian for "swampy land") survived the demise of the lumber era and gave birth to a fishing one. Today fish-houses line the shores of the river although the still-active commercial fishermen find themselves caught in the environmental crunch. A trip off the superhighway to look for the fishermen mending or tarring their nets or to watch the fishing boats come and go at the harbor's mouth is well worth the time.

Suamico is chicken-booyah territory. This stew of French-Belgium origin is made of chicken, beef, and vegetables and boils outside in 55-gallon iron kettles for a minimum of six hours before it's eaten. It is commonly served in summer at local taverns or at church picnics.

PARKS

Brown County Reforestation Camp (E. J. Smith Park)
3 miles west of U.S. 41 in Suamico on County B; telephone: 434–2632. Beautiful 1500-acre park, open year-round, with nature trails, snowmobile and cross-country ski trails, plus trout ponds, picnic areas, playground, and small zoo. There's a new rifle range, reputed to be Wisconsin's finest, and deer hunting in season.

The end of the 12-mile race at the annual dog sled meet in Suamico, Wisconsin, finds two tired dogs riding on the sled.

SHOPPING

Henry House, 1869
1749 Riverside; telephone: 434–0614. Formerly a rooming house for a lumber company. Currently sells antiques, locally made handcrafted toys, flowers. Mon.–Sat., 9–5.

Vickery's General Store, 1897
1765 Riverside; telephone: 434–2131. Every morning, from 6:30 AM, until about 9 AM, mail time, the old-timers gather 'round the potbelly stove to drink coffee and eat doughnuts. You can buy hardware, farm supplies, building materials, and pancake flour. Mon.–Sat., 6 AM–5:30 PM.

SPECIAL EVENTS

Booyah Festivals

Call churches or VFW for exact dates and locations.

St. Benedict's Catholic Church
Telephone: 434–2024. One Sun. in Aug.

St. Edwards and Isadore Parish
Telephone: 865–7677. Two Suns. — early summer and late summer.

VFW Post 9409
Telephone: 434–2237. Sun. in June.

Dogsled Races

Brown County Reforestation Camp (see Parks)
Sponsored by the Knights of Columbus. This is an exciting winter
event. Booyah is served to warm chilled bodies! Last weekend in Feb.

Oconto

Population: 5000   Area Code: 414   Zip Code: 54153
Oconto County Courthouse: County Extension Research, P.O. Box 19; tele-
phone: 834–5322

In 1952, a little boy playing near the Oconto River discovered some strange artifacts in the dirt. That innocent find turned out to be a remnant of a culture dating back 7500 years. Dr. W. F. Libby, a nuclear physicist from Chicago, carbon-dated those artifacts as well as tools and bracelets discovered later. The Copper Culture Indians are now known to have been among the world's first metalsmiths; they were surely the first citizens of Wisconsin, and a fascinating part of a civilization that existed 5500 years before the birth of Christ. Now the town of Oconto has a museum to show off its prizes, and a state park (1960) where an ancient battleground was discovered, strewn with skulls and bones and prehistoric mounds. That park is now considered the oldest cemetery in North America.

Oconto, 30 miles north of the city of Green Bay, was important historically as a lumbering town. The Holt and Balcom Logging Camp, oldest operating lumbering camp in the nation, dates back to 1880. It was called the Depot, and it was in an area of white pine so dense that people said a squirrel could travel from here all the way to Lake Superior without touching the ground.

Oconto has a cross that marks the early mission of Father Allouez (1669), the first Christian Science Church erected for worship services (1886), and the only traffic light in the whole county. The church is on the National Registry.

Oconto — a little town surrounded by marsh, new forest growth, and old farmland — also has a number of beautiful old mansions dating back to the lumber barons.

ARCHITECTURE AND HISTORIC SITES

* Christian Science Church, 1886
Chicago and Main

* Lumber Mill Office, 1854
105 Superior Ave. Now a restaurant, this restored office contains implements of lumber era.

* Governor Edward Scofield Mansion, 1868
610 Main. Another lumber baron's mansion.

St. Joseph's Catholic Church, 1870
Park and Main. Old brick church in original.

St. Peter's Catholic Church, 1899
516 Brazeau Ave. Parish founded in 1857. Site of first public meetings in Oconto County.

Father Allouez Cross
Highway 41 and 22 on Oconto River. Location of Mission of St. Francis Xavier, founded by Father Allouez in 1669.

MUSEUM

Beyer Mansion Oconto County Museum, 1868
917 Park Ave. This museum and its annex include artifacts, displays and home furnishings from the time of the Copper Culture Indians (about 5556 BC), through the John Jacob Astor Fur Trading Post (about 1825), to the restored John Beyer home, the first brick mansion in northeastern Wisconsin. May 30–Sept. 15, daily, 9–5; Sun., 12–5.

PARKS

City

Holtwood City Park
Highway 41 and Mott. This picturesque park with a river running through its 50 acres provides good camping, fishing, swimming, and picnicking.

County

North Bay Shore County Park
9 miles north of Oconto via County Y on Green Bay; telephone: 834–5322. Lovely forested park with thirty-five campsites, swimming, boat launching, hiking.

State

Copper Culture State Park
End of Mott St.; telephone: 732–0101. Indian burial grounds of the "Copper Culture" civilization estimated to have existed between 5500–5600 BC; 41 acres.

RECREATION

Boating

Breakwater in harbor

Newport Marina
County Y at Oconto River.

Fishing

Lake Michigan
Drive your car on the half-mile-long pier to the lighthouse and fish. Great view from out there!

Susie's Hill
1 mile up Oconto River from mouth. Named after an old Indian who used to live there, this is a favorite fishing site.

Golf

Edgewood Golf Course (9-hole)
Rt. 2; telephone: 834–2681.

Oconto Golf Course (9-hole)
532 Jefferson; telephone: 834–9997.

Hunting

Oconto County area is touted as a hunters' paradise, abounding in a wide variety of both large and small game. For specific information call or write to the Oconto Courthouse.

Raft and Canoe Trips

Quick Raft and Canoe Rental
Highway 22 west out of Oconto to Highway 32, west to Mountain; telephone: 715–276–7550. Combine marvelous scenery with plenty of exercise.

Skiing and Snowmobiling

For trail information, call or write to the Oconto Courthouse.

RESTAURANTS

The Chez Doulet
818 Main St.; telephone: 834–4542. Daily, 4:30–10 PM; closed Mon.

Lumbermill Pizza
106 Superior Ave.; telephone: 834–4175. Dine in the historic Holt and Balcom Lumber Office. Summers only.

Oconto Golf Club Restaurant
532 Jefferson; telephone: 834–9997. Mon.–Fri., 11:30 AM–2 PM; Fri., 5–10 PM; closed to public weekends.

SPECIAL EVENT

Lion's Steer Roast
A 1000-pound steer roasted on a spit provides the big attraction! Labor Day weekend.

Peshtigo

Population: 3,250   Area Code: 715   Zip Code: 54157
Marinette County Chamber of Commerce: 601 Marinette Avenue; telephone
735–6681

Peshtigo (Indian for "the wild goose river") once played host to huge
flocks of Canada geese flying south. But the river is not so pure now,
and the geese no longer stop — though Peshtigo is on a flyway, and
one can still see the great V-formations hemstitched across the skies.

Louis Chappee was an early fur trader; important enough to have
some river rapids named for him. In 1835, William B. Ogden, later
mayor of Chicago, helped develop the lumber business in town and
his Peshtigo Company became the biggest woodwork factory in the
U.S. People said "a Chicago businessman was building Peshtigo, and
Peshtigo Lumber, in turn, was building Chicago." There are a lot of
statistics about pails and tubs, clothes pins and barrels, but the thing
that put Peshtigo on the map . . . or almost wiped it off forever
. . . was the worst forest fire in American history.

It started October 8, 1871, the same day as the fires in Chicago and
Manistee. The summer had been a parched one with no rain for three
months and small fires had burst out repeatedly. But that afternoon
the river suddenly turned a bilious color, the sun disappeared, leaving
a strange yellow light, and soundless birds flew away. John Cameron,
a woodsman who survived, described the ash that began to fall, and
then the hideous low moan that turned to a great roar as a hurricane
of fire broke loose. Deer and wolves fled together, and as fire reached
the town, people rushed for the river, the streets a jumble of cows,
horses, humans, and wagons. The factory and the sawmill exploded,
and burning logs were hurled in the water among drowning people.
One lady saved her life by grabbing on to the horns of a passing steer.
In one hour during that night, Peshtigo was burned clean except for
a single house. Eight hundred people lost their lives; 1,280,000 acres
of timber were destroyed. The smoke from the holocaust traveled all
across the lake. When, twenty-four hours later — twenty-four hours
too late — the rain finally came, it quenched a fire that had been far
more devastating than Chicago's. Today some of that burned-over

land is called Sugar Bush Country and has proven productive for
farming. Some of it produces extraordinarily large huckleberries. And
much of it has been planted in trees by schoolchildren hired to help
reforest during the labor shortage of World War II.

Today Peshtigo has a fire museum, fittingly housed in a church
built after the fire. Next to it is a Fire Cemetery (on the National
Registry of Historic Places) with individual stones as well as a mass
grave for 300 unidentified human beings.

Peshtigo, like the phoenix bird, has risen from its ashes, but not
without ups and downs. Its barge and ferry service (Peshtigo and
Chicago) struggled for the first decade of the twentieth century and
failed because of terrible storms and ice conditions on Green Bay. The
sawmills began closing in 1914. The depression hit hard. But today the
Badger Paper Mill turns out 32,000 tons of paper yearly, its profit-
sharing plan a pilot for U.S. industry. Thompson Boats, started in
1904, by six brothers who made canoes at home, is now turning out
fiber glass boats. The ownership has changed hands, but it has been
estimated that there are 400,000 Thompsons on American waters.

Logs awaiting their fate at the Badger Paper Company in Peshtigo,
Wisconsin.

MUSEUM AND CEMETERY

Peshtigo Historical Museum
Ellis and Oconto. A monument in the cemetery and the museum housed in old St. Mary's Church commemorate the terrible October 8, 1871, fire that took the lives of 800 of Peshtigo's citizens. May 30–Oct., daily, 9–5.

PARKS

Badger Park
Along Peshtigo River in Peshtigo. This 100-acre densely wooded park offers thirty-five campsites plus swimming, fishing, hiking, and picnicking.

Peshtigo Harbor Wildlife Area
U.S. 41, 5 miles south of Peshtigo to County Line Rd. Follow east to Green Bay to mouth of Peshtigo River. This lovely wooded nature area provides swimming, hiking, fishing, picnicking.

RESTAURANT

Schussler's
County B; telephone: 582–4962. German food a specialty. Daily, 5 PM–10 PM; closed Mon.

TOUR

Badger Paper Mills, Inc.
East of U.S. 41 from bridge on W. Front Street; telephone: 582–4551. June 1–Labor Day, Mon.–Fri., 9 AM & 1 PM. Age limit, twelve; advance notice for groups of ten or more.

Marinette

Population: 13,500   Area Code: 715   Zip Code: 54143
Chamber of Commerce: 601 Marinette Avenue; telephone: 735–6681
Tourist Information (summers): Stephenson Island, U.S. 41 at Wisconsin-
    Michigan Interstate Bridge

Marinette and Menominee (which follows), referred to as "the two towns" and never the twin cities, share the Menominee River, which also serves as the dividing line between Wisconsin and Michigan. Marinette stretches west, away from Green Bay, and Menominee lies along the lake. Marinette calls itself the midway point between the North Pole and the Equator.

The explorer Nicolet came into this area in 1634, but it was another 150 years before the next white men arrived. They were fur traders and one of them, William Farnsworth, and his wife became leading citizens of the growing town. She was known as "Queen Marinette," the name being a contraction of "Marie Antoinette," who was the royal favorite of the time.

The town was incorporated in 1888. A brief silver and red granite mining boom was followed by such lumbering prosperity that Marinette became the timbering capitol of the world's biggest white pine forest. The Swedish, Irish, Norwegian, and French-Canadian lumberjacks were, like their counterparts elsewhere, hardworking, harddrinking men, and the town museum tells their story, right up to the day that the pine and hardwoods disappeared. (Due to reforestation, there is now lumbering again, with the timber used for paper and wood products.)

Today Marinette has many fine summer homes (always called "camps") in the Cedar River, Michigan, area. It also has both a deer and bear hunting season, during which it is not uncommon to see a great black bear draped across the roof of a car. When spring comes, there are great clusters of wildflowers, and canoe and other boat enthusiasts arrive from all over the Midwest.

Local companies include Scott Paper, the Ansul Company (which manufactures fire extinguishers and runs a famous fire school in techniques of chemical fire fighting), and businesses making gloves, beauty and barber supplies, and boats. The Harmon Knitwear Company is most famous for its designer, Rudi Gernreich, who in 1964 introduced the topless bathing suit, but went out of business in 1975.

Marinette is also known for its archeological digs, where scientists have unearthed relics of both the copper and red ocher cultures.

ARCHITECTURE AND HISTORIC SITES

Carney Home, 1895
2125 Riverside Ave. Home of an early Marinette pioneer built from local lumber.

Hamilton Home, 1915
2115 Riverside Ave. Another pioneer lumberman's home.

Lauerman Home, 1910
1975 Riverside Ave. A beautiful pillared home.

Lindem Home, 1881
2507 Taylor St. The builder of this house built many others in Marinette during the sawmill era.

Senator Stephenson's Wedding-Present Houses, 1880s
1919 Riverside Ave., 1931 Riverside Ave. The senator built these homes side-by-side for his daughters when they married.

MUSEUM

Marinette County Historical Logging Museum
U.S. 41 at Menominee River, Stephenson Island; telephone: 732–0831. Marvelous replica of all phases of a Menominee River lumber camp highlights this wonderful teaching museum. Also interesting display of nests and eggs of birds native to area. Memorial Day–mid-Oct., daily, 10–5.

ORCHARD

Strawberry Petersons
Shore Dr., south of Marinette on Green Bay; telephone: 735–3784. Pick your own or buy them at the farmstand in season.

PARKS

Marinette City Park
Pierce Avenue and Carney Blvd. A 100-acre park with camping, hiking, picnicking.

Camping in a northern Wisconsin forest. *Marinette County Outdoor Recreation Office*

Red Arrow Park
End of Leonard St. and Green Bay. Swim, hike, and picnic on these beautiful 60 acres.

Stephenson Island Park
U.S. 41 at bridge over Menominee River. Fishing and picnicking.

RECREATION
For information on winter sports, hunting, fishing, camping, contact the Marinette County Courthouse, Outdoor Recreation Department, 1926 Hall Ave., Marinette, Wisconsin 54143; telephone: 735-3371.

Bicycling

"Twin City Historical Bicycle Tour"
Ten-mile tour (available at either city's Chamber of Commerce) includes pedaling past the outstanding historical and cultural sites in Marinette, Menominee, and Peshtigo (printed by the Ansul Company).

A raccoon looks out at a Wisconsin morning. *Edgar G. Mueller*

Birding

Sea Gull Bar
Sandspit adjacent to Red Arrow Park near mouth of Menominee River and Green Bay Harbor. This scientific area under the auspices of the state of Michigan is an excellent birding area and flyway. Sandspit extends 1 mile into bay. Accessible by hiking only.

Boating

Little River Boat Landing
County BB at river's mouth and Green Bay.

M & M Launching Ramp
Bay Shore Dr. in Red Arrow Park.

Reimer's Marina
Menominee River at U.S. 41 Bridge. Small craft harbor.

Riverview Park Launching Ramp
U.S. 41 at Menominee River.

Stephenson Island
U.S. 41 at Bridge. Launching ramp.

Canoeing

Outdoor Expeditions, Inc.
P.O. Box 274, Crevitz 54114; telephone: 854–7863. Whitewater and quietwater trips arranged; also ski rentals.

Fishing

Fisherman's Walkway
Hattie St. Bridge at Menominee River.

Lighthouse and Pier on Michigan side
Mouth of Menominee River at Green Bay.

Menominee River
Entire river; especially good from bay to first dam.

Golf

Little River Country Club (18-hole)
Shore Drive, 2 miles south of Marinette; telephone: 735–7234.

Swimming

Runnoe Park in Marinette
End of University Dr. at Green Bay.

RESTAURANTS

Bill Brown's Supper Club
U.S. 41, 4 miles south of Marinette; telephone: 735–9872. Try the homemade soup. Daily, 5 PM–10 PM; closed Tues.

Lolli's
2029 Hall Ave.; telephone: 735–3044. Try the Sunday brunch. Daily, 11 AM–midnight; Sun., 11 AM–2 PM.

Rivergate
River Rd., 1 mile north of Marinette; telephone: 732–0589. Daily, 11:30 AM–midnight; Sun., 5 PM–midnight.

SHOPPING

Art Works Gallery
1520 Main St.; telephone: 732–0379. Gallery in charming old house displays and sells work of local artists.

SPECIAL EVENT

Waterfront Festival

Midwestern Mariner Scouts (nautical arm of the Girl and Boy Scouts) compete in water events — log-rolling, canoeing, swimming, etc. Third weekend in July.

THEATER

Campus Theater

UW Center, W. Bay Shore; telephone: 735–7477. Good summer theater. Call for exact information on schedules.

TOURS

The Ansul Company

1 Stanton St.; telephone: 735–7411. Makes fire extinguishers, industrial chemicals, and operates fire school in summer. Tours must be scheduled in advance.

Marinette Marine Corporation

Ely St.; telephone: 735–9341. Arrange tours of this shipbuilding company in advance.

Scott Paper Company

3120 Riverside Ave; telephone: 735–6644. All Scott paper products manufactured here. Mon.–Fri., 3 PM; arrange in advance.

Michigan

FROM
MENOMINEE
TO
GRAND BEACH

Menominee

Population: 11,000   Area Code: 906   Zip Code: 49858
Chamber of Commerce: 1005 10th Ave.; telephone: 863–2679

The other half of the "two towns" is Menominee (meaning "wild rice"). Long the only city in a county rich in small towns, woods (175,000 acres), lakes, streams, and legends, Menominee is still the gateway to that vacationer's paradise, Michigan's Upper Peninsula.

The Menominee Indians were here before the white men. Though peaceful, they were finally provoked by the Chippewa, who challenged their fishing rights, and the two fought the Sturgeon Wars (there aren't many sturgeon left now; Chippewa or Menominee either). A tablet in town marks the ancient Bay de Nocquet Trail, used by Indians for eons, and by U.S. mail runners too as they headed farther north.

Nicolet came through the area; Father Claude Allouez built a mission on the river; and finally in the 1830s thousands of lumbermen came to strip the pine. Superstitious, they often refused to cut popple (poplar), or sleep in a bed made of it, for it was the wood used to make Christ's cross, and thus accursed. But they cut everything else, and they kept at it long after Menominee was incorporated (1883) and right up to the early 1930s when the last of the mills closed. When the great fires of 1871 almost wrecked Chicago, and devastated Peshtigo, Menominee too was threatened. But all women and children were put to sea in boats and the men stayed behind and saved Menominee. The effects of the conflagration, however, were felt for a long time. The peat bogs over near Cedar River burned for months, and people said that that winter the smoke burned right through the snow.

In its early days Menominee had an opera house, decorated in maroon velvet with seats for 144 and visiting performers like Maude Adams and Otis Skinner. Now a storage house, the opera building is part of a lost culture, just as the dome-shaped kilns one sees around town are part of a lost craft. Menominee was once a major charcoal center, where hardwoods were burned and sent on to blast furnaces to help make steel.

Each spring for twenty-five years, the first boat into Menominee

Charter fishing on Lake Michigan. *Michigan Travel Commission*

harbor has been the *D. C. Everest,* owned by the American Can Company, which makes thirty-five annual round trips to Marathon, Ontario. The ship has both economic and emotional importance to Menominee, for it hauls supplies and many of its Canadian crews have married local girls. Another nautical landmark is the *Alvin Clark,* built in 1846, sunk in 1866, and recovered in 1969. Now it is moored at the riverfront and tourable.

Today Menominee has a diversified economy. The Scott Paper Company is here, as is the Enstrom Helicopter Company, formerly owned by Boston's famous lawyer F. Lee Bailey. Other local products are doll buggies, canned foods, nuclear reactor parts, sporting nets, bridges, and patio furniture. On the lawn of the state tourist center, Menominee keeps its Spirit Stone, a good-luck piece dating from Indian days: when the last of the stone is weathered away, the legend goes, the last of the braves will have gone to the Happy Hunting Grounds.

ARCHITECTURE AND HISTORIC SITES

* Courthouse, 1889
10th St. and 10th Ave.

* First Street Area
From 4th Ave. to 10th Ave. this shopping district boasts a marvelous collection of old limestone and brick buildings.

* The Mystery Ship
Berthed in River Park just east of the Interstate Bridge.

Archeological Digs
North end of 14th Ave. into Riverside Cemetery. University of Michigan and the Oshkosh and Milwaukee public museums have unearthed fifty-two burial pits with evidence of two cultures.

Charcoal Kilns
10 miles west of Cedar River on Highway 352.

MUSEUM

Menominee County Historical Society Museum
904 11th Ave.; telephone: 863–6221. Artifacts and curios from early Menominee families and commerce. Children are allowed to touch! June 1–Oct. 1, daily, 10–5.

PARKS

Air Port Park
4 miles north of Menominee on M-35 on Green Bay. Camping, hiking.

Bailey Park
14 miles north of Menominee on M-35 on Green Bay. Camping, fishing, swimming, boat launch, hiking.

Fox Park
8 miles north of Cedar River on M-35 on Green Bay. Camping, hiking, fishing, swimming.

Henes Park and Zoo
End of 38th Ave. and Green Bay. Swimming, nature trails, deer, buffalo, picnicking on 68 acres.

Kleinke Park
15 miles north of Menominee on M-35 on Green Bay. Swimming, boating, fishing, picnicking.

Rochereau Park
13 miles north of Menominee on M-35 on Green Bay. Camping, swimming, boating, fishing.

J. W. Wells State Park
1 mile southwest of Cedar River off M-35; telephone: 863–9747. Quiet, family-type 974-acre park with 155 campsites, fine beach, fishing, boat launch. Outdoor center can be reserved by groups. Winter sports. Open all year.

RECREATION

Bicycling

"Twin City Historical Bicycle Tour"
Ten-mile tour (available at either city's Chamber of Commerce) includes pedaling past the outstanding historical and cultural sites in Marinette, Menominee, and Peshtigo (printed by the Ansul Company).

Boats

Great Lakes Memorial Park and Marina
End of 10th Ave. at Green Bay. Small craft and yacht harbor and boat launch.

Little River Boat Landing
County BB at river's mouth and Green Bay.

M & M Launching Ramp
Bay Shore Dr. in Red Arrow Park.

Reimer's Marina
Menominee River at U.S. 41 Bridge. Small-craft harbor.

Riverview Park Launching Ramp
U.S. 41 at Menominee River.

Stephenson Island
U.S. 41 at Bridge. Launching ramp.

Fishing

Fisherman's Walkway
Hattie St. Bridge at Menominee River.

Lighthouse and Pier on Michigan side
Mouth of Menominee River at Green Bay.

Menominee River
Entire river; especially good from bay to first dam.

Swimming

Menominee Beach Area in Marina Park
Near pier at river mouth in Green Bay.

RESTAURANT

Jozwiak's
1010 16th Ave.; telephone: 863–2229. Good hamburgers and pizza. Daily, 10:30 AM–midnight.

SPECIAL EVENT

Waterfront Festival
Midwestern Mariner Scouts (nautical arm of the Girl and Boy Scouts) compete in water events — log-rolling, canoeing, swimming, etc. Third weekend in July.

TATTOOING

Ed's Tattooing
607 First St. No minors, the sign says!

TOURS

Enstrom Helicopter Corporation
Telephone: 863–9971. Call in advance for tours.

Menominee Paper Company, Inc.
Telephone: 863–5595. Waxtex products made here. Tours must be arranged in advance.

Escanaba

Population: 15,300   Area Code: 906   Zip Code: 49829
Chamber of Commerce: Delta County Area Chamber of Commerce, 230 Lud-
ington Street; telephone: 786-2192

They call Escanaba the Riviera of the North — it is a charming city with a waterfront almost as lovely as Chicago's — and the banana belt of the Upper Peninsula.

Blessed with neither coal nor iron nor minerals, Escanaba's great resource is, and has always been, water: water for power, for shipping, fishing, lumbering, and recreation. Fortunately, beginning with Eli P. Royce who platted Escanaba in the early 1860s, the city has always kept its shoreline open for aesthetic reasons and for recreational purposes.

Man's life in the area of the Little and Big Bays de Noc, fingers of Lake Michigan, probably goes back 5000 years to the copper culture and the Indians who carved and painted their caves centuries ago. After the copper period, the Woodland Indians arrived — Sauk, Fox, Chippewa, and the gentle Nocs who were around when the French explorers paddled their canoes through the water highways of the Northland. The peaceful Nocs (also spelled Noques, Nokes, Noquettes) avoided war, preferring trade with the French. In time, a series of punitive treaties, and the softening effects of trade with the whites, brought their culture to an end. The few Nocs who survived were absorbed into the Chippewa tribes. Today only their name remains in the bays, and the remnants of their culture in the local Delta County Historical Museum.

In the beginning, Escanaba (then Sand Point) was a vast sweep of dunes, backed by a primeval forest, girdled with a great glut of berries. In the 1830s lumber cruisers arrived, searching for the great fir trees necessary to build an inland America. Rough and ready, these jacks created small settlements where the many rivers met the bay. They set up saw mills and systematically began the greatest plunder of forest ever known. Trees went down and were hauled by sled to the rivers where they were rolled to the nearest mills and awaiting schooners. In late spring, the men arrived in town, money jingling in their

Escanaba harbor at night. *Paul F. Gerard*

pockets. Their desire for "Montana Red Eye" and for the Miss Marys of Thomas Street was limitless. To give an inkling of the values of the day, in 1902 Escanaba had thirteen blacksmiths, twelve lawyers, twenty-four medics, and eighty-eight saloons. Great cargoes of logs, 4000 carloads a year, were shipped out. The Escanaba Manufacturing Company alone packed off two carloads a day of clothespins, toothpicks, butter dishes, and shingles. And when the pine and fir were gone, the men shifted to hardwoods (more difficult to lumber as the trees cannot be rolled in water). Today, 95 percent of the world's supply of bird's-eye maple still lies within 200 miles of Escanaba. The *Queen Mary* alone required 100,000 square feet of the wood.

Vital in the development of Escanaba was the arrival in 1837 of Michigan state geologist Douglas Houghton. In search of minerals, he found the great iron and copper ranges of the Upper Peninsula and the Gogebic range of Minnesota. The challenge became how to unlock this treasure from the earth, and then how to transport the ore to the harbors. The mining era began. William B. Ogden, who had recently served as Chicago's first mayor, and now headed the Galena and Western Railroad, saw the challenge and dreamed of a rail system that would connect the developing mines with the great natural harbor at Sand Point. In 1859, he bought the floundering Chicago, St. Paul and Fond du Lac Railroad, changed its name to the Chicago and Northwestern, and brought a branch of it, the Peninsula Railroad, from the mines to the port. With the outbreak of the Civil War, pressure mounted to extract more ore for munitions and shipbuilding.

Escanaba (renamed by an Indian prince, John Jacobs, in 1863) became a boom town. Lumbermen piled into town. So did rail workers. The ore docks were made higher and longer to service the schooners, and later the steamers and freighters, for their journeys down to the lower Lake. By the 1890s Escanaba billed itself as the largest iron ore shipping port in the world, exceeding even Liverpool. Today Escanaba's ore dock with its mechanical loaders is still a vital link to the steel plants of Chicago and Gary and Burns Harbor.

There was a time when fishing was also a great Escanaba industry. Early accounts tell of nets so filled with sturgeon, pike, trout, and whitefish that they were too heavy to empty. But there have been changes. The lamprey eel wrecked havoc on the whitefish. Sturgeon, once only eaten by the Indians, has now become rare and a delicacy. Today, smelt have come into their own. In April, men march in torchlight parades to celebrate the runs of millions of the tiny fish and huge bonfires brighten the banks of the lake at night. Smelt are not only food for mink and cats but for humans as well. The Hansen Cannery in nearby Gladstone processes millions of pounds of smelt for the local Whitey Cat Food Company.

The greatest day in Escanaba, indeed the whole Upper Peninsula, is November 15, a regional holiday when schools close, stores shut, and 100,000 hunters take to the woods. Fourteen days later 100,000 deer will have been shot and local butchers will be working overtime to cut up the animals for home freezers. The bear season that follows has no such popularity as this.

Escanaba has changed a good deal over the years. Its iron ore docks have been built and rebuilt, and are now mechanized. Lumbering today is largely for wood pulp to make papers for magazines. The fishing fleets have diminished. The biggest employer in town is now the Harnischfeger Corporation, makers of cranes, excavators, and welding equipment.

But Escanaba has its local claims to distinction. It was home for Mary Terry, first woman lighthouse keeper in the nation. It was also chosen as the place to retire by Dan Seavey, the only known pirate on the Great Lakes.

ART CENTER

William Bonifas Fine Arts Center
7th St. and 1st Ave. South; telephone: 786–3833. Changing art and cultural shows. Also, the theater for the Players De Noc, Inc.

FAIR

Upper Peninsula State Fair
12th Ave. north and Lincoln Rd.; telephone: 786–4011. Usually, third week in August; call Chamber of Commerce for exact information.

MUSEUM

Delta County Historical Museum
Lake Shore Dr., Sand Point. Good, though small, local collection of Indian heads, minerals, old bottles, geology and history of area. An active historical society. The museum has a witness tree with the scribe marks left by lumber cruisers as they surveyed the tracts of forest preparing for the onslaught of the lumberjacks. June–Labor Day, daily, 1–9.

MUSIC

Band Concerts
Frank Karas Memorial Band Shell. June (late), July, and August, 7:30 PM.

PARKS AND MARSHES

Ford River Public Access
Where river meets Lake, 7 miles south of Escanaba on M-35. Toilets, fishing, ramp. No camping. 4 miles off in the Lake are 3 limestone slabs that look like an island. They are part of the old logging town of Ford River. Also notice Round Island, a mile out in the Lake, reachable by walking on a very shallow knee-deep shoal. No predators on the island, it is inhabited by ducks, seagulls.

Hiawatha National Forest
Escanaba to St. Ignace; telephone: 573–6155. One million acres, including twenty-one campgrounds, eighteen picnic sites, controlled lumbering. Hunting and fishing, wildlife sanctuaries. One of major

forests of U.S. You may see deer, beaver ponds, bear, and other small game. For information about hunting, animal preserves and Birch Farm, call the Hiawatha National Forest. Maintained by the U.S. Department of Agriculture.

Ludington Park
Lake Shore Dr. Marvelous Lakefront park with beach, bath house, picnicking, tennis courts, marina, boat ramps, lighthouse. Daily, 7:30 AM–II PM.

Portage Point Road Marsh
South edge of Escanaba off M-35. Fishing and several boat launches.

RECREATION

Birding

For information, call Michigan Department of Natural Resources: 786–2351. Waterfowl and marsh birds, sharptailed grouse, dancing grounds, sandhill cranes abound throughout the area.

Fishing

For information on year-round fishing, call Michigan Department of Natural Resources: 786–2351. Ten smelt streams in area. Little Bay de Noc, Big Bay de Noc, Escanaba Yacht Basin, and streams in national forest. Charter boats almost nonexistent in this part of Upper Peninsula.

Horseback Riding

Stoney Acres Farm
10 miles south of Escanaba on M-35; telephone: 786–3500. Riding, lessons, boarding.

Hunting

For information, call Michigan Department of Natural Resources (786–2351) or Hiawatha National Forest (573–6155).

RESTAURANTS

Halstead's Bayside Park, Motel and Restaurant
R.1 Bark River, Michigan, 49807. M-35, 16 miles south of Escanaba; telephone: 786–3763. May 1–November 1, 7 AM–9 PM.

Terrace Motor Inn & Restaurant
U.S. 2 and 41; telephone: 786–7554. Wonderful Lake view. Fresh broiled whitefish. Breakfast, 7–10; lunch, noon–2; dinner 5:30–10; bar.

SHOPS

Bay de Noc Taxidermy
Rt. 1, Box 410A; telephone: 786–9029. For the hunter who wants trophies — fish, game, waterfowl and small mammals can be preserved here.

Deloria Sales
412 Ludington St.; telephone: 786–6097. Everything, but everything in the line of stoves and fireplaces, cook-out cutlery, etc.

Marble Arms
420 Industrial Park; telephone: 428–3710. Manufacturing and retail shop. Largely a wholesaler. Marble is one of the oldest firms in the area, founded in 1898. It makes gunsights, knives, compasses. Around the country there are some 20,000 collectors of Marble Products. Company also makes waterproof matches. Mon.–Fri., 9–4:30.

MiAnne Port & Dive Shop
M-35, South of Escanaba, on Lake; telephone: 786–6740. Dono Hoff sells everything for the snorkel and scuba trade.

TOURS

Mead Paper Company
Off M-35, on the Escanaba River; telephone: 786–1660. Part of Escanaba's economy for half a century, today the company uses pulp to make paper for publishing. Guided tours are available; call in advance.

Saykilly's Candy Factory
1815 3rd Ave. North; telephone: 786–3092.

VIEWS AND DRIVES

Start at Escanaba on U.S. 2/41. Stay on this till you pick up Route 513 on Stonington Peninsula. Head south at Peninsula, until you reach Peninsula Point where you can picnic.

Start at Escanaba, U.S. 2/41 west to Hyde — pick up Rd. 521, south to Ford River, where you pick up M-35 and stay on it to Escanaba.

Northwestern Railroad Ore Docks

M-35. Turn right on Ludington, turn left into Stephenson. At second traffic light, veer right. At Shell oil site, go over two sets of tracks. At dock sign, turn right and continue to a small parking lot. Fine spot to watch the great mechanical loaders filling the freighters. Also, naval ships and passenger craft come to the docks.

Gladstone

Population: 5237   Area Code: 906   Zip Code: 49831
Delta County Chamber of Commerce; 230 Ludington Street, Escanaba; tele-
phone: 786–2192

In 1887 W. D. Washburn, appointed surveyor general of Minnesota by Abraham Lincoln, explored the shoreline of Little Bay de Noc in search of a protected harbor and a good location for rail lines to link the bays with the Mississippi and the Soo. At that time the area had nothing but a hunting lodge on one side and a fisherman's hut on the other, but Washburn established a tent city of 1800 people within five years. Four thousand acres of primeval forest were cut and tons of rock excavated to lay out a town and to build a one-quarter-mile-long dock (capable of holding 80,000 barrels of flour) and an elevator (capable of storing 200,000 bushels of grain.)

Washburn called the new town Gladstone after the great English statesman (some years later he became U.S. senator from Minnesota himself). Those years were boom ones and the little town swelled as millions of logs floated down the Whitefish River to the lumber mills; tons of coal rumbled west; and bushels of wheat steamed east.

When the pine forests were almost depleted, the hardwoods were lumbered. An enterprising forester named Webster Marble invented a safety ax, and established the Marble Arms Company whose products are now used worldwide. A Ford plant, a tannery, and a mining company soon opened up, and for a while Gladstone prospered enough to support a restaurant that employed a famous chef from Boston. But the boom didn't last. The Fords left, and so did the tanners, the miners, and the diners.

Today Gladstone still has a few industries but, like Escanaba, its greatest asset is its water.

CEMETERY

Pioneer Trail Park
U.S. 41 at the bridge. Many pioneers buried here.

ORCHARDS

Daniel Barron
Cornell, northwest of Gladstone off U.S. 2; telephone: 786–7027.
Strawberries.

Victor Ledvina
County 426 (2 miles north of paper mill); telephone: 786–3614. Strawberries.

PARK

Van Cleve City Park
Gladstone Yacht Harbor. Overlooking Little Bay de Noc. Boat ramp,
beach house, swimming.

RECREATION

Golf

The Bluff
Lake Bluff Rd.; telephone: 428–2343.

Gladstone Golf Club
Days River Rd.; telephone: 428–9646.

Marina

Point Marine
On Little Bay de Noc; telephone: 428–4039.

RESTAURANT

Log Cabin Restaurant
Rt. 2, 6 miles out of Escanaba; telephone: 786–5621. Daily, 5–10:30;
closed Sun.

SHOPPING

Hoegh Industries, Inc.
311 Delta Ave., P.O. Box 173; telephone: 428–2151. Hoegh manufactures caskets for beloved deceased pets; some satin-lined and embroidered. From birds to dalmations, from $5–$180. Lots of business with National Association of Pet Cemeteries, and many clients abroad.

Rapid River (Masonville Township)

Population: 600   Zip Code: 49878

Stonington Peninsula

Population: 900   Zip Code: 49878

Nahma

Population: 125   Zip Code: 49864

Garden Peninsula

Population: 340   Zip Code: 49835

Fayette

Population: 20   Zip Code: 49835

Fairport

Population: 150   Zip Code: 49835

Thompson

Population: 100   Zip Code: 49889

Rapid River

This is where the old Indian Trail that the Nocs used as path between Lake Michigan and Lake Superior begins. The U.S. Forest Service now has reconstructed the trail for hiking and riding. The town is on U.S. 2 and County 513.

Winter on Little Bay de Noc from Stonington, UP. *Paul F. Gerard*

Stonington Peninsula

The Stonington Peninsula is the finger of land that divides Little Bay de Noc from Big Bay de Noc. Settled by Scandinavian farmers and fishermen in the last century, today it is largely inhabited by folks from Escanaba and Gladstone who have their summer camps here.

Nahma

Nahma is seven miles south of U.S. 2 on Big Bay de Noc, midway between the Stonington and Garden peninsulas. At the turn of the century it was a booming lumber town with a hotel and 450 townspeople. On July 26, 1951, the last log was sawed at the big mill in town, and a feeling of doom settled over the community. The town was put up for sale . . . one more Upper Peninsula Ghost Town. Then a stroke of luck: the American Playground Device Company of Anderson, Indiana, bought it and made elaborate plans to create a manufacturing and recreational center. So far $14,000,000 has been invested, but terrible storms, inadequate electricity, and other problems have plagued the project. Though equipment is slowly being installed, the 4300 acres of beautiful bayfront land are largely idle.

PARKS

Ten Mile Rapids Park (at Sturgeon River)
4 miles north of Nahma Junction on Forest Highway 13.

Flowingwell National Forest Campgrounds
U.S. 2 and Federal Forest Highway 13. Picnic tables; fishing; ten camping sites.

Garden Peninsula

At U.S. 2 and County Rt. 483 one enters the Garden Peninsula, a pastoral area of rolling meadows, birch and maple woods, small churches, large barns and isolated farms. Side roads wind down to coves, caves, and Lake bluffs and the main road runs through Garden, a tiny town with a couple of churches, a school, and some simple grocery stores. Warning: if you are picnicking or camping, get your supplies here, for eating out is not "in," and the area is short on restaurants. But it is ancient country, its history perhaps dating back to the Copper Culture. Unfortunately the prehistoric paintings and pictographs, well known to archeologists and university scientists, are all on private lands and out of bounds for visitors.

RESTAURANT

Tylene's Restaurant
U.S. 2, at entrance to Garden Peninsula, Cooks, MI 49817; telephone: 644–2283. Daily, 6 AM–10 PM.

Fayette

The magnificently preserved town of Fayette and Fayette State Park are on the National Historic Registry, and they are, in the judgment of many yachters and UP (Upper Peninsula) enthusiasts, among the "must" places to see on the Lake.

Fayette, an old iron smelting town that flourished from 1867 to 1891, was named for the Jackson Iron Company's general manager, Fayette Brown. Brown laid out the company town (an interesting contrast to Pullman in Chicago or Marktown in East Chicago), and oversaw the working of the furnaces and the welfare of the 450 residents of that beautiful but isolated setting.

As early as 1845 a Chippewa chieftain had told the Jackson Company's prospectors about rich veins of iron ore in the UP, and for many years thereafter crude ore was shipped east to foundries to fabricate pig iron.

But the crude ore was full of waste products and expensive to transport, so to cut costs, local smelter sites were sought. Fayette became the second largest iron smelting operation in the UP during the later nineteenth century. Its preeminence was due to the availability of ore, natural deposits of limestone and the hardwoods used to make charcoal, all products necessary to smelting.

The thriving community with its old hotel and opera house, furnaces and kilns, workers' homes and doctor's office, was — and is — scattered over a glorious hilly site. The citizens of 100 years ago were a diverse lot from many countries and faiths who shared the

Old Fayette on the Garden Peninsula of the UP. *Paul F. Gerard*

work and the sense that they were isolated from a larger America. One spoke for all when he wrote, "in winter it is a little dull; sometimes the rest of the world seems a great way off."

With the development of the rails, the great ore docks and blast furnaces to the south, Fayette slipped into history, another reminder of the way life had been lived long ago.

RECREATION

The major recreation area in Fayette is, of course, the state park. For information on the park and its facilities, contact the Visitor Center, County 483 (telephone: 644–2603). The park is open in the spring, summer, and fall from 9 AM to 7 PM; the Visitor Center is open from 8 AM to 10 PM; guided tours are given between 11:30 AM and 2 PM.

Camping

Portage Bay Campgrounds
Bay de Noc Forest (10 miles south of County 483 and Portage Bay Rd.). Twelve campsites, boating, fishing, swimming.

Marina

Snail Shell Harbor Marina
Fayette. A small number of slips. An absolutely glorious site with limestone cliffs across the harbor and the town around it.

Swimming

Sandy Bay
Fayette.

Sac Bay Park
Fayette.

Fairport

Fairport is a charming little fishing village at the end of the Garden Peninsula. The total population is perhaps 100, and most families are involved in commercial fishing, making the isolated area seem a jumble of nets, floats, buoys, and boats.

Thompson

Thompson is a tiny hamlet on the Lake, near the important state fish hatchery, and a popular fishing spot. Blink an eye and you have entered and left town.

Park

Frank F. Rogers Roadside Park
Swimming, picnicking. Beautiful Lake view.

Hatchery

Thompson State Fish Hatchery
7 miles SW of Manistique on U.S. 2 and 1/4 mile N on M-149; telephone: 341–6917. Propagate several varieties of trout, coho, muskies, northern and walleye pike. Fishing licenses provide revenue for fishery. Daily, 8–4:30; closed Sat. and Sun.

Manistique

Population: 4700   Area Code: 906   Zip Code: 49854
Chamber of Commerce: Water Tower, U.S. 2 at bridge (Deer St.); telephone:
341–5010

Manistique ("red ochre river") is the only sizable town between Gladstone and St. Ignace. Now known as "the motel city," it has become a popular four-season area for sportsmen, because of its two rivers and generous woods.

Nicolet was the first to come through here (in 1634) and many believe that La Salle stopped here with his ship, *Griffon,* the first boat on the Lake. But it was in the lumbering era that Manistique flexed its muscles and grew. One lumber king named George Orr determined that his town was not going to be like other "sin cities" of the north, bought up all the land he could to keep things clean — but forgot one piece at the end of the settlement, which naturally became a saloon, and later the central business district of Manistique.

When lumbering was at its height, the jacks came to town to spree, offending the citizens with their carousing and making a great issue for the temperance preachers. (One circuit-riding Methodist who came to preach was the grandfather of actor Fred MacMurray. In time, he became a newspaper publisher, but was so blunt that the many libel suits brought against him forced him out of business.) The big lumber companies, of course, were all for temperance and provided free lemonade for the whole town at Fourth of July celebrations. But on the side of sin were the whiskey boats that anchored off shore and did a lively nightly trade.

The little city at the top of the Lake has had a lot of interchange with the giant at the bottom, including Chicago ownerships of the biggest mills; the limestone quarries; and, today, the largest employer in town, the Manistique Paper Mill (a subsidiary of Field Enterprises, which publishes the Chicago *Sun Times*).

ARCHITECTURE AND HISTORIC SITES

Siphon Bridge
U.S. 2, in town. A Ripley oddity because bridge is really below level of Manistique River and uses water pressure for support.

ORCHARD

Strawberry Acres
M-422; telephone: 644–2761.

PARKS

Indian Lake State Park and Museum
4 miles west of Manistique on County 442. 160 campsites on one side of Indian Lake; 144 on other. Beach, hiking, canoeing. Camping limited to fifteen days. Museum contains Indian displays and artifacts. Daily, June 15–Labor Day, 8–10.

Palms-Book State Park *(Kitch-iti-kipi)*
4 miles west of Manistique on U.S. 2, to County 442, to M-149. Beautiful spring, biggest in Michigan. Marvelous clear water. Picnicking; no camping. Raft rides. Great for kids. Busy.

RECREATION

Fishing and Hunting

This area has state and national lands open to deer and small game hunters in marshlands, small inland lakes. For information, call the Chamber of Commerce. Fishing at breakwater and at Intake Park. Good ice fishing.

Golf

Indian Lake Golf Course (9-hole)
U.S. 2 to 94; 3 miles north, left at schoolhouse, watch signs, telephone: 341–5600. May 1–October 15.

Marina

Marina
One block from downtown. Any size boats.

Snowmobiling

The Haywire
From Manistique to Alger County through wilderness. 33-mile right of way of Manistique & Lake Superior Railroad. For information, call Chamber of Commerce.

RESTAURANTS

Fireside Restaurant
3 1/2 miles east of town, U.S. 2; telephone: 341–6332.

Surf Restaurant
Ramada Inn, 2 miles east of town, U.S. 2; telephone: 341–6911. Lake view.

SPECIAL EVENTS

Schoolcraft County Fair
Manistique Chamber of Commerce. Annual corn roast. August.

Blessing of the Fleet
Once held in Manistique, but now in various towns that volunteer. Held on a Sunday under sponsorship of Knights of Columbus. Outdoor mass, parades, ball, and blessing. August.

TOURS

Manistique Pulp and Paper Company
Manistique River at Lake; telephone: 341–2175. Manufactures wallpaper, craft paper, and newsprint. Make reservations ahead.

Wyman Nursery
East of city pumping station on Indian and Manistique Rivers; telephone: 341–2518. Produces millions of trees to plant on Michigan public lands. Trees also sold to public. Arrange nursery tours with superintendent.

American bittern finds safety in the Seney National Wildlife Refuge, UP. *U.S. Department of the Interior*

Gulliver

Population: 300   Zip Code: 49840

The tiny hamlet of Gulliver is important because it is the home of the Inland Limestone Company, subsidiary of Inland Steel Company of Chicago and Indiana Harbor, Indiana. Great freighters, as many as 200 a year, enter the Port Inland Harbor at the Lake (where Seul Choix Point Lighthouse is situated), and they load up on limestone, a basic ingredient in the making of iron, steel, fertilizer, pharmaceuticals, paint, soap, baking powder, cement, and glass. The plant, opened in 1930, today ships almost 4 million tons of stone.

This rich limestone deposit was formed 325 million years ago when the area that is now the state of Michigan was covered by a warm shallow sea, and in no other place is the material so pure as it is here in Gulliver.

FARM

Truman Cook
3 miles N. of traffic light; telephone: 283–2351. Potatoes.

LIGHTHOUSE

Seul Choix Point Lighthouse, 1890
8 miles S. and E. of Gulliver, County 431. Old French fishing village and very picturesque lighthouse. Means "Only Choice" and was haven for sailing vessels.

PARKS

Seney National Wildlife Refuge
M-77; 3 miles N. of Germfask, 40 miles N. of Gulliver Visitor Center; telephone: 586–9851. Auto tours; marvelous wildlife; breeding grounds of Canada geese. Eagles, bear, deer, sandhill cranes. Great swamp. Observation Tower. Three trout streams. 96,000 acres. A bit off the beaten path. Daily, 8–8.

Green School Roadside Park
4 miles E. of Gulliver. Picnicking.

Wildlife Drive Trail located in the Seney National Wildlife Refuge, UP. *U.S. Department of the Interior*

A coyote, a native of the Seney National Wildlife Refuge, UP. *U.S. Department of the Interior*

Milakian State Forest Campground
Rt. 2 and Milakol State Rd.

Gould City Roadside Park

Big Knob Forest Campground
3 miles E. of Gould City. Marina with launching.

Ted D. Anderson Roadside Park
Beach, picnic, toilets, on Lake.

Biddle Point Roadside Park

Island Point State Forest Campground

SCENIC DRIVE

Between Naubinway and Mackinac Bridge
Glorious drive along Lake. Woods, water, marvelous wildflowers.
Many high vistas.

Epoufette Bay
The Hiawatha Trail cuts in here. Slightly east of Gov. G. Mennen
Williams Roadside Park is the Cut River Bridge with a spectacular
view.

Little Brevort State Forest Campground
The Hiawatha National Forest Campgrounds are east of Brevort.
After Brevort, there is a fine area of Lake, dunes, with the forest to
the north.

Edward D. Suino Roadside Park
Just west of St. Ignace in Gros Cap. A glorious view.

Mackinac Bridge Scenic Turnout
Gros Cap. By maneuvering about, one can get a view of the great
bridge to the east, the islands, and the straits. Wonderful.

TOUR

Inland Lime and Stone
Telephone: 283–2615. An interesting and important quarry that
shouldn't be missed; make reservations.

St. Ignace

Population: 2892   Area Code: 906   Zip Code: 48933
Chamber of Commerce: telephone, 643–8717

The Soo Canal (Sault Ste. Marie)

The Mackinac Bridge

Mackinac Island

Population: 200

St. Ignace

Whenever one talks about Mackinac or Michilimackinac, there is apt to be confusion. Is one referring to the island? The region? The first fort at St. Ignace? The second one at Mackinaw City? Or the fort at Mackinac Island? If it's confusing to you now, it was also confusing to the British, the French, and the Indians from the seventeenth century on. For as you move through this region you are in a triangle of history that was vital in the struggle for a continent. History buffs will be forgiving if we try to tell the story geographically rather than chronologically.

It begins with St. Ignace, on the north side of the bridge, second oldest community in Michigan, and situated next to the Isle Aux Galets lighthouse and Waubonance Point (known only to the natives as Skillagally and Wobbleshanks).

Two missionaries had been here as early as 1641, and thirty years later Father Marquette arrived. He set up his mission, built his small chapel, and waited here for Louis Joliet and his paddlers, so they might go off on their famous probe into the Illinois country and on to the Mississippi. It was to the chapel in St. Ignace that his faithful Indians returned his body in 1676, a voyage he had dreamed of completing himself.

The braves in the St. Ignace area knew of the good father's death, and while hunting in the area of today's Ludington, they discovered the cross, the grave, and the body. In Indian style, they dissected it, washed it in the Lake, and returned to St. Ignace with their burden carefully packed in a birchbark box. The priest at St. Ignace gave the final sacraments, then buried the body under the chapel floor.

Some explorers of that era described St. Ignace as the "tag end of the world," but everyone agreed it was important. From the first it was the center of French trade with the Indians: muskets and beads, knives and brandy exchanged for the furs that were so popular in creating men's hats on the continent. The French voyageurs and traders often married Indian squaws, thus guaranteeing peace for their persons as well as their pursuits. In time the French traders got out of hand, and instead of working for the French crown, they did a bit of free lancing in furs on their own. To control the trade, and to protect the waters of the inland seas, the French finally built Fort Michilimackinac at St. Ignace (even today it is referred to as the *Ancient* Fort, in contrast with the later garrison at Mackinaw City that became the *Old* Fort). But the wilderness was so large, and the bandy-legged traders were so difficult to control, that eventually the fur business began to move down the Mississippi to New Orleans. When that happened, Cadillac, fort commander, was ordered to Detroit to control the remaining trappers. With his departure, the Indians and the last of the traders left. In 1706, two of the last Jesuit fathers made ready to leave, and fearing vandalism and sacrilege to Father Marquette's little chapel, they set it on fire.

In the meantime the English began moving through Canada into the Lake Superior country to do a bit of trading and empire building of their own. The French watched anxiously, and in 1714 decided that they had better replace the fort at St. Ignace with a new one at Mackinaw City, this time on the south side of the straits. For 100 years after that, St. Ignace stood, a lonely little town between the dark woods and the restless waters.

In 1834, St. Ignace began a new spurt of growth. It has been a tourist town of sorts ever since, a place to catch the ferry for Mackinac Island. In 1877 someone decided to begin digging at the site of Marquette's chapel, and found his grave. Part of the relics were sent to Marquette University in Milwaukee; the rest were assigned to his final grave, the marble monument and cross that now stand in Marquette Park on the St. Ignace highway.

ARCHITECTURE AND HISTORIC SITE

Fort DeBuade Museum, Inc.
334 N. State St.; telephone: 643–8686. Concentrates on early French and Indian periods. Daily, 9–9.

FERRIES TO MACKINAC ISLAND

Arnold Line
On Waterfront, Downtown Michigan State Dock; telephone: 847–3938. Closed in winter.

PARK

Straits State Park
3/4 mile southwest of St. Ignace on U.S. 2 from I-75. 120-acre park on high bluff overlooking Mackinac Bridge. Swimming, picnicking, hiking. 322 campsites.

SPECIAL EVENT

Black Gown Tree Pageant
Kiwanis Beach. Dramatization of life of Pere Marquette. Labor Day weekend.

SCENIC VIEW

Gros Cap
This lovely high bluff area, a few miles west of St. Ignace, is the site of a legendary romance. A young Indian maiden, disconsolate at her approaching marriage to an elderly chieftain, purportedly threw herself off the high bluffs. As she hurtled downward, she was caught by a young brave, taken in his arms to an awaiting canoe, and carried off to St. Helena Island where the two lived in harmony ever after. Legend has it that wherever the two wandered on the island, great clusters of blue gentians have grown ever since.

The Soo Canal (Sault Ste. Marie)

Although the Soo is out of our territory, 40 miles north of Lake Michigan, we include a visit to the Soo Canal and the locks because it is an ideal way to get an overview of the great water highways of Lakes Huron and Superior. Just as all commerce between Lake Michigan and the other lakes must ultimately pass through the Straits of Mackinac, so all shipping between Lake Superior and her four smaller sisters must use the Soo. These two great passages are vital links in the St. Lawrence Seaway, and bring ships and sailors from all over the globe to the mills and manufacturing centers of Chicago, Gary, and Milwaukee.

When canal talk started in the mid-nineteenth century, Henry Clay scoffed in Congress. "What! Build a canal up there at the end of nowhere? The federal government might as well build a canal on the moon."

Charles T. Harvey, who eventually built the canal, had such resistance from the French and Indians at Sault Ste. Marie, that he had to import 400 workers from Detroit. It immediately became apparent that it was essential to overcome the rapids of the St. Mary's River and the 22-foot drop they create between lakes Superior and Huron.

Soo Locks at Sault Ste. Marie. *Michigan Travel Commission*

A canal was needed to connect the iron mines of the Upper Peninsula with the mills and markets of ports to the east and south, for as Andrew Carnegie said, "Gold may be precious, but iron is priceless."

To begin the canal, an old Chippewa graveyard had to be moved, and Indian drums began rumbling ominously around the Lake. Nonetheless, in 1855, one and a half months ahead of schedule, Harvey's marvelous canal was completed . . . and for under $1 million. Prior to the canal, 1400 tons of ore had gone through the waterway a year; in 1856, it handled 800 times that amount.

Today there are four American locks and one Canadian. They enable lumber barges, iron ore carriers, boats hauling limestone, taconite, and grain to make the passage. Without the locks the new 1000-foot-long boats could not exist. The much ridiculed Soo now carries more tonnage than the Panama, Suez, and all the other canals of the world combined.

The Mackinac Bridge

When the Mackinac Bridge ("Mighty Mac") was completed in 1957 to connect Mackinaw City and St. Ignace, an irate taxpayer wrote a letter to the governor of Michigan. "Why," he asked, "would anyone build the most spectacular bridge in the world at the top of Michigan instead of at Detroit where everyone could see it?"

A lot of bridge buffs knew the answer and had written for tickets to the ceremony a year in advance. That first year 2 million tourists went over: 6000 cars an hour, each 5-mile crossing taking ten minutes. Before the bridge opened, at the height of the deer season, with traffic dependent on the highway ferries, the back-up was often 17 miles with waits as long as twenty-eight hours. As one legislator said, "The north and south of our state have long been engaged. They now have a wedding ring." Economically and geographically the Straits of Mackinac are the crossroads of water transportation, and the bridge is good dowry for both partners to the marriage.

From the time of the earliest trappers, men have dreamed of a connection between the lower and upper peninsulas, and now the dream is a $100 million reality. One of the most beautiful bridges ever built, it is the longest suspension bridge in the world. The Mighty Mac was the creation of Dr. David B. Steinman, a poor boy who grew up in view of the Brooklyn Bridge and dreamed of one day becoming a bridge engineer. (Mac was his four hundreth bridge on five continents.) Steinman had serious problems to overcome — terribly turbulent water, wind velocities up to 78 miles an hour, a gorge 295 feet deep — and he mastered them all. More tons of steel and cubic yards of concrete were used than in the Empire State Building. He created a four-lane highway of enormous grace, with a three-foot protective rail, yet a view of the straits, the islands, and both lakes. Among the workmen carrying out his plans were Indians whose ancestors had fought the French and the Americans for 350 years.

When the final concrete was poured, the state legislature was so impressed that they put a bill in the hopper that hereafter it would be a misdemeanor to print a map of the state without showing both halves of Michigan . . . symbolic proof that this was a marriage destined to endure.

An aerial view of Mighty Mac. *Michigan Travel Commission*

The annual Labor Day Walk over the 5-mile length of the
Mackinac Bridge. *Mackinac Bridge Authority*

The Grand Hotel with its large veranda dominates Mackinac
Island. *Michigan Travel Commission*

Mackinac Island

Except for summer, Mackinac Island is one of the relatively quiet,
unchanged places of the country. No cars are permitted, and one can
either fly in or take the ferry from St. Ignace or Mackinaw City. Once
arrived, travel is by foot, bike, or in a fringed carriage, an island
trademark.

Natives call visitors "fudgies," because almost all of them depart
with a box of fudge from a string of shops.

Mackinac sights include the fort (moved here from Mackinaw City
by the British in 1780 when they wanted to secure their holdings), the
lilacs (brought by the French in the seventeenth century), the Mission
Church, the Beaumont Memorial (named for the first doctor who was
able to study the gastrointestinal tract because his patient had a
gunshot wound that wouldn't heal), the Grand Hotel (built in 1887
with the world's largest veranda on which a good portion of the
world's dignitaries have rocked), and the three cemeteries dating back
to 1690.

The island, 9 miles round, has been a beautifully cared for state
park since 1895. It is the summer home of the governor of Michigan,

Mackinac Island's busy yacht harbor. *Michigan Travel Commission*

All motor vehicles are banned on Mackinac Island. *Michigan Travel Commission*

and the winter home of some 200 year-round stalwarts. Summer days are so balmy and the nights so short, that they claim a Mackinac hopvine once grew eighteen inches in twenty-four hours. The place is hay fever–proof and almost free of mosquitos. From the island's heights one can see Father Marquette's statue overviewing the harbor, or preview a marvelous procession of freighters going under the great bridge.

Over the years a lot of people have stopped here: French explorers in search of China, Jesuits, traders, trappers, lumberjacks, copper prospectors, soldiers of three flags, and waves of hopeful immigrants. Among the many were two prominent in the growth of Chicago: Gurdon Hubbard, fur trapper, who helped launch the Illinois and Michigan Canal; and John Kinzie, later to become the first white settler.

High, beautiful, and green, Mackinac perches on steep limestone bluffs. One nineteenth-century traveler remarked that its waters were so clear that a white napkin could be seen 30 fathoms deep. The fish were so abundant and delicious that each spring the Indians gathered from miles around to feast upon them. In his journal, Father Marquette had called the area the home of the fishes and the place where the lakes toss the wind back and forth like a ball. The Indians who came here to worship (Ottawa, Objibway, and Huron), believed the spot sacred and made it their burial grounds. Here they believed the Great Manitou had invited the earth, water, and wind to make their resting place. They called the island Michilimackinac because that was their word for the sacred turtle, who gave the island its shape. They also believed that the creation of Adam and Eve had taken place in this paradise.

Mackinac's history under the white man has been a fast shuffle between the French, the British, and Americans, reflecting what was happening in the country at large.

In the beginning the French used the island as a trading post, a base for supplies, and the Indians became so dependent on this material way of life that it all but ruined their culture. In 1779 the British, fearful that they could no longer protect the mainland fort at Mackinaw City against American raids, built a new fort on the Island for better control. After the Revolution it passed into American hands, only to seesaw back to the English in 1812, and finally back to the

Americans in 1815. The fort is easily invaded now for a tour.

In the mid-1800s the island was headquarters for the Astor fur operation, which became a veritable monopoly when Governor Cass of Michigan ruled that only Americans might now trade in furs. The Astor, Biddle, and Stuart and Beaumont houses can all be visited today on Market Street. In time the elaborate trading patterns resulted in a glut on the fur market. The Astors turned to hotels and land holdings in New York. But Astor House in Mackinac is a memorial to greed, a reminder that beaver and mink and stylish hats in Europe played more than a little part in the building of a continent.

Mackinaw City

Population: 1000   Area Code: 616   Zip Code: 49701
Chamber of Commerce: 310 S. Huron; telephone: 436–5574. Mon.–Fri., 9–5;
* summer: 9–9; closed Sun. and weekends, Christmas and New Year's day.*

Mackinaw City perches along a 5-mile strip of land on the straits. It is the northernmost town on Michigan's lower peninsula. "Where else," people ask, "can you sit all day and still see the sun rise on one lake and set on another," and it's true, for this town of 1000 people is the land link between lakes Michigan and Huron.

Like the bridge, the island, the various forts, coats, boats, and everything else named Mackinac, the city's name comes from *Michilimackinac,* which meant "sacred turtle to the Indians." And no matter how it's spelled, it's always pronounced as though it ended *aw* to rhyme with *paw.*

Mackinaw was at first an Indian camping and fishing ground. Then in 1714 the French shifted their fort and trading posts here from St. Ignace across the water. For almost fifty years they did great business with the Indians of the surrounding areas: Fox, Sauk, Huron, Ottawa, Chippewa, and Menominee. But their empire began to crumble after the British victory at Quebec and England's claim to all the lands of North America. Fort Michilimackinac at Mackinaw was taken over as well.

Unlike the French, the British were rather clumsy in their relations with the Indians, and one day during a lacrosse game being played at the fort, the Indian lady spectators pulled tomahawks out of their blankets, handed them to their braves, and an awful massacre followed. A number of Englishmen were taken prisoner, and some unfortunates were boiled and eaten. One, Alexander Henry, was saved because in prior years he had had a good relationship with an Ottawa chief named Wawatam. He lived to write a famous account of the affair, and the brotherhood between the two lives on in two prestigious ice-cutting boats: the *Chief Wawatam,* which keeps shipping lanes open at the straits, and the Canadian cutter *Alexander Henry,* at the Soo.

That all happened in 1763 and was instigated by Chief Pontiac, but the English returned again in 1764 and stayed for seven years. During the Revolutionary War, the British Regiment, which had garrisoned the fort, was sent on to Boston. In April 1775, they turned out to be the very redcoats who attacked at Concord and Lexington and spurred Paul Revere on to his famous ride. The fort was finally moved to Mackinac Island during 1780–81; part of it (including the Church of St. Anne) was pulled over the ice, and the rest was sailed over the next spring in the sloop *Welcome* (currently being restored for placement in the marina at the rejuvenated Fort Mackinaw). The English made the move because of security, for they were justifiably nervous about American naval power in the straits. From then until 1902 when the fort site became a state park, the place lay desolate and abandoned.

Today Mackinaw City has about 1000 full-time residents, a number that explodes with the arrival of summer tourists (and, though it has a lot of beds to accommodate the visitors, reservations are tight). The modern town was platted in 1857. In 1870 the first permanent settler, Charles Stimson, built his log cabin and eventually enlarged it to a hotel, which still exists as a lodging and bus depot.

Mackinaw City has had a varied life as a lumber center, fishing area, and summer resort. The Michigan Central Railroad (now the New York Central) arrived in 1881, and the Grand Rapids and Indiana (the current Pennsylvania road) in 1882. The coming of the rails brought more people, but the tourist boom really started in 1957 with the opening of the bridge.

After the old fort site became a state park, it was used as a camping ground until the restoration of the fort was undertaken in 1959. Two million dollars' worth of revenue bonds were sold to begin the meticulous rebuilding, and archeological digging in the area is still going on. There are moments of amusement in the process, however. At the fort the sexton at the church excuses himself once an hour and rushes off to his other job of firing the musket at the gates. It's not that the man of God isn't a pacifist; it's just that help comes higher now and minding the store may also require securing the fort.

FERRIES TO MACKINAC ISLAND

Arnold Line
Telephone: 847–3988.

Shepler's
Telephone: 436–9891.

Straits Transit, Inc.
U.S. 23; telephone: 436–5542.

MUSEUMS

Fort Michilimackinac
At bridge; telephone: 436–5563. 27 acres contain lighthouse museum, orientation center, French village, and boats representative of every period on Lake. Daily, May 15–October 19, 9–5.

Tysen's Talking Bear Museum
416 S. Huron (above Tysen Cafeteria); telephone: 436–7011. Good private collection of Indian culture, beautifully displayed. Also, cases on lumbering and assorted indigenous history. Oral tapes. Daily, May 20–October 20, 9–10.

PARK

Wilderness State Park
11 miles west of town on Scenic 1 (Trail's End Bay on the Lake shore). Picnic, swim, fine hiking. 6409 acres of land acquired by state after end of timber era. Big lumbering companies farmed the land they could, refused to pay taxes on the rest. Result, land reverted to Michigan for parks. Camping, hiking, boat launches, gorgeous beaches and dunes.

RECREATION

Marina

Mackinaw City Public Marina
At Lake.

Snowmobiling, Cross-Country Skiing, Ice Fishing

For information, call Chamber of Commerce. Caveat: ice breakers keep shipping lanes open so care must be taken at straits to avoid open channels even when some areas are frozen 3-feet deep.

Swimming

Municipal Beach
6 miles north of Town Wilderness Drive or Scenic Rt. 1.

RESTAURANTS

Downing's
314 Nicolet; telephone: 436–9631. Daily, July 1–September 5, 8 AM–
10 PM.

The Fort
400 N. Louvigny; telephone: 436–5453. Daily, April 1–December 1.
7:30 AM–10 PM.

Neath the Birches
1 mile south on old U.S. 31; telephone: 436–5401. Daily, May 15–
October 15, 7 AM–11; 4–10 PM.

Tysen's Cafeteria
416 S. Huron; telephone: 436–7011. Three generations. Current Tysen
got experience at Harding's in Chicago. Daily, June 20–October 20,
6:30 AM–9:30 PM.

SCENIC DRIVE

Wilderness Drive
County 81 (also called Scenic 1), south from Mackinaw City through
Bliss to Lake Michigan where it becomes M-131. Marvelous woods
and dunes — also, at some points, marshy Lakeshore.

SPECIAL EVENTS

Fort Michilimackinac Pageant
Reenactment of events, 1715–1781. Last weekend in May.

Labor Day Bridge Walk
Bus takes walkers to St. Ignace end of bridge. Up to 25,000 people,
all ages, walk the 5 miles back. Some go on bikes, wheelchairs, stilts.
Celebration started in 1950s, led by Governor G. Mennen Williams.

Cross Village

Population: 100   Area Code: 616   Zip Code: 49723

The Indians called this area *Waganakisi;* the French traders, *L'Arbre Croche.* Both names describe the crooked tree, high on a bluff, which was a marker for passing canoes. But it was Father Marquette, or one of his padres, who placed a great cross high on a bluff and gave Cross Village its current name.

Cross Village is part of an ancient area, full of mystery, which embraced Indian settlements all the way south to Harbor Springs. The earliest inhabitants were the Mascoutens ("Little Prairie people") who were driven out by the Ottawa tribe that arrived almost simultaneously with the French missionaries. These French ties involved the Indians with the early frontier wars, and they played a role in the defeat of General Braddock in 1755. Good farmers as well as warriors, the Ottawa traded maize with the English at Fort Michilimackinac, and this connection helped save the lives of four British VIPs in the sack of the fort in 1763.

Cross Village was always a hub of Catholic mission work from the circuiting Jesuits to the large seventeenth- and eighteenth-century missions. The list of priests' names reads like a Who's Who of Catholic missionaries, but no religious figure quite matches the incredible Father John Bernard Weikamp who arrived in 1855. A Prussian by birth, Weikamp quarreled with his bishop in Chicago. He left there and came to Cross Village where he put his business acumen and mystical streak to work, administering a self-sufficient 2000-acre institution, where he manufactured everything from wooden shoes for his teaching nuns to currant wine. He also slept with his coffin next to his bedside and descended daily into his already-prepared grave for meditation.

In the early days the Ottawas (and there are still several thousand of them as well as Chippewa in the Emmet County area), bringing prisoners over the waters, let out great war whoops to inform the folks on shore how many captives they had taken. There are old settlers today who claim that Indian spirits still roll their muffled drums when the waters claim another death.

Father Weikamp's mausoleum in Cross Village, Michigan. *Michigan Travel Bureau*

In addition to its Indians and its padres, Cross Village had its lumbering era, a brief encounter with blueberry farming, and maple sugaring. Today its natural beauty is still its greatest asset. The drive from the village to Harbor Springs is probably the most spectacular on the Lake.

ARCHITECTURE AND HISTORIC SITES

Redpath Memorial Presbyterian
South end of village on M-131. Picturesque church named for a local pioneer missionary pastor.

Holy Cross Catholic Church
North end of village on M-131. This Indian Mission church built in 1895 has a carved angel in center of altar that is rumored to have been taken from a raid on the Mormon Church at Beaver Island.

Town Hall
Street two blocks east of M-131. Formerly schoolhouse where Father Weikamp's sisters instructed Indian children of village. One of the few original buildings surviving a series of devastating fires.

CEMETERY

Old Indian Cemetery with Father Weikamp's Mausoleum
Two blocks east, behind Indian Museum. Look through windows of Father Weikamp's Mausoleum and notice the skulls and crossbones and other objects obviously used by the Father in his curious meditations.

MUSEUM

Great Lakes Indian Museum
East side of M-131 in middle of village. Crafts and handwork of Great Lakes and Plains Indians on exhibit and for sale. Small library. Also check here for location of early Indian mound burial sites. Daily, June 15–September 4, 9 AM–6 PM.

RESTAURANT

Legg's Inn
M-131, overlooking Lake Michigan, north of Cross Village; telephone: 526–5087. Unusual decor of driftwood and roots. Summer.

SCENIC VIEWS AND DRIVES

Lighthouses

Skillagalee
8 miles west of Cross Village (at flashing white light).

Gray's Reef
Northwest of Cross Village (at flashing red light).

White Shoals
Farther northwest of Cross Village (at flashing white light).

Harbor Springs

Population: 1662   Area Code: 616   Zip Code: 49740
Chamber of Commerce: Bay Street; telephone: 526–2761

Harbor Springs, alias Little Traverse, was first part of an area called L'Arbre Croche (the Indian territory that included lands from near Mackinaw City, through Cross Village, Middle Village, and Good Hart). It is conjectured that ancient mound builders came through here on their way from Mexico to Lake Superior, but the Indians who remain today (and there are some 2000) are Ottawa and Chippewa whose great-great-grandfathers fought in all the wars from the French and Indian to the Battles of 1812. They were generally allied with the French, for, beginning in the seventeenth century, the traders were sent down from Mackinac Island with baubles and trinkets to exchange for furs. The cultural gap between the sophisticated Continentals and the Woodland Indians must have been enormous, but the French took to the woods with gusto, often taking squaw wives. "It was easier," someone commented, "to make an Indian out of a Frenchman than the reverse." But no matter, the two managed to get along well.

Harbor Springs had its day in the lumbering era when it was a busy port, having one of the deepest natural harbors on the Lake. The land in the area was for many years protected by early treaties with the Indians, but in 1874–75 when the Homestead Law was passed, the frontier opened, and the homesteaders, resorters, and hayfever victims arrived.

Today Harbor Springs has a population of 1662 people. Its beautiful white frame homes are set high on bluffs, surrounded by pine and birch woods. The houses, the shops, the yachts all look expensive and, indeed, they are. And the most expensive and exclusive part of the whole area is Harbor Point, originally bought for $100 by Father Weikamp (whom we met at Cross Village). He sold the Point in 1878 to some prosperous gentlemen from Lansing, Michigan. You can't see Harbor Point, except across the harbor, because there is a security gate — and to pass through your name must be Ford or Libby or Procter or Gamble. There are no cars at the Point, and the possessors of the magic names either walk, bicycle, or move about in horse-drawn carriages, a bit of nostalgia from the nineteenth century.

In the era when the super rich began arriving, there were steam-ships galore, gone now because all those Ford cars revolutionized transportation. There were also many elegant hotels built, ostensibly to house the overflow when the super rich had spectacular events. Some of them remain, and like the horse-drawn carriages, some are longer on nostalgia than comfort. On the east side of Harbor Springs is another conclave, the Wequetonsing Association, built by Pres-byterians who, like everyone else, wanted to escape the heat and the pollen and enjoy the Lake.

Exclusiveness is only part of the story, however. Harbor Springs is charming, with eager shops and welcoming restaurants. Moreover, for many people it is the kick-off point for the color tour that takes place each fall. Even local people take the drive up to the straits. Everyone — Indians, Fords, Presbyterians, and agnostics — agrees with the English author from the last century who said, "In the autumn the whole country goes to glory," or the lady from Charlevoix who wrote to a friend, "Come up soon when the lights go on in the woods."

Downhill skiing at Nubs Nob in the Harbor Springs–Petoskey area. *Michigan Travel Commission*

ARCHITECTURE AND HISTORIC SITE

Holy Childhood Catholic Church

Main and State. Indian mission church. Indian school on same grounds. Built in 1820s.

MUSEUM

* Chief Blackbird Indian Museum

M-131; telephone: 526–2104. Site of first post office. The chief was postmaster. Indian artifacts, quilts, baskets, blanket work. (Building that houses dress shop next door is also on the National Historic Registry.) Daily, July 1–Labor Day, 10-noon, 1–5; free admission.

ORCHARDS

Bill Corey

U.S. 31 north of Harbor Springs; telephone: 526–6196. Strawberries, raspberries. July, August.

Dave Johnston

6 miles north of H.S. off U.S. 131, on Terpening Rd.; telephone: 526–5322. Raspberries. July, August.

PARK

Josephine D. Ford Park

Bay St. (behind Chamber of Commerce). Lakefront picnicking.

Recreation

Boats

Irish Boat Works

400 E. Bay St.; telephone: 526–2145. Has list of available charters. Boat storage and repair. Sailboat rental.

Fishing

Fish any place on harbor, but only rock bass. Trout in inlets.

Golf

Harbor Pointe Golf Course (9-hole)

Shore Dr. (M-131); telephone: 526–2951.

Sail Surfing

Check with Chamber of Commerce for specifics.

Snowmobiling

Moose Jaw Safari Trail
North of Harbor Springs on M-131. Popular and well marked. Call Chamber of Commerce for specifics.

RESTAURANTS

Arboretum
Lake Shore Dr. (2 miles west of town); telephone: 526–6291.

Harbor Inn
Little Traverse Bay, Beach Drive and M-109; telephone: 526–2108. Memorial Day–Labor Day, December–February, weekends.

The Harbor Pier
102 Bay St.; telephone: 526–2571. View of Little Traverse Bay and yacht basin. Open year round, daily, 5–11; Sun., 12–10.

Juilleret's
120 State St.; telephone: 526–2821. Great ice cream. Closed end of September–May 15.

SHOPPING

Bluff Gardens, Inc.
658 W. Bluff; telephone: 526–5571. Charming vegetable stand, featuring all miniature vegetables. Specialize in Northern Michigan products. May–Christmas; closed Sun.

The Patrician
373 E. Main St.; telephone: 526–5524. Antiques with a leaning toward glass and porcelain. American, English, French, Oriental.

Bay View

(No permanent population)

Petoskey

Population: 6330   Area Code: 616   Zip Code: 49770
Chamber of Commerce: 401 E. Mitchell; telephone: 347–4150

Bay View

Just to the north of Petoskey is Bay View, a charming little village created and organized by nineteenth-century Methodists who longed for a retreat in the woods. The church people sent emissaries to scout the area in 1875. The emissaries became advocates and ended by building their own house, Barclay Cottage, in the unbroken forest. Within a few years a great many Midwestern Methodists followed "god's prophets," and the number increased steadily when the Grand Rapids and Indiana track reached Petoskey in 1876. Chautauquas, revivals, and prayers were the order of the day. The main street is still called Encampment Avenue. People lived in rustic surroundings, ate their meals in a huge tent, spent their evenings at camp meetings, encircled with great torches. Behind everything stood a group of silent Indians. Rustling leaves mingled with the weeping of penitents. And famous people came to stir the gathering, Helen Keller and William Jennings Bryant among them.

Eventually many people wanted permanent homes. Someone has said, "Land was changing hands so fast, all one had to do to get some was reach in the air and catch a deed going by on the breeze." Today the village consists of endless cottages, fashioned with marvelous fretwork, carpenter Gothic, and big porches.

The prayer meetings are a thing of the past now, the amen corner is gone, but the community has excellent speakers, good musical affairs, and a very creditable summer liberal arts program.

Petoskey

If Little Traverse Bay were considered a neck chain, Petoskey would be its locket, for the town hangs like a pendant at the edge of the bay. It is famous for its spectacular sunsets, and for the stones found on its beaches. The Petoskey stone is a coral fossil, formed 305 million years ago when the whole area was a warm salt water sea. The official stone of the state of Michigan, they wash ashore endlessly to the delight of rock hounds who spend hours searching for them on the beach.

Forty miles south of the Straits of Mackinac, this town of 6300 people is the trade center for a region ten times that size. Petoskey sits on limestone bluffs. One still finds old burners and ovens where the stone was once cooked (to get rid of impurities) along the shore and in the woods.

The town got its name from a Chippewa Chief Pe-to-se-ga ("Rising Sun") who was one of the large landholders in the area. He grew up in Harbor Springs, and married a local Catholic girl. When he, a Methodist, shipped their sons off to a Protestant school, she left him. He remarried, moved down to the Petoskey region, and fathered fourteen children in all. In old age, he missed his first wife so badly that he made a settlement on wife number two, and remarried the bride of his youth.

Petoskey, Harbor Springs, and Cross Village were all slow to develop as towns because the central government had made a treaty with the Chippewa and Ottawa in 1836, holding the lands at this northwest portion of the state as their reservation. At the end of twenty years the Indians were supposed to vacate to lands west of the Mississippi. They refused and were eventually given acreage. Under the Homestead Law of 1874, the unused Indian lands were open to other claimants as well, and hundreds came, although many had to be satisfied with woodlands because the Indians had first claim on Lake property. Some of the white men were so poor that first winter that they lived in holes dug in the hillsides and survived on squirrel stew. But a miracle of sorts occurred: the skies darkened one day and a flight of millions of passenger pigeons came to nest in the area. The birds not only made good eating, but were shot and shipped to the Chicago markets as a delicacy. With the proceeds, many settlers had enough capital to start their farms. (The last of the world's passenger pigeons, a doomed species, was gone by 1914. Some claim that they had at one time accounted for one third of the bird life of North America.)

The first permanent settlers in the area were R. H. and William Little who started out in a tent and then spent time in the already existing Catholic mission. A Methodist mission had been set up in 1863 at Greensky Hill; the church still stands. This had once been the sacred ground where thirty Ottawa chieftains had gathered to plant their council trees. As long as those trees grew, they vowed, there would be peace in the area.

The coming of the Grand Rapids and Indiana Railroad was, of course, a great stimulus to immigration. By 1878 Petoskey was incorporated as a village and by 1896 as a city. Landlookers of all sorts, from ladies with parasols to burly lumberjacks, rented rooms in boarding houses until they could build permanent homes, and Petoskey's population soon reached 4000.

Today the area has several large industries, among them Penn Dixie Cement. Wooden butcher blocks are locally produced, as are all manner of nuts and washers and plastic bags. The outlying farms produce hay, winter wheat, potatoes, and fruit. Petoskey is the major medical center for northwestern Michigan, and its excellent hospitals, including the Burns Clinic, are often referred to as Little Mayos. Once primarily a summer resort, it has become the center of a thriving ski business. Between Christmas and New Year's, Petoskey does such an enormous business that it makes its winter profits in seven days.

ARCHITECTURE AND HISTORIC SITES

St. Francis Solanus Indian Mission, 1859
On W. Lake St., six blocks west of Howard St. Church in good repair. Old Indian cemetery adjoins church. Mass celebrated once a year on St. Francis Feast Day, July 13.

Indian River Shrine
Petoskey area, off beaten path. Bay View, take Rt. 68 to Indian River, 27 miles east. World's largest crucifix and outdoor shrine. Cross 55 feet high, bronze corpus weighs 7 tons.

Skin Diver's Underwater Shrine

Bottom of Little Traverse Bay (U.S. 31), 65 feet down, 500 feet off-shore (west of lighthouse). Hand-carved white marble figure of Christ put in water by Michigan Diver's Club and the Coast Guard. Prayer attached to statue begins "Those who would pray, let them come to the sea."

MUSEUM

Little Traverse Historical Museum (in Railroad Depot), 1892 Petoskey Waterfront; telephone: 347–2620. Indian artifacts. Early settlers, along with memorabilia of authors Ernest Hemingway and Bruce Catton. July, August, Mon.–Sat., 1–5. Free admission.

ORCHARD

Wilbur Brown

Off U.S. 131 on Epples Rd.; telephone: 347–3383. Cherries all summer long.

PARKS

City Park

West Lake St. Charming site overlooking marina; great view of Lake, nice picnic spot.

Mineral Well Park

West Lake St. Great drinking water.

Petoskey State Park

6 miles north of Petoskey on M-131. Swimming, picnicking, ninety campsites.

RECREATION

Biking

Jake Jakab

Telephone: 347–8277. Maps for weekend excursions and tours available at Chamber of Commerce.

Boats

Marina

At Waterfront. Eighty slips; room for larger boats.

Golf

Petoskey Bay View Country Club
Bay View; telephone: 347–2402.

Wilderness Golf Course (36-hole)
3 miles west of Carp Lake; telephone: 537–4973.

Skiing

Excellent snow-making equipment. Listed north to south. Call Chamber of Commerce for specifics.

Nub's Nob
Between 131 and 31, East of Cross Village, north of Harbor Springs.

Boyne's Highlands
Off 131, south of Nub's Nob above Harbor Springs.

Boyne Mountain
South of 39 and west of 131, just east of East Jordan.

RESTAURANTS

Jesperson's
215 Howard St.; telephone: 347–3601. Daily, 8–4 PM; closed Sun., Mon., and the month of March).

Vic's of Petoskey
712 Pleasant St.; telephone: 347–8383. Daily, 11:30–3, 5–10; closed Sun.

Park Garden Café
432 E. Lake; telephone: 347–8251. Mon.–Sat., 11–2 AM.

Perry-Davis Hotel
Bay and Louis St.; telephone: 347–2516. Bar. Great Lake view. Mon.–Sat., 8 AM–10:30 PM; Sun., 8–1 PM; 6–9:30 PM.

* **Stafford's Bay View Inn**
U.S. 31 North; telephone: 347–2771. Breakfast, 8:30–10; lunch, 12–2; dinner, 6–9. Smorgasbord on Thursday. Old English brunch Sunday 10–2. Good-neighbor buffets Fri.–Sat. nights.

SHOPPING

Gaslight Area
Lake, Howard, Bay, and Petoskey Sts. Absolutely top-notch specialty shops in center of town. Don't miss!

Maus & Hoffman
321 E. Lake; telephone: 347-3621. You can buy neckties here that cost as much as $3 thousand — yes *thousand!* Summer only.

Ed Behan's Tweed Shop
200 Howard; telephone: 347-8107. Exclusive patterns and designs. Open June through Christmas.

Rock Shop
411 E. Lake; telephone: 347-5580. Specializes in Petoskey stones.

Underwater Systems, Ltd.
411 E. Lake; telephone: 347-9612. Super boat store with all accessories.

SPECIAL EVENT

Emmet County Fair
Check with Chamber of Commerce for details. Last week of August.

Charlevoix

Population: 3520   Area Code: 616   Zip Code: 49720
Chamber of Commerce: 408 Bridge Street; telephone: 547–2101

Charlevoix has always been a top-drawer summer community, attracting wealthy families from New Orleans, St. Louis, Cincinnati, and Chicago. Many families have been coming for six generations to live in fine white houses (always called cottages) on high bluffs overlooking the lakes: Charlevoix, Michigan, or Round lake. In the palmiest days there were more coachmen than closets, more nursemaids than central heat. In the afternoons people got into their carriages, took in the good air, and made formal calls.

In the old days it mattered how long your family had been on the scene. The grandest dame of all was Julia Scott, guiding light in the Daughters of the American Revolution and the Women's Christian Temperance Union, and great-great-great-aunt to Senator Adlai Stevenson of Illinois. She and her sister won national fame when they entertained President Grant in Charlevoix, and served him iced lemonade when he requested whiskey. Julia bristled when the town wanted to put sidewalks along the length of *her* Michigan Avenue, and she lobbied so ferociously that the last 200 feet of the street have no sidewalks to this day.

Propriety was important to other people too, including the Baptist minister who expressed his outrage in a 1914 news column:

> Backward, turn backward, oh time in your flight.
> Give us a girl with skirts not so tight.
> Give us a girl, no matter what age,
> Who won't use the streets for a vaudeville stage . . .

But the young bloods kept to the styles, and they came back with their monogrammed steamer trunks to tango at teas, and to gamble at nearby casinos. Ernest Hemingway was around for a while. So was the shy poet Sara Teasdale. And Dudleigh Vernor, organist at the Methodist Church, won his share of fame with his song, "The Sweetheart of Sigma Chi."

Charlevoix was named for a famous French missionary, but it had a troubled birth. In 1850 some Irish fishermen from the general area fought the Mormon followers of "King" James Strang in the Battle of Pine River. The first permanent settlers arrived in 1854. But the two events that triggered the development of the town were the coming of the Grand Rapids and Indiana passenger train as far as Petoskey in 1874, and the passage of the Homestead Act in 1875, which opened Indian reservation land to claims from whites as well as Indians.

The effect of these events brought the Methodists to Bay View in 1876; the Episcopalians to Harbor Point two years later; the Presbyterians to Wequetonsing; and the Baptists and Congregationalists of Chicago to Charlevoix to form, respectively, the Belvedere and Chicago Clubs.

Today the grandchildren of the grandchildren are still coming. Many of them have winterized their homes and have returned to live full time . . . with lots of closets, no coachmen, and far less formality.

ARCHITECTURE AND HISTORIC SITES

Greensky Hill United Methodist Church
4 miles from Charlevoix take US 31 north, turn right on Boyne City Rd. (C-56), then left on old U.S. 31. Site of ancient Indian Council. Services in English and Objibway on Sunday. Outdoor platform for worship under trees. Famous autumn harvest dinner. *Vosiman ishpimieawn, mano tukikitu auinjigade in kidizhin kazouin.* (First line of the Lord's Prayer in Objibway.)

Fairy-Tale Stone Houses
South end of Charlevoix along Lake Michigan on Park Ave. between Clinton and Grand. Notice vegetation growing on some roofs.

FERRIES

Beaver Island Boat Company
102 Bridge St.; telephone: 547–2311. Call for exact schedule: April 14–December 29, weekdays and Sun., 8–4 PM; June 18–September 15, 7 AM–6 PM. Change without notice if weather poor.

ORCHARDS AND FARMS

Dhaseleer's Farm
U.S. 31 south to Barnard Rd.; telephone: 547–9544. Strawberries, peas, beans, corn.

Kitely Farm
3 miles south of Charlevoix on Wickersham Rd.; telephone: 547–2318. Asparagus and other vegetables.

Rosenthal's Orchards
U.S. 31 to Barnard Rd.; telephone: 547–4350. Apples, cherries, plums, pears, apricots.

Smith's Little Acres
1 mile south of Charlevoix on U.S. 31; telephone: 547–2920. Blueberries, corn, apples, cherries.

PARKS

Fishermen's Island State Park
On 31, south of Charlevoix. Forty-one camping sites.

City Park on Lake Michigan
Along Park Ave. (Lakeshore Dr.). Picnic tables and swimming beach.

RECREATION

Beach

Lake Michigan side of Charlevoix
A fine public swimming beach with a playground, picnicking.

Boat Rentals

Irish Boat Works
Stover Rd.; telephone: 547–9967. Sailboat rentals, charters, bare-boat charters for weekends or longer; repair. Mon.–Sat., 8–5.

Charters

James Bishop
P.O. Box 232; telephone: 547–9071.

Ward's Charter Service
Foot of Antrim St.; telephone: 547–2371.

Mark White
316 Mason St.; telephone: 547–6618.

Golf

Antrim Dell's Golf Club (18-hole)
10 miles south of Charlevoix on U.S. 31; telephone: 599–2679.

Belvedere Golf Course (18-hole)
1.5 miles southeast of Charlevoix; telephone: 547–2512. Home of the Michigan Amateur Golf Tournament (held third week in June).

Charlevoix Municipal Golf Course (9-hole)
Central Ave.; telephone: 547–2171.

Marina

Municipal Boat Park
Ferry and Stover Sts.; telephone: 547–9752. Public boat launching.

RESTAURANTS

Grey Gables Inn
308 Belvedere, Charlevoix; telephone: 547–9261. Dinner only, 8.

The Jordan Inn
Highway 66 and City 48, 228 Main St., off beaten track at East Jordan; telephone: 536–2631. Year round, daily, 6–10; Sun., 4–8; reservations only.

Rowe Inn
County 65 and County 48, off beaten track at Ellsworth; telephone: 588–7351. Reservations; worth a trip.

SCENIC DRIVE

Boyne City to Boyne Falls Scenic Train Ride
Off beaten track, but 7 miles of beauty, from Charlevoix, take M-75 to County 56; telephone: 582–2232. Mid-May to mid-Oct., three round trips daily.

SHOPPING

Bolt's Grange Hall Print & Pottery Shop
3 miles south of Charlevoix on C 65; telephone: 547–4855. Ceramics, prints, paintings. Year round, 10–6.

Great Lakes Shipwreck Company

Rt. 31, south of Charlevoix; telephone: 547–2694. Interesting furniture made from Lake Michigan shipwrecks. Year round: summer, daily 10–6; evenings by appointment.

Staffel's Pottery

Bonnie and Bill Staffel. U.S. 31, 7 miles south of Charlevoix; telephone: 547–2409. Handcrafted stoneware. Year round.

Todd Warner's Tree Toad Gallery

1 block north of Bay Shore on U.S. 31; telephone: 347–6131. Hand-carved toys, animal sculpture. Year round.

Yacht Shop

Round Lake (next to city docks); telephone: 547–9811. Outfitters for all boating needs.

SPECIAL EVENTS

Lakeside Hobbycraft Show

East Park. Second week in July.

Venetian Festival

Fourth weekend in July.

Beaver Island

Population: 200   Area Code: 616   Zip Code: 49782
Beaver Island Civic Association: telephone, 448-2211

Off the coast of Charlevoix, 32 miles by air or an hour by ferry boat, lies the Emerald Isle, 14 miles long, 5 miles wide, and 70 square miles of dramatic history.

Beaver Island's period as a kingdom in the mid-nineteenth century is unique in American history. The "king" was James Strang, who became a Mormon through baptism by Joseph Smith, the great Mormon leader. When Smith was assassinated six months later, Strang declared himself the chosen successor, basing his claim on revelations as well as the necessary letter from Smith, and 2000 believers willingly followed him from Wisconsin to the Beaver Islands where he immediately had himself crowned king. He gave religious names to everything: the highest dune became Mt. Pisgah; the major river, the Jordan; the only town on the island, St. James; the bay on which it was located, Paradise. And so the saints came marching in from 1847 until 1856. Despite feuds with the local Irish fishermen and occasional rumors about murder and Mormon theft, Strang continued in power (even entering the Michigan legislature) and led his people — until two of them shot him to death. The acknowledged murderers were never brought to trial, but with the king gone the Mormons were driven away by the fishermen. Strang left behind twelve children and four pregnant wives. One of the wives later declared the great Chicago Fire was a punishment for her husband's murder.

The fishermen remained in Beaver Island, and today whitefish caviar is shipped off to Charlevoix in fifty-gallon drums. This island has also been host to Girl Scouts who have come to the more isolated areas occasionally for survival training. For the most part, however, the island lives off the memories of the Mormon Monarchy. It has two museums, two stores, two bars, a marina, and numerous inland lakes. But where there were once twenty-three cattle farms, there are now two, and the permanent population, once over 2000, is down to 200.

Beaver Island is part of an archipelago (Lake Michigan island groups are also found off the Garden Peninsula and the Door Penin-

Rustic charm on Beaver Island off Charlevoix, Michigan. *Michigan Travel Commission*

sula). The Beavers consist of the Manitous off Sleeping Bear Park; the Foxes; Squaw Island where a wicked Indian lady, banished by medicine men, is said to walk headless at night; Hog (also called Marion), once used by Indians to fatten their cows and now owned by Henry Ford II; Garden, site of Indian burial grounds with latticed huts over the graves; and High, sometimes called the Siberia of Michigan, since it was reported to be the penal colony for miscreants from the House of David in Benton Harbor (a bit of fantasy according to historians, but the Davidites did farm here on what are now public lands). In addition the archipelago has six unsurveyed islands.

MUSEUMS

Beaver Island Museum, 1848
Main and Forest, St. James; telephone: 448–2212. Old Mormon lore, sponsored by local historical society. July, August, daily, 11–4.

Marine Museum
St. James waterfront. Fishing history.

PARKS

Beaver Island Wildlife State Research Area
East Shore Dr., 7 miles southeast. Southern part of island. Free camping.

St. James Township Park
West of St. James — Donegal Rd. Free camping.

RECREATION

Boats

Beaver Haven Marina
Telephone: 448–2300.

Island Rental Service
Telephone: 448–2289. Offers sunset cruises and island tours.

Fishing

Beaver Island (north) has good fishing off docks, piers, along shoals. Inland lakes for family fishing. For licenses, call: 448–2266.

Golf

Beaver Lodge (9-hole)
St. James; telephone: 448–2396.

Hunting

Deer, small game, birds in season. For licenses, call: 448–2266.

RESTAURANTS

Circle M Lodge
1 1/2 miles south of St. James Harbor; telephone: 448–2318. Planes taxi to door from Welke's Airport. Year round.

Shamrock
Downtown St. James; telephone: 448–2278. Overlooks bay. Year round.

SPECIAL EVENTS

Annual Homecoming and Dinner
St. James. Second Sunday in August.

Fly In
St. James. October.

TOURS

For island tours by air, contact Welke Aviation (telephone: 448–2326); call 448–2300 for information on bus tours; and, for information on ferry, see Charlevoix.

The East Arm of Traverse City Bay

Eastport

Population: under 200   Zip Code: 49627

Kewadin

Population: under 200   Zip Code: 49648

Elk Rapids

Population: 1249   Zip Code: 49629

Acme

Population: under 200   Zip Code: 49610

Eastport

Several small communities are strung along the eastern shore of Grand Traverse Bay on U.S. Route 31. At the top of East Bay lies the village of Eastport, which was one of the stops made by the schooner that took workers down to Elk Rapids to work in the mills and mines of the Dexter and Noble Company. One of the most famous lumbering cooks at that time was a Mrs. Conklin. Before daylight she would whip up a "bushel of cookies and a thousand fried cakes; beans, bacon, fat salt pork from a barrel . . . all staples of the lumbering era."

PARK

Antrim County Park
U.S. 31 at Lake Michigan. Swimming and picnicking.

RESTAURANT

Brownwood
E. Torch Lake Dr. — M-88 — in Central Lake; telephone: 544–5811.
Try the homemade cherry butter. Open year round: summer, Mon.–
Sat., 11:30 AM–3:30 PM, 5 PM–11 PM; Sun., noon–11 PM; winter, Mon.–
Sat., 5 PM–10 PM, Sun., noon–10 PM.

Kewadin

Today Kewadin is in the middle of resort country, near the famous
Chain of Lakes. Its name means "northwest wind," and comes from
a Chippewa chieftain who lived to be 100 and was buried in the old
Indian cemetery nearby. All the things he might need in the future
went with him to the grave: maize, his hunting knife, cloth, and even
a tool to help him scale the walls in case he came to the Happy
Hunting Ground and couldn't mount the fence. The Indians of the
area today are struggling to revive old Indian arts and cultural tradi-
tions.

RECREATION

Harbour Lights Marina
7164 Cherry Ave.; telephone: 264–8914.

Elk Rapids

This handsome town started in 1852 but got its real growth spurt when
Wirt Dexter and Henry Noble joined forces and went into business
in 1856. They were the commercial phenomena of the north woods.
At the height of their remarkable careers they owned a blast furnace
and shipped out tons of high-grade pig iron (the first ever exported
from America). Their sawmill dressed 75,000 board feet of lumber
daily; their grist mill produced 100 barrels of flour. They made wood
alcohol, tar products, acetic acid. They owned 24 scows, 3 tugs, and
had a cash-and-carry general store that had more merchandise in that
era than the Marshall Field store in Chicago.

All this activity in a town of 600. At the time they called the
Hannah & Lay Company in Traverse City "the dukedom"; and Dex-

ter and Noble "the principality." But in time the lumber thinned out, the iron smelting faltered. Today one can see the ruins of the smelting plant next to the Iron Works Restaurant at U.S. 31 near the new bridge. Today Elk Rapids is vacation country, with a nice park and marina.

RECREATION

Golf

A-Ga-Ming Golf Course
9 1/2 miles north of Elk Rapids to Barnes Rd.; telephone: 264–5081.

Elk Rapids Golf Club
724 Ames; telephone: 264–8891.

Marinas

Elk Rapids Public Marina

Chain of Lakes Marina (commercial)

RESTAURANT

Iron Works Restaurant
U.S. 31; telephone: 264–5671. Bar and dining room. Tues.–Fri., 11–2; Mon.–Sat., 5–10.

SHOPPING

Ed Gray Gallery
10774 U.S. 31 south; telephone: 264–9977. Metal sculpture, fine pottery, oils, acrylics. Daily, 10–6; Jan.–April, 10–4.

Acme

A gentleman named L. S. Hoxie was the prime mover in Acme's early days. He built a sawmill that flourished till the lumbering ended. He also had a woolen mill, and sold blankets to the asylum in Traverse City. Goods from the mill were so excellent that one man said of his Hoxie material, "it nearly outwore me." Eventually new mills opened in Traverse City with higher pay for the workers. The Petobego Swamp, north of town on U.S. 31, was a rich source of marl, which was used in the making of local cement. Where the cement company once stood, land has been cut up and sold for scores of summer homes.

RECREATION

Golf

Grand Traverse Golf Club
4263 M-72; telephone: 938–1620.

Marina

Acme Cutty Sark Harbor

RESTAURANT

The Embers
M-31 north; telephone: 938–1300. Overlooks East Bay. Famous for one-pound pork chop. Daily, 11:30–10:30 PM; Sunday, 4–10; closed 2:30–5:30.

SHOP

Millers Antiques
From Acme, take Rt. 72 to Williamsburg, continue to County Rd. 347 north to Rapid City. Watch for antique sign. Telephone: 331–6104. Books, primitives, furniture. A must. Weekends or by appointment.

Traverse City

Population: 16,387   Area Code: 616   Zip Code: 49684
Chamber of Commerce: 202 Grandview Parkway, P.O. Box 387; telephone:
   947–5075
Up-to-minute snow conditions: 947–5075. Mon.–Fri., 9–5.

Cherries, Cherries! Traverse City is the cherry capital of the world. Each year the area produces millions of pounds of tart red and sweet cherries, one third of all the cherries on this globe. There are morel mushrooms and Petoskey stones up here, coho and marvelous water sports, ski slopes and dog sled races. There is even oil in the eastern part of the county. But nothing compares to the beauty and booty produced by cherries. One flies into the Cherry Capital Airport, sleeps in a cherry-something motel, attends a cherry theater. Well, everything here comes up cherries. And the climax of it all is a magnificent July cherry festival in which a cherry queen is crowned in order to take a cherry pie to Washington to present to a sometimes chary president.

It wasn't always that way, of course. In the beginning there were the Indian mound builders (one of their burial sites can be seen at the corner of 8th and Boardman streets). The tribesmen were followed by the usual trappers and traders, a smattering of French priests, and by a Presbyterian missionary named Reverend Peter Dougherty, who came down from St. Ignace in 1839 to spread the Good Word and to establish the first white settlement at Old Mission Peninsula, where one can still see a full-scale replica of his school. In 1847 Captain Boardman, a farmer from Naperville, Illinois, arrived, bought the land where the city now stands and put his son into the sawmill business. Parts of that old slab town remain. What isn't called cherry is therefore apt to be called Boardman, and if not Boardman, then Hannah and Lay. For Perry Hannah was actually the city's founding father. A first-class lumber baron, he also owned the bank, general store, and railroad. In the 1840s the Traverse City area was a glorious forest of white and Norway pine, but by 1900 the lumber was gone. Lean days followed until someone discovered that potatoes would grow in the local soil. Better yet, the B. J. Morgan family discovered

Aerial view of Traverse City, Michigan. *Michigan Travel Commission*

that cherries would flourish. Unlike Door County in Wisconsin, where the top soil was so thin that it had to be dynamited to plant the trees, Traverse City has a deep alluvial soil. This light soil and the endless fingers of water that tended to protect the land from heavy frosts, resulted in a peninsula of unbelievable beauty. But the orchardists had heavy risks — winter kill, pests, etc. In 1923 the churches of the Grand Traverse Bay region were asked to set aside a Sunday in May, a time when the bloom is at its peak, to have a Blessing of the Blossoms. This became the forerunner of the National Cherry Festival.

Since then the area has been a happy blend of cherries and tourists. Traverse City has a permanent population of 16,387. In summer the number swells by a factor of twelve. The town nestles in a corner of West Bay, but the greater Traverse Bay area covers 263 square miles of parks, woods, beach, and orchards. It has best been compared to a woman's bosom, West Bay forming one breast as it follows the curve of the Leelanau Peninsula; the other, East Bay, is contoured by Rt. 31 going north. Old Mission Peninsula (the greatest cherry producing area of all) forms the cleavage. Interestingly Old Mission Lighthouse is that point halfway between the North Pole and the Equator.

This is boom time in cherryland. One orchard, a big one (and big may run up to 350 acres), sold 1000 tons of cherries in 1978 (at 43 cents a pound). New tree orders are backed up three years (a cherry tree takes ten years to reach maturity and full production). New methods of trickle irrigation are proving important. But the big change, the one that has brought a cultural revolution in its wake, is the shaker. First tried in the 1960s this remarkable $20,000 machine has become the cotton gin of the cherry kingdom. In the old days thousands of migrant workers came into the area for the summer months. Each cherry had to be hand-snipped with a clipper, then shipped, stems on to avoid crushing, to Chicago for further processing. Today a shaker moves through the orchard, shaking down each tree in a little more than a minute. Every last cherry is released without damage to the trees. The cherries are packed, processed, canned, or frozen in the area, so transportation of the delicate fruit is no longer necessary. Cherries are used for pies, for wine, for preserves. They are glaced for

Cherry harvest in Traverse City, Michigan. *Michigan Travel Commission*

ice cream, and maraschinoed for Manhattans (the maraschino undergoes a ninety-day bleaching process, with color and flavor added afterward). One resourceful soul has even discovered that cherry pits make fine gravel for driveways.

Many early settlers on the Mission Peninsula were homesteaders and their deeds frequently bore Abraham Lincoln's signature. In recent years land prices have skyrocketed, and the question is no longer whether you have property on the water, but whether you even have a *view* of the water. The governor of Michigan and one of its former U.S. senators both call Traverse City home, and many theatrical people and artists commute on a regular basis to New York. There are reputedly more architects, doctors, and lawyers here per capita than anywhere in the country. Their average earnings are lower, but that's a trade they make voluntarily in order to live the good life on the bosomed bays in the land of the cherries.

ARCHITECTURE AND HISTORIC SITES

* Perry Hannah House, circa 1891
305 6th St. Built for $40,000, has forty rooms. Hannah was a lumber baron. Story went that the house was built of brick, then re-covered with wood because of the amount of criticism. Now home of Reynolds-Hansen Funeral Home.

Henry Hull House, 1894
Northeast corner of Washington and Wellington.

Morgan House
State and Wellington.

Opera House
Front St.

6th and 7th Streets
Interesting old lumber baron homes.

MARITIME ACADEMY

Great Lakes Maritime Academy
1701 E. Front; telephone: 946–5650. Only state academy on Lakes for training officers for marine industry and shipping. Three-year training. Become pilots on Great Lakes or engineers for salt or fresh water shipping.

ORCHARDS

Small

Gallagher's Farm Market
3 miles west on M72; telephone: 947–1689. Pick your own cherries.
Fruit, baked goods, jams, jellies. June 12–Labor Day.

Lars Halvarsen
County Route 633, north of Traverse City on M22; telephone: 946–
7906. Sweet cherries. June 10–July 10.

Southview Orchard's Farm Market
167 N. Garfield Rd.; telephone: 946–5867. Cherries, fruits, vegetables,
baked goods, cider. June–December 1.

Large

Cherry Growers, Inc.
Grawn, Michigan (9 miles southeast of Traverse City on U.S. 31);
telephone: 276–9241. See the whole cherry process.

Morrison Orchard and Storage Facility (Uba Coop also)
Rt. 2 — Williamsburg (NE of Traverse City on M72); telephone:
264–8175. A very large cherry and apple orchard. Splendid to visit in
July and early August when picking, processing, freezing, and packing are at height. July 15–August 10, twenty hours a day, subcontract
maraschinos.

PARK

Clinch Park
Grandview Parkway at waterfront. Has marina, beach, Con Foster
Museum (mainly Indian artifacts), and a very mediocre zoo. Indians
of area put on pressure to have Indian skeletons given a decent burial.

In whole Traverse City area, note beautiful mute swans. There are
now 600, all descended from one pair brought from England.

RECREATION

Charters

P & K Charter
13258 W. Bay Shore Dr.; telephone: 947–2530.

Boot-Z
Captain Ric Zehner, 516 6th St.; telephone: 947–8038. Scenic cruise to Marion Island, evening fishing as well as usual charters. Call before 6 AM or after 9 PM.

Golf

Elmbrook Golf Course (18-hole)
Hammond Road, between Garfield and 3 Mile Rd., 1 mile south of Airport; telephone: 946–9180.

Sugarloaf (18-hole)
18 miles northwest of Traverse City near Cedar on Route 1; telephone: 228–5461.

Marinas

Clinch Park
Grandview Parkway at waterfront.

Elmwood Township Marina
13051 W. Bay Shore Dr.; telephone: 946–9773.

Harbor West Marina
12917 W. Bay Shore Dr.; telephone: 941–1800.

Skiing

CROSS-COUNTRY TRAILS

For more information, call Department of Natural Resources; telephone: 373–2199.

Betsie River Trail
Betsie River State Forest. 30-mile trail.

Boardman Valley Trail
Kalkaska State Forest, 25 miles from Traverse City. Trails vary from 7 miles to 28 miles.

DOWNHILL TRAILS

Crystal Mountain
Approximately 29 miles southwest of Traverse City; telephone: 378–2911.

Hilton Shanty Creek
Approximately 40 miles northeast of Traverse City on M-88; telephone: 533–8621.

Schuss Mountain
Approximately 40 miles northeast of Traverse City on M-88 in Mancelona; telephone: 587–9162.

Sugarloaf
18 miles northwest of Traverse City near Cedar on Route 1; telephone: 228–5461.

Timberlee
5 miles northwest of Traverse City on Route 3; telephone: 946–4444.

Traverse City Holiday
5 miles east of Traverse City on Holiday Rd.; telephone: 946–5035.

RESTAURANTS

Coach and Four
900 E. Front; telephone: 947–4100.

Dill's Olde Towne Saloone
423 S. Union (Old Town); telephone: 947–7534. One-hundred-year-old lumbering saloon. Singing waitresses. Lunch and dinner, Mon.–Sat., 11 AM on.

The Ice Cream Shoppe
810 E. Front (U.S. 31); telephone: 946–4191. Good ice cream. Light food. Daily, 11 AM–11 PM.

The Omelette Shoppe
124 Cass St.; telephone: 946–0912.

The Pinestead — Reef
On East Grand Traverse Bay, 1265 Shore Dr.; telephone: 800–528–1234 (toll-free). Great Lake view.

The Saw Mill
236 E. Front; telephone: 946–9160. Entertainment nightly. Light foods. Genuine 1830s sawmill aura. Luncheon daily.

Louie Sleder's Family Tavern
717 Randolph; telephone: 947–9213. In slab town, old lumber section of town. Tavern built in 1882. Flavor of lumbering days. Friday afternoons, evenings jump with teachers, lawyers, and town professionals. Lively, colorful. Good hamburgers. Closed Saturday night.

Top of the Park
Park Place Hotel; Park Pl.; telephone: 946–5410. Ten stories up . . . gorgeous view of city and the bays. Top place in town, and highest. During cherry festival, a cherry smorgasbord. Next to Cherry Orchard Playhouse.

SHOPPING

Babel & Buchbruder Inc.
10285 Cherry Bend Rd., three blocks west of M-22; telephone: 941–1222. Cruising and racing sailboats of all sizes.

Devonshire Antiques
West Front St., to Cedar Run Rd., turn on Barney Rd.; telephone: 947–1063. Seven days a week.

Gaslight District (a complex of shops)
Front and Union Sts. (West Bay, Union between 7th and 8th Sts.). Stained glass, photography, stoves, arts and crafts.

Glen of Michigan Outlet Store
122 Cass; telephone: 946–0260. Mon.–Sat., 10–5:30; Friday, evenings.

Logan's Landing
Boardman River at S. Airport Rd.; telephone: 947–6234. Weavers, women's wear, bed and bath, needlepoint — on both sides of river with enclosed foot bridge.

Scuba North, Inc.
13258 W. Bay Shore Dr.; telephone: 947–2520. All sorts of scuba equipment.

SPECIAL EVENTS

Dog Sled Races
Up-to-date material on date, time, and place of races (January and February) can be had by calling Department of Natural Resources.

National Cherry Festival
Second week in July.

Traverse Bay Outdoor Art Fair
Northwestern Michigan College. First week in August.

Northwestern Michigan Fair
First week in September.

THEATERS

Civic Center Complex
1125 W. Civic Center Dr.; telephone: 941–2246. Eight baseball fields, jogging course, golf, music pavilion, indoor pool, racquetball courts. Closed to public at 6:30 PM, while local teams play. 8 AM–11 PM.

Cherry County Playhouse
Park Place Motor Inn, P.O. Box 661; telephone: 947–9560. Call for current schedule of plays. July 4–September 3.

Community Players
Cass and 8th, old First Christian Church. Consult Chamber of Commerce for calendar.

TOURS

Chef Pierre
Box 1009; telephone: 947–2100. Fabulous place. Turn out 40,000 pies in eight hours . . . 20 million yearly. Favorites: apple, cherry, rhubarb. Now part of Consolidated Food, this business started in a family kitchen in Muskegon. Every bit of process is mechanized, and anything defective goes to plump the pigs in local pig farms. Write ahead for tour, c/o personnel office.

Leelanau Wine Cellars
5 mi. south of Traverse City, 1 mi. north of junction U.S. 31 and M-37; telephone: 946–1653. Wine-making and tasting.

West Arm of Traverse City Bay

Bower's Harbor

Population: under 200   Zip Code: 49673

Old Mission Peninsula

Population: under 200   Zip Code: 49673

Sutton's Bay

Population: 522   Zip Code: 49682

Peshawbestown

Population: under 200   Zip Code: 49674

Omena

Population: under 200   Zip Code: 49674

Northport

Population: under 200   Zip Code: 49670

Bower's Harbor

Route M-37 provides access to Old Mission Peninsula, which divides
the East Arm from the West Arm of Grand Traverse Bay. There, in
November, 1851, the schooner *Madeline* pulled into the cove now
called Bower's Harbor. Five young men were aboard, and they were
determined to spend the winter on their ship and improve their educa-

tion while awaiting spring. They created a schoolroom aboard the schooner, hired a teacher, and carried on what was to become the first educational institution in the whole area. Today Bower's Harbor is a favorite stopping point for water lovers and cross-country skiers ... who say that several hours of hard work permits them to indulge in the French-fried ice cream for which the local Bower's Inn is famous.

Off Bower's Harbor is Marion Island, once a stopping point for excursion boats and now a favorite of yachtsmen.

Old Mission Peninsula

In 1851 when Perry Hannah first saw from his schooner the Old Mission Peninsula and the area where the town of Old Mission stands today, he was enchanted with the vista. He wrote of the many white-washed wigwams, the old Indians sitting with their pipes, and the children "wallooing" in great play. Reverend Peter Dougherty's lovely white mansion stood on a high point, and the Indian ponies were tethered together, each with bells on its neck. Old Mission served as an early post office for the whole area. For years the land was reserved for the Indians, but when the reservations were opened to other settlers in 1852, Dougherty and his Indian parishioners moved to the west arm of Grand Traverse Bay. The good reverend was always called *Mikoos* ("little beaver") by his followers.

Two famous shipwrecks still lie off Old Mission Point: the schooner *Metropolis,* which went down in 1886, and the *A. J. Rogers,* which was sunk in 1898.

ARCHITECTURE AND HISTORIC SITES

Old Mission Church and School
M-37, south of Old Mission Village. Authentic full-scale replica of original built by Reverend Peter Dougherty in 1839.

Old Mission House
1/2 mile north of village. Restoration of first building in Grand Traverse region, 1842. Displays of early local culture.

Old Mission Lighthouse, 1870
Tip of peninsula.

CEMETERY

Cemetery
M-37, Ogdensburg. Some of gravestones date back to 1850s.

ORCHARD

Underwood Orchards
360 E. McKinley; telephone: 947–8799. Daily, 9–6. July and August, cherries and apricots; September, apples and peaches; October to December 23, apples and cider.

PARK

Lighthouse Park
Tip of peninsula. Picnicking, swimming.

RECREATION

Biking

50-mile Bike Tour
Get information and map at Traverse City Chamber of Commerce.

Marina

Bower's Harbor
Swimming, picnicking.

RESTAURANT

Bowers Harbor Inn
13512 Peninsula Dr.; telephone: 223–4222. Beautiful bay view. Year round: Jan.–April, weekends only.

SHOPPING

This Old Barn Antiques
7 miles out M-37, Old Mission, turn west on Nelson Rd.; telephone: 223–4833. Daily, 10–5:30.

Suttons Bay

H. C. Sutton was the first man to own land in the beautiful area around Suttons Bay on the West Arm of Grand Traverse Bay. That was in 1865, but in 1871 a missionary priest, Father Heratrit, laid out the village. The waters of the bay open into the Lake here. There is a pier and good fishing. Glacial hills look down on a water world. This is cherry and apple country with twenty-two fruit warehouses in the area. Many residents today work in Traverse City.

ORCHARDS

Mawby's Farm Market
M-22; telephone: 271–3028. Fruit, vegetables all year.

Patrick Hawkins' Market
M-22; telephone: 271–3750. Strawberries, cherries, cider, jams, jellies, vegetables. June 15–September.

RECREATION

Sutton's Bay Public Marina
M-22 at Lakefront.

SHOPPING

Rod Conklin Studio
Solar Barn Studio; M-22 to Shady Lane, west 1/2 mile to Elm Valley Rd., north 1/8 mile; telephone: 271–6844. June–Labor Day, Mon.–Sat., 10–5.

Peshawbestown

The good Father Mrack ministered to the Ottawa in the settlement once called Eagletown and now called Peshawbestown. He was of vital importance to the whole Traverse area because of his respect for and knowledge of Indian customs. Shortly after Sitting Bull upset General Custer and stirred up unrest among tribes everywhere, a council of Indians was called at nearby Boot Lake. Chief Petoskey attended and so did chiefs Ahgosa and Blackbird and the chief from Cross Village and scouts representing Sitting Bull. It was a frightening period and white families throughout the area bolted their doors, called their children close, and had meat cleavers in readiness. One family reputedly had its pet bear loose in the kitchen. Father Mrack had been invited also, and fortunately for everyone his gentle persuasion convinced the local chieftains to seek peace and not to follow the red power tactics of Sitting Bull. Mrack founded the Immaculate Conception Church, which later burned and was replaced. Late in the century Franciscans from Petoskey took over the Peshawbestown Mission.

ARCHITECTURE AND HISTORIC SITE

Immaculate Conception Church
M-22. Note poured-glass windows, which let in light but are opaque.

Omena

When Reverend Dougherty moved his mission from the Old Mission Peninsula he came to Omena and started his new church. New England in design, it has a bell of copper alloy, created out of the thousands of British pennies that the Chippewa Indians collected and contributed to the new mission. The word *Omena* is Indian for "it is so," the response that Dougherty made to almost everything said to him. Dougherty's Chippewa followers embraced his Presbyterianism, but over the years there was hardly an Indian family that did not intermarry with Father Mrack's Catholic Ottawas. Everyone lives peacefully and poorly around the beautiful beaches of Omena Bay. The poverty does not extend to the whites who also live here in a very attractive small community.

SHOPS

Tamarack Craftsmen Gallery
Telephone: 386–5529. Pottery, prints, glass, sculpture, etc. Year round.

Wendy Knob
Between Omena and Northport, M-22; telephone: 386–2761. Quill boxes, Indian baskets, pine-cone wreaths.

Northport

For some unknown reason the Reverend George N. Smith did not get along well with the Hollanders who settled in the Black River country. So the Congregational cleric, with his faithful Indian followers, set out in 1849 by schooner and moved into the unbroken wilderness of the Leelanau Peninsula. The settlement they chose was called Waukazooville, because it had been inhabited by the Waukazoo tribe and named for their chief. Until 1886 the Indian lands were protected by treaty, but once that period ended, Northport grew. Today it is a charming town and it still has its Waukazoo Street.

ARCHITECTURE AND HISTORIC SITE

Grand Traverse Lighthouse
Tip of peninsula on Rt. 629.

PARK

Northport State Park (Leelanou State Park)
Tip of peninsula. Camping, swimming, picnicking.

RECREATION

Charters

Lake Trout Charters
Camphaven Rd., 1 mile south of Northport on M-22; telephone: 386–5416.

Marina

Northport Village Marina
105 S. Rose; telephone: 386–5411.

RESTAURANT

The Beech Tree
202 Waukazoo; telephone: 386–5892. Superb; reservations required. Memorial Day-Labor Day, dinner.

SHOPPING

Cedar Chest Gift Shop
Features locally made Indian baskets.

The Pier Group
1 block north of marina; telephone: 386–5371. Built on site of cherry canning factory whose chimney remains. Great Lake view. Gallery, variety of shops, and a restaurant. Late May–September 1, 10–6.

Leland

Population: under 200   Area Code: 616   Zip Code: 49654
Leelanau County Chamber of Commerce: Suttons Bay; telephone: 271–3542

Leland (originally spelled *Leeland* because of its protected position on the shore) is a tasteful town with large concerns about conservation and avoidance of the usual tourist clutter. Someone once described it as "the other side of ritziness because of its impeccable good taste."

The earliest arrivals were French; Antoine Manseau and John Miller, who searched for a mill site and built a dam on the Carp River (now the Leland River), which is the connecting waterway between the big Lake and inland Lake Leelanau. In 1870 Father Mrack, the Catholic missionary to the Indians, built Holy Trinity Church here.

For fifteen years the Leland Lake Superior Iron Company operated in the area, and after that came lumbering. When the railroad finally connected Chicago and Traverse City, the summer settlers arrived — wealthy families from Detroit and other Midwestern cities — and they built their homes in a section called the Indiana Woods and along the shores of both lakes.

Far earlier, however, mound builders lived in the area and occupied a hill at the south end of today's town. Despite their advantageous location, they had at least one battle — at Nedow's Bay — the site where the now-private golf course reaches down to the shore of Lake Leelanau.

The best-known section of Leland is Fishtown, a cluster of gray fishing shanties now on the National Historic Registry. Many of the buildings date back to the turn of the century. Some are fish houses or ice houses, and some have been converted to smart shops. The area is a charming blend of nets and buoys, paralleling a protected harbor that is filled all summer with yachts from all over the Lake.

The adjoining town of Lake Leelanau was drilled for oil during a period in the 1860s. Instead up came a marvelous though temporary spurt of good mineral water. Everyone brought jugs and kegs and figured that they were bottling good health. The settlement, once French, is now an area of farms, many owned by Polish families, giving the place its name Polltown.

ARCHITECTURE AND HISTORIC SITES

* Leland's Fishtown
Main St. on Leland River at Lake. A must.

FERRIES

Manitou Mail Service Boat
108 Hill; telephone: 256–9116. Ferries to Manitou Islands. Charter trips for fishing, year round. Winter trips, Tuesday and Friday, November–April.

MUSEUM

Leelanau Historical Museum
Chandler and River Sts. In old county jail. June 30–Labor Day, Mon.–Sat., 10–3.

ORCHARDS

Manitou Market
2 miles south of Leland on M-22; telephone: 259–9900. Fruit, vegetables. June 15–September 1.

Robert Swanson Market
8 miles south of Leland on M-22; telephone: 228–5677. Strawberries, sweet cherries.

PARK

Leland Public Park
Pearl St. and Public Park. Picnicking, beach, pier.

RECREATION

Boat Rentals

Stander Marine, Inc.
On the river; telephone: 256–9231. Fishing boat and canoe rentals.

Marina

Leland Township Harbor
Telephone: 256–9132.

RESTAURANTS

The Bluebird
Telephone: 256–9081. Porch overlooks river. Mon.–Sat., 12–3, 5–10; Sun., 12–8.

Fishermen's Cove
On dam overlooking Fishtown; telephone: 256–9866.

Leland Lodge
Overlooking country club; telephone: 256–9498. May 1–October 31.

Riverside Inn
Overlooking Leland River; telephone: 256–9971. Breakfast only, daily, 7–12.

SHOPPING

Carlson Fisheries
Fishtown; telephone: 256–9801. Commercial fishing — fresh and smoked fish.

Connoisseur
Telephone: 256–9894. Antiques and fine gifts. Hours by chance or appointment.

Nautic Antiques
Lake Leelanau, about 4 miles southeast of Leland; telephone: 256–9954. Furniture, glass, Americana. Mon.–Sat., 10–5:30; Sun., 12–5:30; closed Thurs.

TOUR

Boskydel Vineyard
County Highway 641, about 4 miles southeast of Leland; telephone: 256–7272. Table wines. Samples and tours available.

North Manitou Island

Population: under 200

South Manitou Island

Population: under 200

Glen Arbor

Population: under 200

Empire

Population: 409   Zip Code: 49630

North Manitou Island

This lovely island is in the process of becoming part of Sleeping Bear Park like its fellow cub, South Manitou. Today, it is still in private hands, managed by the Manitou Island Association, which controls the number of beds as well as the permissible fish catch. North Manitou is a choice preserve, 15,000 acres of natural beauty, which is a reminder of what most of Michigan must have been before the fury of the lumberman's saw. There is a clump of ten white birch nicknamed the Ten Commandments and a specimen elm so huge that it takes five people, finger-to-finger, to span its girth.

In early days the island was used as a fueling stop by Lake steamers. In 1843, the intrepid New Englander Margaret Fuller stopped off to see what had happened to some Unitarian leaflets given out to woodsmen the prior year. She found few converts among the cutters.

Later a few Germans dug in to fish, farm, lumber, and earn a fine reputation for their splendid cherry orchards and, briefly, for local cattle as well.

Today, North Manitou's fine inland lake makes it a fisherman's paradise. Large flocks of wild turkey and great numbers of deer also make it a hunter's delight. No more than fifteen hunters are allowed in the woods at one time and each is allotted a range of 600 acres. Transportation to Manitou must be arranged through private charters from Traverse City, private planes, or a bit of pleading with the captain of the mailboat that leaves Leland each day.

For more information on the island, call or write to Marvin Fruelling, Manitou Island Association, Leland, Michigan; Traverse City Mobile Operator: YJ28493–083.

South Manitou Island

Every morning from mid-May to late September a ferry boat leaves at 10 AM from Leland for South Manitou Island. This 16-mile trip is a passageway to the wilderness, a reminder of a land so sacred to the Indians that they never used it. For here, they believed, the Great Spirit (their Manitou) dwelled.

The southernmost island in the Lake Michigan archipelago, this jewel of the waters contains 5250 acres of woods and fields, 12 miles of beach, and dunes that soar 350 feet. In 1970 when Congress authorized the Sleeping Bear Dunes National Lakeshore, South Manitou was included.

Indian legend tells of a great fire that blazed long ago on the Wisconsin shore, and of a mother bear and her two cubs who tried to escape by swimming to the Michigan side. The mama made it, but her cubs sank into the water. The Great Manitou, aware of the bear's grief, lifted her cubs' heads so that she, now the great sleeping bear, might always see them. More scientifically, the bear cubs, North and South Manitou, are the remains of a limestone tilt that existed long before there was a lake. The heads of the cubs are the glacial debris left on the limestone 10,000 years ago as the ice retreated northward, having carved out the basin that became Lake Michigan. Soil has built up on top of the debris, plant life has flourished, and today a virgin forest of white cedar grows on the island with one all-American champ reaching a height of 111 feet. The island also contains a champion maple and elder as well, and rare plants such as the walking fern and the green spleen wort. Bird life is abundant, but animal life is so minimal that one traveler remarked that even the mosquitos avoided the place, so little was there to bite.

The terrible bite of Lake storms, however, has made South Manitou a haven for ships and sailors. In earlier days, a settler wrote: "Father was plowing and I saw from a hill nearby 24 schooners going east and west at one time. It was a beautiful sight." That same man wrote of seeing five sailing ships dashed against the shore in one devastating storm in 1880. One recent shipwreck, the *Francisco Morizon,* still lies on the island's south side, a major attraction for today's hikers.

With the opening of the Erie Canal in 1825, and with the arrival of lumbermen in the 1840s, South Manitou became an important refueling station for the new woodburning steamers. So busy were the jacks cutting wood and loading it onto the ships, that passengers claimed they used bushel baskets to hold their money until they had the time to stash it away.

South Manitou has been used in several other ways as well. The ginseng plant was gathered here for export to China where it served medicinal and aphrodisiacal purposes. The Great Lakes Naval Reserve held summer maneuvers of the fleet here because of the island's fine natural harbor. The pollen-free island also has served as an experimental station for growing pure strains of various seed crops. And finally South Manitou always has been a prime nesting ground for Lake Michigan's herring gulls and ring-billed gulls. Today's visitors are asked to view the colony from the island's north side to avoid endangering gull chicks.

The lumbermen and the farms are gone now. Today the Coast Guard station houses a park ranger. There is one commercial motor tour of the island daily which leaves the dock shortly after the ferry arrives. There is a marina with a restaurant that provides light meals. But mainly this is an island for hikers, campers, boaters, and lovers of the outdoors. As one author said, "Nature has reclaimed Manitou. Perhaps it never should have been settled. It was a preserve of the Great Spirit . . ."

Glen Arbor

Glen Arbor is a little village nestled between the great Sleeping Bear Point to the west and Pyramid Point to the east. It was once the place where the early steamboats picked up wood as they moved along the coast. It was settled in 1854 by four men, all named John. The village was originally started on the shore, but the weather was so rough that it was moved inland and situated in a glen of pines and hardwoods whose trunks were covered with twisting grape vines. Settlers considered it nature's glen arbor.

Dr. William Walker, an early pioneer, was a central figure in the town's development when he cultivated a thriving cranberry business just outside the village. And the D. H. Day family were among the first in the lumbering industry to experiment with selective timber harvest. The Day Forest estate is now a national campground. In the early days scores of black bears lumbered through the area, and so the inland lake behind the town was first called Bear Lake. It is now called Glen Lake, and many consider it as beautiful as Lake Como in Italy. Its marvelous shadings of blue and the hills around it have captivated travel writers and artists for years. It is best seen from the top of Sleeping Bear Dunes National Park.

OBSERVATORY

Leelanau Observatory
South of Leland, turn into Drive for Homestead off M-22; telephone: 334–3072. June 15–August 31, Thurs., 9–11:30 PM.

RECREATION

Boats

Crystal Harbor Canoes
1 1/2 miles NE of Glen Arbor, on County 675; telephone: 334–3991. Boat and canoe rentals. Crystal River canoe trips.

Horseback Riding

Circle H Farms
3 miles north of Glen Arbor on M-22, 4250 Thoreson Rd.; telephone: 334–4761. Trail rides overlooking Sleeping Bear Bay

RESTAURANTS

The Homestead
1 1/2 miles north of Glen Arbor on M-22; telephone: 334–3041. Three meals daily; Sunday brunch; seven days in summer, weekends only in winter; closed November and March.

Point Betsie lighthouse station between Empire and Frankfort.
Michigan Travel Commission

The Red Pine
Downtown Glen Arbor; telephone: 334–3555. Breakfast, lunch, dinner.

SCENIC DRIVE

Leland to Sleeping Bear
Gorgeous views of inland lake, Lake Michigan, fine woods.

Empire

In 1865 the schooner *Empire* was locked in by ice for the whole winter near the Sleeping Bear, and the few settlers around took advantage of the event and set up a school on the schooner. In time they gradually named their town Empire after the nautical schoolhouse. In 1873 one of the students built a dock and sold cordwood to passing ships, establishing the Empire Lumber Company, which eventually cut 20 million feet of board a year and shipped a good part of it to Chicago. There were 1000 people around then — twice today's population. When lumber diminished, many individuals and some of the mills turned their acreage into orchards, and the land that belonged to the Empire Lumber Company became a community park.

The current town is important for its radar station run by the Air Force, and the bluffs at Pyramid Point, which are used for soaring. Lovers of ghost towns may want to visit Aral at Empire on the Platte River.

RECREATION

Shore-to-Shore Trail
From Lake Michigan to Lake Huron. Trail begins at Empire's post office on Main St. 150-mile trail, clearly marked with "S-to-S" symbols. Reserved for hiking, cross-country skiing, snowshoeing, and horses (no motor vehicles or snowmobiles).

Sleeping Bear Dunes National Lakeshore Park

Headquarters: 400 Main St.: telephone: 352–9611

Frankfort-Elberta

Population: 1500   Area Code: 616   Zip Code: 49635
Chamber of Commerce: Main St., Box 352; telephone: 352–4601

Sleeping Bear Dunes National Lakeshore Park

The great bear, sitting 400 feet high, searches the lake for her two cubs, North and South Manitou Islands. She is spectacular: a great desert of sand between Lake Michigan and Glen Lake (on Route M-109), 10 square miles of unspoiled beauty. When the park, which was authorized October 21, 1970, is finally complete, it will include 30 miles of Lake Michigan shoreline and 60,000 acres. A better bruin was never born.

Eventual plans call for bike trails, snowmobiling, horseback riding, canoeing, and sailing; and already one can hike and ski the trails, and enjoy some of the finest beaches in the nation.

The bear is the result of four great glacier periods, which brought millions of tons of ice (some a mile thick), carving out the basins that eventually became our Great Lakes. Young in the history of the world, the whole miraculous birth occurred a little more than 10,000 years ago. As the glaciers began to melt and retreat, they left rock and sand and silt which eventually became the ridges and hills that surround today's lakes. Hiking inland one can see evidences of old shorelines of ancient lakes higher than the present one. The high places, Pyramid Point, Sleeping Bear Point, and Empire Bluff resulted because the glacier had scalloped edges, and between the scallops rock material piled up and formed high ridges. Where the ice scallops covered the area, the bays or embayments developed. Constantly there is a battle between wind and water. In 1971, for instance, the water ate away tons of sand from Sleeping Bear, dropping the material into the Lake. At other times wind attacks the beaches (sand can be swept as high as 450 feet), and piles it in new dunes high up on the bluffs. The ever-moving sands creep up and bury forests, and then, perhaps hundreds of years later, blow out and leave tree graveyards. Because there are so many ecological settings — shore, bluff, swamp, wood — there are plants and trees that are particular to each: quaking bogs of sphagnum moss, clumps of white birch, areas of beech and maple, and clutches of pine. Two hundred and twenty species of birds have been identified, and animal life varies depending on the habitat. Porcupine thrive on the green inner bark of young trees and deer cluster in aspen thickets.

The Sleeping Bear Park is a gift of the American people to themselves — a national heritage and one of the country's great outdoor museums.

Empire Bluffs, the south end of Sleeping Bear Dunes National Lakeshore Park. *Michigan Travel Commission*

HEADQUARTERS

Visitors Contact Station
County Route 109, about 3 miles south of Glen Haven; telephone: 334–4017. Conducted tours, publications, hikes, self-guided tours. Also a headquarters office in Frankfort; telephone: 352–9611. Ask here for specifics on canoeing, beaches, skating, cross-country skiing, hiking, snowshoeing, and three areas with trails. Daily, June–Sept.; weekends, May–Oct.; Jan. and Feb.

RECREATION

Camping

Platte River Campground
(South end of park) on M-22. Open all year.

D. H. Day Campground
(North end of park) on County R. 209. Open all year.

Hang Gliding

Empire Bluffs
Permission necessary in person from Platte River Campground office at south end of park.

Pyramid Point
Permission necessary in person from D. H. Day Campground office at north end of park.

Water Sports

Glen Lake
M-109. Swimming, picnicking, great dune climbing.

SCENIC DRIVE

Stocking Nature Trail
Begins where M-109 joins M-22. This drive meanders through dunes, forests, goes past scenic overlooks.

Frankfort-Elberta

Frankfort is a lovely town with Lake Michigan at its front and the Frankfort River and Lake Betsie (a corruption of Bec Scies or "sawbill duck") at its side. The town was platted in 1859, had a brief period of Mormon settlement, and a far longer period of logging. During the 1880s Norwegians came to fish and raise cabbages on land where the airport stands today. And other settlers found peaches grew splendidly, and named the little town across the river, Elberta, after the variety of peach that flourished the best.

Frankfort has been a water center . . . and a tourist favorite . . . for generations, with the best ice-free harbor on the east shore of the lake. Its Coast Guard station was brought over on a scow from Chicago when its operator was transferred to Frankfort, and its main lighthouse is one of the last manned lights on the Lake today.

Artists find Frankfort paintable because of the famous Point Betsie lighthouse. Kids love the place because the Ann Arbor car ferries operate out of Elberta across the harbor. The small towns around beautiful Crystal Lake — Benzonia, Beulah, Crystalia — are charming, and at Interlochen 20 miles away, the air at the National Music Camp is saturated with Bach and Bartok. Divers visit and turn greedy when they study shipwreck maps and discover the buried wealth along the Frankfort coast. Historians (and the late Bruce Catton was one who spent most of his summers here) are still debating whether Father Marquette really died on the beach at Frankfort or at Ludington down the way.

But everything Frankfort is, was, or ever will be, pales beside its role as a soaring center. During 1938 and 1939 when it became host to the national gliding meets, the town literally "soared on wings of glory." Ever since from April to October it has been commonplace to see cars and vans, topped with hang gliders, rolling into town from everywhere.

Soaring began in Germany, and came to America via Cape Cod and Elmira, New York. By 1920 when there were some 900 pilots in the country, someone discovered the wonders of Frankfort-Elberta. The Lake, the bluffs, the unlimited landing facilities of the beach, the special glimmer of the surf, even at night, made it a perfect spot. And

Soaring from the Elberta Bluffs outside Frankfort, Michigan.
Michigan Travel Commission

Frankfort, it seemed, because of its unique winds, had more soaring days a year than any other place.

The town realized what soaring could do for Frankfort, and they asked the gliders what the town could do for them. The outcome was the development of the Frankfort Sailing Manufacturing Company, and its offshoot, the gliding school. Local druggists, bankers, doctors, and undertakers each bought shares and made the business possible. The whole town got into the act. Mature men became terribly involved with southwest winds and their understanding wives kept roasts warm when the soaring was good. The truant officer checked the gliding field before he visited homes, and if the milkman was late everyone knew it had more to do with air currents than errant cows.

When the first national meet was held, one of the highlights for the crowd was watching Ted Bellak, a famous pilot, complete his 54-mile flight (Sturgeon Bay, Wisconsin, to Frankfort), the longest ever over water. The next year, when Helen Montgomery, the women's champion, could not compete for endurance records because her two-month-old daughter had pressing feeding demands, she delighted the crowd by taking the infant along, between feedings, and doing a mother and daughter flight.

Although the sailplane factory moved to Joliet, Illinois, many years ago, and the early instructors scattered, the town is currently having a soaring renaissance. In 1978 it hosted the 6th Annual National Soaring and Hang Gliding Festival. Pilots came from everywhere. So did the crowds. And the cooperative town with the wonderful beaches celebrated with fish bakes, dances, parades, and a sense that everyone was gliding in up draft currents.

ARCHITECTURE AND HISTORIC SITES

In Frankfort, alleys are wonderful places to find architectural points of interest. Notice the little houses that locals moved into when they rented their big houses in summer to vacationing families from Chicago and Cincinnati in early 1900s.

Pere Marquette Memorial
Pere Marquette Circle at Lakefront.

Point Betsie Lighthouse Station
M-22 between Empire and Frankfort; telephone: 352–4242. Beautiful Tiffany-like light. Tours: Sat., Sun., 11–3.

FERRIES

Ann Arbor Railroad Company and Car Ferry Service
1224 Furnace, Elberta; telephone: 352–7571. Carferry to Kewaunee, Wisconsin and Manitowoc. Reservations recommended.

ORCHARDS

Jim Mead Orchard
4373 Crawford; telephone: 882–5554. Peaches. August–September.

Nugent Farms
Off U.S. 31; telephone: 352–9580. Strawberries. July.

Bruce Walton Market
2671 Frankfort Highway; telephone: 352–7679. Apples, cherries, pears.

PARKS

Mineral Springs
At waterfront in Frankfort. Tennis, picnicking, playground, lovely sandy beach.

Market Square Park
Overlooks the Lake in Elberta. Swimming, picnicking.

RECREATION

Canoes

Waterwheel Canoe Livery
M-22 at Platte River (north of Frankfort on Lake); telephone: 325–3620. Rent canoes, motor boats, bikes. March–December.

Charters

Ronn Beyette
Telephone: 352–7624.

Mike Bradley
Telephone: 352–7515.

Jim Hooker
Telephone: 352–4267.

Delbert Parsons
Telephone: 352–7970.

Harry Putney
Telephone: 352–9493.

Earl Soderquist
Telephone: 325–4551.

Robert Wilkens
Telephone: 352–4637.

Fishing and Ice Fishing

Lots of fishing on the 3000-foot Lake Michigan Breakwater, and trolling and bait casting in Betsie Lake and Betsie River (Crystal Lake). For information, call Chamber of Commerce.

Golf

Crystal Lake Golf & Country Club (9-hole)
U.S. 31 at Beulah; telephone: 882–4061.

Frankfort Public Golf Course (9-hole)
M-22 overlooking the Lake; telephone: 352–4101.

Interlochen National Music Camp, south of Traverse City and east of Frankfort. *Photo by Brill*

Music

Interlochen
U.S. 31, east of Honor (off beaten track); telephone: 276–9221. In 1928 Joe Maddy founded the National Music Camp with 150 charter campers. Today there are 3500 plus an academy that runs during the school year. The famous camp was begun on money borrowed from National Association of Band Instrument Manufacturers. Today there are bands, orchestras, choral groups, dance, art, drama. There is the Corson Auditorium for Performing Arts, the Grunow Theater. Hotel reservations can be checked out by calling the camp, and season schedules are available.

Marinas

Elberta Marina
Lakefront; telephone: 352–4434.

Frankfort Marina
Waterfront. Excellent for small pleasure boats and large yachts. Launching facilities.

Soaring

Elberta Bluff
South over Frankfort Bridge, M-22 to M-168, then at Bye St. go up steep hill to far end of beach.

Swimming

Elberta Beach
South over Frankfort Bridge, then take M-22 to M-168, at Bye St. go up steep hill to beach. Marvelous wide beach.

Seventh Street Beach Park
Crystal Lake.

RESTAURANT

Frontenac Dining Room
Pere Marquette Cir. (on Lakefront); telephone: 352–9431. Summer, 7 AM–10 PM; winter, 11 AM–2:30 PM, 5–10 PM.

SHOPPING

Gwen Frostic Prints
6 miles east of M-22 on River Rd. out of Frankfort (off beaten track). Original block cuts. Presses operate Mon.–Fri., 9–4:30, year round. A beautiful sprawling shop with grasses growing from roof. 250 acres in wildlife sanctuary on Betsie River. Nature poetry and prints for sale, paper doilies, napkins, etc. Miss Frostic twice named by Michigan legislature as woman of year. Daily, from last Sun. of May to first Sun. of Nov.; 9–5:30; rest of year, Mon.–Sat., 9–4:30.

Eco Flight Hang Gliders
Benzonia; telephone: 892–5070. Full-service hang gliding establishment — sales, parts, lessons. Information on where best gliding spots are.

Vigland Pottery
U.S. 31 in Benzonia (off beaten track); telephone: 882–4958. Alan and Susie Vigland, potters. June–August, Mon.–Sat., 10–5.

SPECIAL EVENT

National Glider and Soaring Festival
Check Chamber of Commerce: telephone; 352–4601. Last week in June to July 4.

TOUR

Platte River Anadromous Fish Hatchery
From Frankfort take M-115 east to U.S. 31 to Honor. Birthplace of the Michigan coho salmon with rearing ponds for Chinook, rainbow, brown, and steelhead trout. Seven million fish per year. Daily, 8–4:30 (provided pamphlets make self-guided tours possible).

Arcadia

Population: 525   Zip Code: 49613

Onekama

Population: 638   Zip Code: 49675

Arcadia

One of the smallest and loveliest villages on the Lake is Arcadia, with a fine beach, marina, and natural harbor. Parts of the area are known as the Arcadian Marshlands, and 3 miles south of town, off M-22, is a waterfowl sanctuary.

Arcadia became a village in 1880, and an early German pioneer became a millionaire by cutting the heart out of the nearby hardwood forests. For years the Missouri Synod of the Lutheran Church convened here summers to build their bodies and expand their souls. Synods and cynics alike ever since have been charmed by the bays, the bluffs, and the great grove of American chestnut trees that grow here.

Onekama

Nobody is sure what Onekama really means ("place of contentment," "lake of many springs," or "man lost in a canoe"), but it is the town on Portage Lake which, in turn, is connected to Lake Michigan by a tiny creek. In early days the Porter and Bates Company of Chicago built a mill and a dam near the creek. The dam kept the water of the inland lake high, often so high that the backlands were impossible to farm. Half the time the settlers could sail a boat through the woods, and almost all the time people suffered from the ague. So the community got together, and during the night secretly cut a channel between the two bodies of water. The results were phenomenal: the water rushed out of Portage Lake, lowering it 12 feet, and a great many large trees went rushing out with it. The story goes that an old captain, making the run from Traverse City to Manistee, was so confounded at finding his Lake boat surrounded by a floating forest, that he turned course and whipped off to the Wisconsin shore. Ever since then the farmers around Onekama have been raising excellent apples and strawberries, as well as a huge crop of pickles. The Portage light now stands at the entrance to the channel, and sailors today find the tricky entrance into the inland lake more easily.

PARKS

Glen Park Mineral Springs
Erdman Rd., 2 miles north of Onekama.

RECREATION

Camping

Dorner Lake Campsite
Sand Lake National Campgrounds. For information, call Manistee County Chamber of Commerce: 723–2575.

Fishing

Portage Lake and long pier to Lake Michigan

SCENIC DRIVE

M-22, 4 miles north of Onekama (lookout).

SPECIAL EVENTS

Bloomer Memorial Cup Races
August.

Manistee County Fair
Great agricultural event. End of August.

Onekama Days
Parades, fireworks, dancing. July.

Manistee

Population: 8000   Area Code: 616   Zip Code: 49660
Chamber of Commerce: River Street at Bridge, P.O. Box 159; telephone: 723–
2575

Manistee ("spirit of the woods") is a town that looks loved and cared for with its face lifted, yet all its Victorian charm intact. It was, in its day, one of the lumber capitals of the country with more millionaires than any other town its size on the Lake. And it is, in this day, the salt capital of the world.

Two great river systems come together here, the Big and Little Manistee. They flow into Lake Manistee, which, in turn, has a channel into Lake Michigan deep enough to support oceangoing vessels. Recently Mrs. Carter, speaking for beautification, cited Manistee's harbor and new marina as one of the four handsomest in the country.

In 1840 when Joseph and John Stronach arrived here by boat from their home in St. Joseph, Michigan, there were only Chippewa Indians to greet them. Friendly, they helped the two white men scout for a good site to locate a lumber mill. Then the Stronach brothers set sail for home, gathered their families, collected their tools, and came back the following year to kick off the lumber era. In those days, as now, the little settlement was surrounded on three sides by a vast forest of pine and hemlock. All communication depended on Lake Michigan. Indians would arrive in their boats (the squaws rowed; the braves sailed). They brought potatoes and mococks (packets of maple sugar). Mail was brought by boat from Grand Haven or Milwaukee, and horses and cattle came in from Wisconsin and Illinois, were unloaded and allowed to swim to shore. Winter was long, and when the first white sails appeared in April, the community literally danced for joy.

Within a few years 100 saw mills were in operation, and the town had earned a reputation for hardwood and hard liquor. Ministers pleaded for men to keep the sabbath, and they did . . . for brawling. They would come out of the woods to celebrate, and in one evening spend a winter's earnings. Sometimes they drank communally from a barrel or an old boat filled with whisky. Whoever refused was shoved head first into the container. Ears were bitten off in battle. Deaths were common. And one minister earned minor fame for eulogies delivered for men who had left this world, cursing till the last breath: "Brother, thou wert mild and lovely,. gentle as a summer breeze . . ." Though the lumbering days are over in Manistee, the town still has a disproportionate number of bars, some dating back to times when men gathered to brew, brawl, and bellow the old Lake chanteys.

The great fire of 1871 blazed through Manistee as it did so many Lake communities. Flames raced across the tinder-dry state all the way to Lake Huron, and they destroyed 1 million acres of trees. One provident family buried all its summer canning in the sand, but never could find it again. Eleven hundred families were homeless. But the community realized that others had shared in the disaster when a townsman, returning from a trip to Pentwater, mounted a dry goods box and announced that Chicago, too, had been destroyed.

Happily, in the early 1880s, a man named Charles Reitz decided to drill for oil. He sank a well 2000 feet and hit a vast layer of salt. Shortly before this Dr. Douglas Houghton, the state geologist, had been trying to get a bill through the state legislature offering a bounty of ten cents for every bushel of salt found in Michigan. But the lure became ludicrous, for it turned out that Manistee was almost at the center of a saline formation, laid down millions of years ago and containing magnesium, limestone, marl, gypsum — a fortune in minerals and salt — in inexhaustible supply. The vast Hardy and Morton salt companies are operating full force today, turning out salt for dozens of industrial and agricultural purposes, as well as for the table, and they've been at it long enough so that the Morton Salt girl has been redressed and restyled five times since 1921.

Modern Manistee has considerable industry. Century Boats (fiber glass) are made here, Martin-Marietta has a plant, and Ex-Cells manufactures machine tools and foundry castings. The Packaging Corporation on Lake Manistee at nearby Filer City is one of the largest manufacturers of corrugated board and packaging in the country.

Since Manistee's prevailing winds are from the south and west, and the water is very deep in the area, it has a tendency to gather and retain the summer heat making winters less cold, summers less hot, and conditions almost perfect for the growing of certain fruits. Manistee County has two of the state's largest apple and cherry orchards; 50 percent of Michigan's apples are processed here, and the yield of strawberries per acre is the highest east of the Rockies. Although major lumbering is over, the area still ships out shingles, bark, and cord wood.

Manistee is headquarters for the U.S. 11th District Life Saving Service. For years the Pere Marquette boats sailed into the local harbor, and for all those years young men from Manistee trained to earn their livelihoods on those boats. Those days are gone now, and with them most of the passenger boats on the lake. But in the last years a lot of young people are returning home from the bigger cities of the lower lakes.

ARCHITECTURE AND HISTORIC SITES

* First Congregational Church, 1892
412 4th St.; telephone: 723–5361. Note Johnson tower clock, made in Manistee. These clocks were sold all over the world.

Guardian Angel Catholic Church, nineteenth century
371 5th; telephone: 723–2165. Tower clock.

* Historic Ramsdell Theater
101 Maple, P.O. Box 32; telephone: 723–9948. Built in 1903 by T. J. Ramsdell, well-known Manistee pioneer, this Edwardian brick structure contains many unique theatrical and architectural features. Manistee Civic Players perform here. February to November.

* Our Savior's Evangelic Lutheran Church, 1869
West U.S. 10. Oldest Danish Lutheran Church in America.

St. Mary's of Mt. Carmel Catholic Church
260 St. Mary's Parkway; telephone: 723–3345. Ultra modern. Designated a shrine.

MUSEUM

Holly Water Works 1881
425 River; telephone: 723–5531. Open daily during summer months.

Lyman Drug Company Building Museum Annex
425 River St.; telephone: 723–5531. Wonderful cataloging job of old photo plates — can find ancestors and homes in folders on museum's

center table. Wide variety of exhibits including much material on heyday of lumbering era, Indian relics and artifacts, antique photo exhibits. Open daily year round.

ORCHARDS

Agles Fruit
Northwood Highway, Bear Lake; telephone: 889–5563. Variety of fruit. June through November

Fruit-ful Acres Farm Market
Bear Lake off U.S. 31; telephone: 889–4197. Fruits, vegetables, baked goods. June through September.

Jebavey-Sorenson Orchard
3642 Orchard Highway; telephone: 723–3559. One of the largest orchards in Michigan.

Martin Miller, Jr.
Off U.S. 31; telephone: 723–5073. Open June through September.

Marvin Hummon
Off U.S. 31; telephone: 864–3568. Summer.

PARKS

Manistee National Forest
Call 723–2211 for information on specific areas in this vast park, which extends from Pierport in the north, south to North Muskegon. Morel mushrooming, deer and small game hunting in season, 200 miles of snowmobile trails, horse trails, hiking, skiing, tobogganing, camping, and ski trails.

First Street Beach
Beaches, playgrounds, picnicking, and great view of incoming salt and ore boats.

RECREATION

Camping

Orchard Beach State Park
Lakeshore Rd., 3 miles north of Manistee. Nature trails. 8 AM to 10 PM.

Lake Michigan Recreation Area
On Lake Michigan, 7 miles south of Manistee. Ninety-seven camp sites.

Udell Rollways National Forest Campground
On Manistee River, 7 miles east of Manistee on M-55. Twenty-three camp units.

Marinas

All marinas are stretched out along the river in Riverside Marina Park.

Fisherman's Center

Joslin Marina

Moonlite Marina

Municipal Marina

Solberg Boat Yard

RESTAURANTS

Dry Docks
25 Caberfae Highway; telephone: 723–4661. April–December, 5–10; closed Sun.

Victorian 1888
399 River; telephone: 723–4774. Mon.–Sat., 9–9.

House of Flavors
284 River St.; telephone: 723–2233. Part of a chain from Ludington. "Everybody eats here." 6 AM–midnight.

SCENIC DRIVE

On U.S. 31 turn east at Filer City sign, and drive to the high point on Filer City Rd. Great view of Morton and Hardy factories and the vast area filled with logs of the Packaging Corporation of America.

SHOPPING

Glen of Michigan
Clay and Hancock. Women's sportswear, fabric by yard. Mon.–Sat., 10–5.

Little Red Shoe House
Cypress and 6th, U.S. 31. Mon., Tues., Wed., Thurs., Sat., 9:30–5; Fri., 9:30–9; closed Sun.

SPECIAL EVENTS

For specific information on special events, call the Chamber of Commerce.

National Forest Festival
Log rolling, wood sawing. First week in July.

International Day
Second week in August.

Ludington

Population: 9566   Area Code: 616   Zip Code: 49431
Chamber of Commerce: Ludington at James Street; telephone: 843–2506

There is a white cross on the peninsula between Pere Marquette Lake and Lake Michigan that marks the spot where, in 1675, Father Marquette reportedly breathed his last. His name has loomed large in the area ever since, and Ludington itself when deeded in 1840 was called Marquette, as were the inland lake, the river, the early railroad, the biggest lumber company.

In 1859 a Milwaukee capitalist named Ludington came, looked, and platted the town. He also conducted a thriving lumber business there, and put a lot of money into the new community, evidently with the stipulation that his name would replace Pere Marquette's. It did, and the first names of his brothers, cousins, and his father still grace the streets. His own name marks the major intersection in town: James and Ludington streets.

A stiff-necked fellow, Ludington declared, "So long as I can control the matter I will not allow a liquor saloon to live in the town that bears my name." So he inserted into the deed of every lot he platted the condition that no liquor be allowed on the premises.

The Lake has always had a tremendous influence on this town that stands equidistant from Chicago to Detroit, and from Chicago to Mackinac. After the Civil War, the idea of steamboat travel between Wisconsin and Michigan caught on, and the Goodrich line (and in 1897 the C&O) used Ludington as a major Michigan port. The commerce around Ludington was matched only by the severity of its storms, and during one fifteen-year period eighty-eight shipwrecks were identified between Little and Big Point Sable lighthouses. In 1880 a less terrible fate overtook the *Mars,* a lumber schooner trapped suddenly in a northwest wind. Her captain had no time to lower her sails, and the ship simply whisked down Main Street on the crest of a huge wave.

Today Ludington is having a major renaissance as a fishing center, as have most of the towns on Lake Michigan's eastern shore. The coho salmon seeded into Ludington's rivers, the Pere Marquette and the

S.S. *Spartan* entering Ludington Harbor. *Chicago Historical Society, photo by J. Sherwin Murphy*

Sable, are mature and in the millions, and the big ones congregate at a sharp drop-off of the Lake near the Big Point Sable Lighthouse. Ludington is host to the American Salmon Derby, the biggest fishing event on Lake Michigan, with a purse of $50,000. The dunes and the water near the Big Point Sable lighthouse have been chosen by Outward Bound as the site for one of its survival schools. And the Marine Inspector's office, responsible for examining ferries and freighters, also has headquarters at Ludington.

For many years the lumbering business boomed in the area (its municipal building stands on land still called "the chip yard" near a street marked "Sawdust Trail.") As the timbering waned, the Pere Marquette Lumber Company tried unsuccessfully to manufacture salt, and to turn the town into a health spa area with baths and fine drinking water.

Over the first decade of the century with the help of the federal government, a breakwater was built to protect the harbor, and dredging goes on regularly to keep the channels clear for large boats.

The Dow Chemical plant and Pumped Storage (the world's largest power plant) are the town's top industries. The gorgeous Ludington State Park, considered by many to be the queen of all Michigan's parks, was built by the Civilian Conservation Corps in the 1930s. It has high dunes, a dam, and inland Hamlin Lake, which in trout season has a lottery to determine who fishes — and when.

Perhaps the most significant name in modern Ludington is Hawley. For four generations Hawleys have raised fruit, run schools, owned banks; but equally important they have created museums and restored pioneer villages so that their town will not lose a sense of its past.

ARCHITECTURE AND HISTORIC SITES

Court and Lavinia Sts.
Green gingerbread house of lumber era.

Church of Christ
201 N. James St.

Courthouse, 1893
E. Ludington Ave. and Rose St. Beautiful inside.

Ludington and Lavinia Sts.
House built by Cartier, descendant of famous explorer. Second story designed so he could address crowd after gubernatorial race. He lost.

Court and Park Sts.
Ship captain's house.

Melendy and Filer Sts.
House slid across Lake winter of 1900.

Pere Marquette Shrine
South Lakeshore Rd., south off junction U.S. 10 and U.S. 31, until you cross Pere Marquette River. After turning right you will find a clearly marked route to shrine. This illuminated cross marks the spot where Pere Marquette died in 1675. Indian tradition: Annually, on May 18, service conducted here by priest to commemorate Marquette's death place, which lends credence to fact that *here* is where he actually died.

CEMETERIES

Cemetery of 1866
Chauves and Lake Shore Dr., south of Ludington, toward Pentwater.

Lakeview Cemetery

North of Ludington on M-116. One plot purchased by Interlakes Steamship for thirty-three members of *Novodoc*. Some men unidentifiable . . . so company established a memorial.

FERRIES

Chesapeake and Ohio

C & O Dock; telephone: 843–2521. Ludington to Manitowoc, daily, summer only.

MUSEUMS

White Pine Village

1687 South Lakeshore Dr., in the area known as Buttersville, P.O. Box 1776; telephone: 843–4803. Restoration includes first Mason County home, built by Chicagoan Caswell; lumber museum, town hall, blacksmith shop, school, chapel, barn, and general store. Caswell became a judge and donated the first floor of his home for a courtroom. Memorial Day–Labor Day, Mon.–Sat., 11–5; Sun., 1–7.

Rose Hawley Historical Museum of Mason County

305 E. Filer St.; telephone: 843–2001. Collections include farm and lumber tools, marine exhibit, local history, typical 1890s Ludington home. Summer, Mon.–Sat., 10–noon, 1:30–4; fall and spring, Mon. and Fri., 1:30–4:30; winter, by appointment. Free admission.

ORCHARDS

The Blueberry Patch

Jebavy Dr., 3 miles to Fisher Rd., then east 3/4 mile; telephone: 845–6832. Open late summer.

John Wagner

Off U.S. 31, Johnson Rd.; telephone: 845–5268. Strawberries, late June.

PARKS

Ludington State Park

End of M-116, north of Ludington between Lake Michigan and Hamlin Lake; telephone: 843–8671. 4120 acres. Hiking — eight separately marked foot trails totaling 25 miles; wildlife — large flock of Canada geese make this their year-long residence; picnicking; boat launch; fishing; cross-country skiing; swimming; mushrooming; birding (200 varieties); biking; snowmobiling (3000 acres of park open for snow-mobiling); camping (398 camping sites); Nature Center (contains huge relief map of area), daily, 10–4. Very imaginative children's area with touch-me bags and some live specimens. Helleborine orchid grows here. Superlative! Open year round.

Stearns Park
Lake Shore Dr. and foot of Main St. Playground, 1/2 mile of sandy swimming beach, fishing off breakwater, picnicking. Lovely spot. Lighthouse at end of breakwater.

RECREATION

Fishing

Hamlin Lake

Pere Marquette Lake

Pier at Lake Michigan

Charters

Tamarac Sportfishing Dock
105 Water St.; telephone: 845–5987.

Ludington Charter Service
1963 S. Lakeshore Dr.; telephone: 845–6048.

Golf

Lincoln Hills Golf Club (18-hole)
M-116, 1 mile north of Ludington; telephone: 843–4666.

Ludington Hills Golf Course (18-hole)
5369 W. Chauvez Rd.; telephone: 843–3660.

Marina

Tamarac Harbor
2875 N. Lake Shore Dr.; telephone: 843–4990.

Music

Wednesday Night Band Concerts
Lakefront Park. Sometimes in conjunction with the music there are ice cream socials. Mid-June–mid-August.

Winter Sports

Call Chamber of Commerce for specifics on snowmobiling, ice fishing, cross-country skiing, and hunting.

RESTAURANTS

Gibbs Country House
U.S. 31 and U.S. 10, between Ludington and Scottville; telephone: 845–5086. Homemade everything. Dance and drink in the barn. 11 AM–10 PM.

House of Flavors Ice Cream Parlour
402 W. Ludington Ave.; telephone: 845–5785. Ice cream factory where it's all made next door! Home base for chain House of Flavors. Daily, 10–10.

Scotty's Harbor House
East Ludington Ave.; telephone: 843–4033. Daily, 8–10; Sun., 9–8 PM.

SHOPPING

Ken's Safari Den
1/2 mile east of U.S. 10 and U.S. 31 junction; telephone: 843–4141. Taxidermist.

Ludington Fruit Exchange
U.S. 31, 4 miles south of Ludington. Summer time, harvest time.

SPECIAL EVENTS

Ludington Salmon Derby
Telephone: 845–5018. Last week in August, first in September.

Western Michigan Fair
Fairgrounds. Second week in August.

Pentwater

Population: 983   Area Code: 616   Zip Code: 49449
Chamber of Commerce: 347 S. Hancock; telephone: 869-4150

The name Mears is to Pentwater what Ford is to Detroit, only instead of building cars Mears was involved in producing clay, timber, shingles, and the saw mills and kilns that produced them.

Charles Mears platted Pentwater, casting it in the image of the New England village from which he came. Mears found a fine clay deposit at one end of Lake Pentwater, and soon his Pentwater common brick was the finest in the area. He also cruised the woods and his lumbering operations dominated the coast from Manistee to Muskegon. Mears even took an interest in farming, and his cranberries, like his lumber, were soon carried to all the Lake ports, primarily to Chicago where he kept his permanent home.

In Pentwater (the name refers to the water pent up by sandbars separating the big Lake from the inland one), there were records of

Fishing off Pentwater, Michigan, often yields a lunker. *Michigan Travel Commission*

settlers by 1849. Early stories mention wolves gnawing at the handles of saws and axes, and bears so tame that they fed alongside the cattle in local barnyards. The first big migration came in 1857 when 1300 Ottawa Indians arrived, driven north from lands in southern Michigan that the whites had taken over after the Treaty of Detroit. The Indians settled on the edges of town, fishing, picking large quantities of blueberries (which still grow in profusion), and making baskets; a few Indian families still live in the area today.

After the Civil War Mears established his mill near the ferry boat that carried people across the channel, building a large hall called Middlesex (after his native county in Massachusetts) to house his lumbermen. The lumbering boom came to a temporary halt in 1871 with the flare-up of a smallpox epidemic at just about the time that the terrible fires burning across the Lake in Chicago and Peshtigo could be smelled in Pentwater.

In 1872 the Chicago, Michigan and Lake Shore Railroad reached Pentwater, and many people came to explore its charms — a number that increased considerably when a passenger boat in 1900 advertised round-trip excursions to Chicago for $1.50. Numerous Chicagoans arrived, among them a group of University of Chicago professors led by the philosopher, Will Durant, who founded a community at Oceana Beach.

Pentwater figured in a major shipwreck on the Lake. When a ship called *Novodoc* floundered in a dreadful storm offshore the Pentwater-based *Three Brothers* went to its rescue, and both vessels were lost with their crews.

Today Pentwater is a quiet, charming town, courteous but mildly indifferent to tourists.

ARCHITECTURE AND HISTORIC SITES

Little Sable Lighthouse
B–15, 15 miles south of town, on Natural Beauty Rd., Silver Lake. Beautiful red brick lighthouse. Sailor's landmark.

St. Vincent's Church
Clymer and Sixth; telephone: 869–2601. Oldest church in area.

PARKS

Mears Park
North of Pentwater on M–31. Acreage donated by Carrie Mears, in honor of her lumber-baron father. Great beach, camping, cross-country skiing, snowmobiling.

Silver Lake State Park and Campgrounds
BR-31 south of town until junction with B-15 to Silver Lake; telephone: 873–3912. 250 campsites, swimming, boat launching, fishing, and trails on 2000 acres.

RECREATION

Charters

Bob Barko
Telephone: 845–5832.

Gary Besser
Telephone: 869–5941.

Beachcomber Company
Telephone: 869–5941.

Bob Maynard
Telephone: 869–7751.

Dune Buggy Rides

Bill's Dune Rides
Silver Lake; telephone: 873–2511.

Mac Woods Dune Rides
Silver Lake; telephone: 873–2817. Seasonal.

Golf

Oceana Golf Course (18-hole)
3333 W. Weaver Rd., Shelby (south of Pentwater on U.S. 31); telephone: 861–4211.

Marinas

Brass Anchor
233 Sixth; telephone: 869–8311. Launch.

Channel View
347 S. Hancock; telephone: 869–5941. Launch.

Lakeside Sail Point
9 E. Lake; telephone: 869–7551. Sailboats only.

Snug Harbor
616 S. Hancock; telephone: 869–7001.

Village Pier
Lakefront. Launch.

Music

Village Park Band Concerts
Hancock, in center of town. Summers, Thurs., 8 PM.

RESTAURANTS

Boardwalk Pantry
327 Hancock St.; telephone: 869–8951. Daily, 11–9.

Nickerson Inn
262 W. Lowell; telephone: 869–8241. Daily, Memorial Day–Labor Day, 8–10:30 and 6–9 PM.

SHOPPING

Celebration Candle Shop and Factory
508 Hancock; telephone: 869–8691. Michigan's biggest. Also lessons and supplies.

The Dunes
2 1/2 miles north of South Pentwater, exit on U.S. 31; telephone: 869–5815. Ceramics, painting, mobiles, etc. Specializes in driftwood. Daily, June–October, 10–5; closed Mon.

West Michigan School of Diving, Inc.
347 Hancock; telephone: 869–5326. Professional instruction — scuba diving for old wrecks. Complete equipment rental and service.

SPECIAL EVENT

National Asparagus Festival
U.S. 31, Box 66H, Hart. Second week in June.

Muskegon

Population: 157,426   Area Code: 616   Zip Code: 49441
Muskegon County Chamber of Commerce: 1065 Fourth Street, Muskegon;
  telephone: 722–3751

Muskegon is the largest city on Lake Michigan's eastern shore. Including suburbs, it spreads along 30 miles at the Lake's coastline and
boasts a good harbor, three state parks, three inland lakes, and,
around Big Point Sable Lighthouse, some of the deepest water on the
Lake (878 feet). Historically the city's two most important features
were the Muskegon River, and what was once one of the finest hardwood forests in the world. Nicolet saw this land as early as 1634;
Josette Lamframboise traded furs here in the early 1800s, and so did
Gurdon Hubbard. Martin Ryerson came here as a boy of sixteen to
trade in furs and stayed to buy up pine forests and build a fortune.
His philanthropist son Martin made good use of the Ryerson fortune
a generation later by purchasing El Greco paintings for Chicago's Art
Institute.

Muskegon was really the kickoff point for the lumbering era, which
began here in 1837 and eventually moved up the coast, on to Wisconsin, and finally over to Minnesota. Fifty years later the town was
known as the Lumber Queen of the World. Forty-seven mills operated
full force, and 665 million feet of lumber were cut each year. The
forests of Michigan helped build an infant Chicago and 100 other
woodless prairie towns as well. For a time at least the lumber era
carved a lifestyle so wicked that it rivaled the West at its wildest. In
those days Muskegon had six solid blocks of "unspeakable whore-
dom" known as the "sawdust flats," where the girls worked for the
grand sum of a dollar a day.

In its heydey Muskegon was madly destroying the forest with little
thought for the future. Get-rich-quick was the watchword of the time.
Many did. Though there were reputedly forty millionaires in town,
Charles H. Hackley surely spread his name the farthest: today there
is a Hackley Hospital, bank, school, library, art museum, boulevard,
and a Hackley Heritage Foundation. He gave much and was remem-
bered well, but the townspeople stoutly refused to change the town's
name to Hackley.

Muskegon was generally settled by Scandinavian and Dutch and other seafaring immigrants, attracted to the area by the water and the Lake vessels. One captain, Jonathan Walker, became a national figure and is buried in Muskegon. Walker, an ardent antislavery man, attempted to sail several slaves to freedom in the Bahamas. He failed, was captured, jailed, and tried in federal court. One of his punishments was the branding of his hand with the letters *SS* (slave stealer). John Greenleaf Whittier wrote a poem about him, "The Branded Hand."

Today the Coast Guard sends young recruits to Muskegon for summer training. The city is a popular boating and fishing area whose visitors have included Buster Keaton and Harold Lloyd and Amy Semple McPherson who came in 1928 to stir a great outdoor audience with her evangelistic sermon. Dressed in flowing white, she promised them when the preaching was over that she would walk on water. Unfortunately the person who had been paid to submerge a row of pilings forgot. The golden voice from the golden west was baptized, and never returned.

Modern Muskegon has sixty major manufacturing plants, among them Brunswick Balke and Continental Motors, which makes Rolls-Royce engines.

Unfortunately Muskegon's largest sand dune was mined out over a period of twenty years by an Ohio glass company, and almost as sad, the ferry boats gave up the ghost in 1978.

ARCHITECTURE AND HISTORIC SITES

Aquarama
Ship in dock on Lake since 1966. Biggest cruiser that ever plied Great Lakes.

Captain Jonathan Walker Monument
"The Man with the Branded Hand." Near the entrance to Evergreen Cemetery on Irwin Ave.

Hackley House
484 W. Webster; telephone: 722–7578. Volunteers are restoring this fine Queen Anne House. May 25–Labor Day, Wed., Sat., Sun., 2–4. Free admission.

Old Indian Cemetery
In Muskegon's downtown district on Morris Ave.

Old Town Fishing Village
Channel Dr. and Fulton Ave. Dates from 1880s — charming houses, old smokehouse. (Only one commercial fishing boat left.)

St. Francis de Sales Church
2929 McCracken, North Shores. 90 feet high; half million board feet of lumber. Very modern.

FARMS

Aftermath Blueberry Farm
5232 Lakewood, Whitehall; telephone: 894–4530. July.

Boca Blueberry Farms
4165 Whitehall Rd. (Old U.S. 31); telephone: 766–2066. July.

Sodini's Blueberries
2345 Weber; telephone: 766–3667. July.

William Hawkins
Mt. Garfield St.; telephone: 798–2801. Strawberries. June.

MUSEUMS

Hackley Art Museum, 1912
296 W. Webster; telephone: 722–6924. Designed by Chicago architect S. S. Beman, this art museum was the first public art gallery in any U.S. city or town of under 30,000 inhabitants. Small but good collection. Mon.–Sat., 9–5; Sun., 2–5. Free admission.

Hackley Public Library, 1890
Webster Ave. at Third St.; telephone: 722–7276. WPA mural in young people's department worth seeing. Wonderful old building, inside and out. Mon.–Thurs., 9–9; Fri. & Sat., 9–5.

Muskegon County Museum
30 Muskegon Ave.; telephone: 722–0278. Relics and items from lumbering era as well as Indian artifacts and pioneer utensils. Excellent early photo collection. June–Sept., Tues.–Sat., 10–4; Sept.–June, Tues.–Fri., 10–5, Sat., 10–3.

White River Light Station Marine Museum
(In old lighthouse) White River Channel, Whitehall. Note frame structure of old shipwreck on beach.

PARKS

City Parks

Bronson Park
End of Sherman Blvd. on Lake Michigan. Beach area and picnic.

Hackley Park
4th St. and Webster Ave. Scenic flowers, park benches, shade trees.

Lake Michigan Park
Lakeshore Dr. and Beach St. 2 1/2 miles of Lake Michigan beach.

McGraft Park
Lakeshore Dr. to Addison St.; telephone: 722–3751. Outdoor summer concerts, Wednesday nights, June 15–Labor Day.

Mona Lake Park
Off Seaway Dr. on Mona Lake. Swimming, boating, picnicking.

Pere Marquette Park
Beach St. at Muskegon Lake. Lighthouse and old pier that extends 1 mile into Lake. Picnicking, swimming beach.

County and State Parks (north to south)

Meinert County Park
B-15, 10 miles south of Silver Lake. 29 acres on Lake. Beautiful dunes and swimming.

Duck Lake State Park
BR-31, Scenic Drive Rd. Unimproved 312-acre state park on Lake Michigan and Duck Lake. Good fishing, beach, picnicking.

Pioneer County Park
BR-31; telephone: 744–3580. 2200-foot Lake Michigan beach; 215 campsites, hiking trails, WPA lodge; 146 acres.

Muskegon State Park
BR-31 on Lake Michigan, 3560 Memorial Dr.; telephone: 744–3480. Huge camping grounds (346 sites), beach, boat launch, hiking; historic block house; 3560 acres.

Hoffmaster State Park
On Lake, B-31, to Grand Haven Rd.; telephone: 798–3711. 333 campsites, beach, trails, picnicking.

RECREATION

Canoes

Happy Mohawk Canoe Livery
351 Fruitvale Rd., Muskegon; telephone: 894–4209. Canoe rental.

North Brand Boat and Canoe Livery
500 Causeway, North Muskegon; telephone: 744–1119.

Charters

Bear Lake Channel Marina
345 Bay Lane Dr., North Muskegon; telephone: 744–3146.

Chalmer's Marina
127 N. Thompson, Whitehall; telephone: 893–3944.

Chinook Charters
607 W. Sunset Dr., North Muskegon; telephone: 744–4493.

Grain's Boat Charter
1921 Lake Ave., North Muskegon; telephone: 744–3091.

Keith Charter Service
2964 Lakeshore Dr., Muskegon; telephone: 773–5247.

Margie-J Charter Service
6097 Ridgeview, Muskegon; telephone: 798–1038.

Muskegon Charter Service
485 N. Whitehall Rd., North Muskegon; telephone: 744–9032.

Captain John Simila
119 Tulgeywood La., Whitehall; telephone: 894–6041.

Skipper's Landing
4464 Dowling, Montague; telephone: 893–4525.

Golf

Chase Hammond Municipal Golf Course (18-hole)
2454 N. Putnam Rd., North Muskegon; telephone: 766–3035.

Fruitport Country Club (18-hole)
6334 S. Harvey St., Fruitport; telephone: 798–3355.

Hickory Knoll Golf Course (18-hole)
3065 W. Ellis St., Whitehall; telephone: 893–9247.

Old Channel Trail (18-hole)
7945 Old Channel Trail, Montague; telephone: 894–5076.

Oyler Golf Port (18-hole)
2480 Duck Lake Rd., Montague; telephone: 766–2045.

Marinas

Balcom Marina
2964 Lakeshore; telephone: 755–1332.

Hartshorn Marina (Muskegon Municipal)
920 W. Western; telephone: 722–3361.

Seaway
3126 Lakeshore; telephone: 755–1522.

Snowmobiling

Map of trails are available at the Chamber of Commerce.

RESTAURANTS

House of Chan
Business U.S. 31, one block west of Seminole, 375 Gin Chan Ave., Norton Shores; telephone: 733–9624. Tues.–Thurs., 11:30–10; Fri., 11:30–11; Sat., 5–12; Sun., 12–10.

Lakeside Inn Resort
Murray Road and Scenic Dr.; telephone: 893–8315. Daily, May–mid-Oct.

Lakos Steak House
428 W. Western Ave.; telephone: 722–2250. Daily, 11–11; Sat., 5–11; closed Sun.

Lost Valley Lodge
Off U.S. 31 at Fruitvale Rd., Montague; telephone: 893–1785. Great view of dunes and Lake Michigan. Mon.–Sat., opens at 5.

Michillinda Beach Lodge
5207 Scenic Dr., Whitehall; telephone: 893–1895. Overlooks Lake.
June 20–Sept. 15, breakfast, lunch, dinner.

Olaf's
1384 W. Laketon; telephone: 755–4800. Swedish. Daily, 8–8; closed
Sun.

Old Channel Inn
6905 Old Channel Trail, Montague; telephone: 893–3805. Tues.,
Wed., Thurs., Sun., noon–10 PM, Fri., & Sat., noon–2 AM.

Tohado House
450 W. Western Ave.; telephone: 726–4377. Tues.–Sun., 11:30–2:30
and 5:30–11:00; Sun., 5–10; closed Mondays.

SHOPPING

Fife and Drum
214 E. Colby, Whitehall; telephone: 894–8200. Antiques.

Muskegon Farmer's Market
700 Yuba St., off U.S. 31; telephone: 722–3251. June–Oct.

Muskegon Heights Farmer's Market
Center St. off Peck St.; telephone: 733–1351. June–Oct.

Muskegon Mall
Downtown; telephone: 726–6129. Mon.–Fri., 10–9; Sat., 10–5:30; Sun.,
12–5.

Pack Rats
116 W. Slocum, Whitehall; 893–6885. Antiques.

The Whippoorwill
2962 W. Lakewood Rd., Whitehall. Primitives; antiques

Grand Haven

Population: 11,850   Area Code: 616   Zip Code: 49417
Chamber of Commerce; 1 Washington Avenue, telephone: 842–4910
For summer information only: Beacon Boulevard; telephone: 842–5930

Grand Haven is the only one of the tri-cities (which include Ferrysburg and Spring Lake), located on Lake Michigan. The town has been called Coast Guard City USA, because in World War II the Coast Guard escort, *Escanaba,* was torpedoed and went down with all hands from Grand Haven. The town raised enough money to purchase a second cutter, carrying the name *Escanaba.* Each August 4, its commander lays a memorial wreath on the Atlantic, where the boat is assigned. Today Grand Haven celebrates an annual Coast Guard Festival the first week of August. It begins solemnly with dedication and prayer, but the pace quickens with parades, water shows, and finally a special performance of the world's largest outdoor fountain. Color and lights, ever-changing water patterns (the fountain is electronically controlled and capable of millions of formations), music, and applause. A water tribute in a water city.

Although Grand Haven was laid out in 1835, its history began 200 years earlier with the Ottawa Indians who trapped and traded furs, harvested wild rice, and helped further the career of an ambitious Frenchman Charles de Langlade. De Langlade came down from the north to recruit braves to fight against Braddock and Washington in the French and Indian Wars, and his reward was the monopoly for all the fur trade of the Grand River Valley. Another Frenchman, Astor Trader Joseph Laframboise, arrived in the early 1800s, only to be shot by Indians while kneeling in prayer. Magdalene Laframboise, his Indian wife, buried him in Grand Haven, got herself a trader's license, and for the next twelve years came down each winter from Mackinac Island to trade. Her daughter, Josette, married the commander at Mackinac (Magdalene attended in full ceremonial dress). In time Josette's new brother-in-law, Franklin Pierce, became president of the United States.

Grand Haven was a lumbering center in its day, and when that era ended, mineral springs were discovered. W. C. Sheldon's Magnetic

Springs Resort and several other hotels boomed and promised to draw tourists. In those days a little ferry took one across the Grand River, which connected the three cities (later an interurban electric trolley did the job).

Grand Haven was the home of Dr. Aaron Vanderveen who attended Lincoln at his assassination. The doctor lived in the highest house in town (known as the DuBee House), whose tower light alerted local people to ships entering the harbor. The warning at least once proved insufficient when Captain Dan Seavey pirated a fully loaded jack ass schooner right out of the harbor (jack ass schooners have the middle of their three masts cut out to hold more cargo in the hatch). Seavey was a well-known character in local saloons where he often appeared carrying a bag of skulls collected at various places in his wanderings. He also collected — and sold — anything else he could lay his hands on, from lumber to oxen.

Today the tri-cities area is pleasant resort country, but also boasts 133 diversified industries. Spring Lake is an excellent place to fish for bass, bluegill, and pike, and the Grand Haven pier is a favorite spot to catch perch.

The Grand Haven beaches have a reputation for being one of two places in Michigan with "singing" sands (the other is Ferrysburg).

ARCHITECTURE AND HISTORIC SITES

Drive down Lafayette and Sheldon Terrace to see old frame houses from lumbering era. Also, the Castle, a private home at end of Lake St. with commanding view of area, is well worth seeing.

ART CENTER

Community Center for the Arts
421 Columbus St.; telephone: 842–2550. Plays, concerts, monthly changing art and craft exhibits. Free admission.

MUSEUM

Grand Haven Historical Society Museum
1 North Harbor Dr., in the Old Grand Trunk Railroad Depot. Tri-Cities History Society has set up a fine museum in 1870 depot. Nicely marked. Quality pieces. June, July, August, Wed.–Sun., 3–9.

ORCHARDS AND FARMS

The Berries
M-104 to Nunica, Michigan, turn left at flasher; telephone: 837–6235.

Blueberry Hill
M-104, 6 miles east of Grand Haven, Nunica, Michigan, telephone: 842–4950.

Reenders Blueberry Farms
U.S. 31, 5 miles south of Grand Haven, telephone: 842–5238 or 842–6675. Also a commercial venture — visit handling and packing shed.

The Shack
West on Leonard St. to 84th, turn left on 84th, 1 1/2 miles on right side of road; telephone: 837–8877. Also has picnic area.

PARKS

Escanaba Park
Parallels channel. View ships docking and *Hains* (Corps of Engineers hopper dredger; Coast Guard cutter *Mackinaw;* University of Michigan's *Inland Seas* (floating lab). In summer, can tour Coast Guard *Raritan.* Note memorial of S.S. *Escanaba* in park.

Grand Haven State Park
End of Harbor St. at Lake Michigan. Pier fishing, swimming beach, accommodations for trailers, campers, and tents; 48 acres.

RECREATION

Charters

Bolhouse Charter
Holiday Inn, 940 W. Savidge, Spring Lake; telephone: 846–1076.

Emmert Charter
19040 North Shore Dr., Spring Lake; telephone: 842–0287.

Tom Pegg's
1016 Harbor Ave., Grand Haven; telephone: 842–9573.

Whitney Charter
15170 155th Ave., Grand Haven; telephone: 846–6640.

Golf

Grand Haven Golf, Inc. (18-hole)
1700 Lincoln; telephone: 842–4040.

Marinas

Barrett Chris Craft
821 W. Savidge, Spring Lake; telephone: 842–1202.

Grand Haven Municipal Marina
201 N. Harbor; telephone: 842–4910.

Grand Isle Marina
N. Beacon Blvd., Grand Haven; telephone: 842–9330.

Holiday Inn Boat Marina
940 W. Savidge, Spring Lake; telephone: 846–1000.

North Shore Marina
18275 Berwyck, Grand Haven; telephone: 842–1488.

Riverbend Marina
900 W. Savidge, Spring Lake; telephone: 842–4824.

The Wharf Marina, Inc.
500 N. 2nd, Grand Haven; telephone: 842–5870.

Music

Grand Haven's Musical Fountain
On Dewey Hill on Grand River. World's largest musical fountain.
Nightly, Memorial Day & June, 9:30 PM; July & Aug., 9:45 PM. Free
admission.

Outdoor Hymn Sing
Waterfront Stadium. July and Aug., Sun., 8:30 PM.

RESTAURANTS

Bil-Mar Inn Supper Club
1223 Harbor Dr., Grand Haven; telephone: 842–5920. Bar is part of
old ship; charming; on Lake Michigan. Mon.–Thurs., 5–9:30; Fri. &
Sat., 5–10:30.

Lord Peppermill
2 Washington; telephone: 842–0550. Daily, 11 AM–10 PM; closed Sun.

Holiday Inn
U.S. 31 at M-104, Spring Lake; telephone: 846–1000. This Holiday Inn is beautifully situated on a historic site overlooking Spring Lake and the marinas.

Paddington & Worthmore's Deli
22 S. Harbor Dr., Grand Haven; telephone: 842–7930. Mon.–Sat., 7–9; Sun., 9–6.

Shaker Good Room
406 W. Savidge, Spring Lake; telephone: 846–4282. 7 days, 3 meals daily.

SHOPPING

Flea and Farm Market
At drive-in theater on M-104. Every Friday, June–Oct.

The Gallery
Washington St.; telephone: 842–2320. Local artists; sponsored by Lakeland Painter Association.

Glen of Michigan Patchwork Store
1st and Washington; telephone: 842–6290. Factory outlet. Mon.–Sat., 10–5; Fri., evenings.

The Guild of Shaker Crafts
401 W. Savidge; telephone: 846–2870. Produce and sell furniture, fabric, and items of Shaker design. Also repair and restore original Shaker pieces.

Marushka
17771 W. Spring Lake Rd.; telephone: 846–3510. Screen printed textiles, fabrics and wall hangings. Watch the screening. Outlet store. Daily, 11–6; closed Sun.

Moser's Dried Flower Barn
M-104 Spring Lake, 4 miles east of Spring Lake Bridge; telephone: 842–0641. Upside-down exhibit of drying herbs, plants, etc. Mon.–Sat., 9–5:30; closed Sun.

Reichart

222 Washington; telephone: 842–6202. Six-shop complex.

SPECIAL EVENTS

Coast Guard Festival

Information Center on South U.S. 31. Memorial service for men lost. Parades, fireworks, special performance of world's largest fountain. Coast Guard Cutter *Raritan* and Ice Breaker *Mackinaw* open for tours. Blessings and fireworks at Waterfront Stadium. First week in August.

Venetian Night Boat Parade

Spectacular display of decorated cruisers and boats pass down waterway from Lake Michigan to Spring Lake Holiday Inn and back again. Late August.

Holland

Population: 30,000   Area Code: 616   Zip Code: 49423
Chamber of Commerce: 3 East 8th; telephone: 392–2389
Tourist Information Booth: 16th & U.S. 31; telephone: 396–2824

Holland is the only town on the Lake settled exclusively by refugees. During the 1840s there was a period of political and religious repression in the Netherlands. Seeking a way out, sixty Dutchmen, led by Reverend Albertus Van Raalte, were refused emigration to Java, but were permitted to sail from Rotterdam to form a new *kolonie* in America. On February 12, 1847, they arrived at Black River Valley in Michigan. That date has become as important as Plymouth Rock for all their descendants. "God be thanked," one of them wrote home, "We have arrived in the haven of our desire."

But Michigan was a strange promised land. Full of great forests and swamps, the area was an anamoly for the farming Hollanders. It took almost two weeks for these nonwoodsmen to fell enough trees to build their first cabin, and by that time hundreds of new immigrants had arrived. They too were fleeing oppression, and had responded to the propaganda of the Michigan agents who had been sent abroad to find good settlers. The remarkable Van Raalte struggled to feed them all, to build shelter, to clear land for raising crops, and to buoy up flagging spirits. Dysentery and smallpox ravaged the Dutchmen that first year. Many died and had to be buried in sheets in shallow graves under the trees. In sadness and in unity, the survivors agreed that that burial ground would become their Pilgrim Home Cemetery and beside it they would build their new church.

Cooperation saved them from the start. When they realized the number of parentless children left by the epidemics, they built an orphanage, but before it was completed every child had already been taken in by a settler. The orphanage became a schoolhouse. As the cabins grew in number and the community in size, the sea-minded Hollanders saw the necessity of building a channel so that trade might go on with other communities around the Lake. This meant that their inland Lake Macatawa needed a channel connecting it to Lake Michigan and other ports on the Lake. They asked the government for help,

Young and old wear Dutch costumes during annual Holland Tulip
Time Festival.

but it was late in coming, so the citizens gathered picks and shovels and dug through the obstructive sandbars themselves. As a group they built their first bridge over the Black River and bought a community boat for early transportation. (The Dutch had little to do with the Indians who were few in number and nomadic, and left in 1850, claiming the new arrivals had appropriated the troughs they used for maple sugaring to feed Dutch cattle.) A century later when they turned their old market square into Centennial Park, they were still cooperating. Each family planted its own memorial trees and shrubs (marked with metal tags).

The memory of home was important to them so they built a windmill with an 80-foot tower from which they could see the big Lake. New Dutch arrivals, as they settled the area surrounding Holland, gave their new towns names from home: Zeeland, Harlem, Graafschap. When the Dutch queen came to visit in 1950, she was charmed by the retention of old-country names, juxtaposed as they were with Indian titles. Even today these ties with home remain. Each summer, for instance, Dutch choirs arrive from Holland to sing and to stay with local families.

But important as memory has been, so has been adaptation to the new land. Van Raalte began learning English crossing the Atlantic, and he insisted his fellow *kolonists* do the same. Early he built Holland Academy to train seminarians, and today that has become flourishing Hope College.

The Dutch were good to the land, and it responded with wheat, potatoes, onions, peppermint, and one of the largest celery crops in the world. The area became a great fruit belt and still produces enormous quantities of apples and blueberries.

Today Holland is a city of 30,000 people, and has industry as well as farms. Chris-Craft, Heinz pickles, furniture factories, and GE all have plants here. The Holland Hitch (or Fifth Wheel), which connects trucks and trailers, was developed in the area.

In May of 1929 a local biology teacher suggested the possibility of a Tulip Festival. For fifty years now that idea has been a reality, making Holland a great tourist center as well. Last year 400,000 people came to see the parades, the dances, and the great tulip plantings. They watched the streets being swept and the mayor playing his introductory role. What most of them failed to realize was that Tulip

Time has become an integral part of community life. Children in gym classes practice their dances year round. Home economics students sew costumes. City councilors budget enormous amounts for 3 million tulip bulbs. It gets bigger and better and busier each year. One thing remains constant: no matter how much fun, Wednesday through Saturday, most everything closes down on Sunday. You are invited to stay over and sing psalms at Hope College, however. For the Dutch still say, "God be thanked."

ARCHITECTURE AND HISTORIC SITES

Dimnent Chapel of Hope College, 1920s
12th & College; telephone: 392–5111. 120-foot bell tower; 2,932 pipes in organ.

Hope Reformed Church, 1862
77 W. 11th; telephone: 392–8818. Founded as English-speaking church.

Pillar Church, 1856
College & 9th; telephone: 392–8686. A Christian Reformed church built under leadership of Van Raalte. Rooster on belfry symbol of many Calvinist churches in Netherlands. Michigan Historic Registry.

Third Reform Church, 1874
12th & Pine; telephone: 392–1459. Carpenter's gothic by Dutchman John Kleyn.

Van Vleck Hall, 1858
Center of Hope College Campus. Old Holland Academy. Used as chapel, classroom, dorm. Still used by Hope College. Michigan Historic Registry.

CEMETERY

Pilgrim Home Cemetery
Historic Marker, 370 E. 16th St.

MUSEUMS

Baker Furniture Museum
Sixth St. & Columbia Ave. Tools for furniture-making, European originals, furniture galore. Early May–mid-Oct., daily 10–5; closed Sun.

Windmill Island in Holland, Michigan. *Michigan Travel Commission*

Netherlands Museum
12th at Central. Chronicle of Dutch life in new world. Museum store sells Delft china. Daily, May–Sept., 9–5; Sun., 11:30–5.

ORCHARDS AND FARMS

Arnell VanderKolk Blueberries
152nd St. and Butternut Dr.; telephone: 396–6248. Closed Sun.

Aussicker's Blueberries
15985 Quincy, telephone: 399–6267. Closed Sun.

Brewer's Berry Fields
4330 148th St.; telephone: 396–5518.

J. G. Brower Blueberry Farm
3221 Beeline Rd.; telephone: 396–4134.

Leon Vanderyacht
6427 Butternut Dr.; telephone: 399–6216. Blueberries and raspberries. Closed Sun.

Windmill Blue
5352 Butternut Dr.; telephone: 396–8834.

PARKS

City

Centennial Park
10th, 12th, Center and River area.

DeGraaf Nature Center
Enter at 26th from Graafschap Rd. 15 acres with nature center.

Kollen Park
South shore of Lake Macatawa. 25 acres; two public ramps, docking.

Joe Moran Recreational Center
21st, 22nd, Pine and Maple.

Windmill Island and "De Zwaan"
7th & Lincoln; telephone: 396–5433. Moved from Netherlands in 1964.
May–Oct.; check schedule with a phone call.

State

Holland State Park
7 miles west of Holland. Frontage on lakes Michigan & Macatawa;
141 acres; great beach, camping, picnic, bath house.

RECREATION

Fishing Charters and Sailing

Holland Charter Fishing Service
769 S. Shore Dr.; telephone: 335–3397.

Lake "Mac" Charters
221 Brooklane Ave.; telephone: 396–1170.

Macatawa Bay Yacht Charters
136 E. 14th St.; telephone: 392–1973.

Golf

Clearbrook Country Club (18-hole)
135 Ave. Saugatuck, 1 mile off I-196; telephone: 857–2000. Open Sun.

Crestview Golf Course (18-hole)
96th Ave. at Port Sheldon Rd.; telephone: 857–8101. Closed Sun.

Holland Country Club (18-hole)
51 Country Club Rd.; telephone: 392–1844. Open Sun.

West Ottawa Country Club (18-hole)
U.S. 31, 6 miles north of Holland; telephone: 399–1678. Open Sun.

Winding Golf Course (18-hole)
8600 Ottagon; telephone: 688–5293. Open Sun.

Marinas

Bay Haven
1862 Ottawa Beach Rd.; telephone: 399–9440.

Bay Shore
1896 Ottawa Beach Rd.; telephone: 399–3331.

Ottawa Beach Marina
2316 Ottawa Beach Rd.; telephone: 399–9340.

Perrin's Marina
561 Crescent Dr.; telephone: 392–5971.

Scott's Marina
1826 Ottawa Beach Rd.; telephone: 399–9420.

Music

Band Concerts
Kollen Park, South Shore of Lake Macatawa (entrance at west end
of 10th St.), Tues. evenings in summer.

Sand Dune Schooner Rides

Goshorn Lake Dune Schooners
Exit 41 off I-96, go west 1 block and follow signs. Enjoy Lake Michigan's sandy slopes and valleys via dune schooner. Daily, June–Labor
Day, 9 AM.

RESTAURANTS

Cobble Stone Kitchen
204 W. 34th St.; telephone: 396–6260. Daily, 6–11 PM; closed Sun.

Hatch
2 miles east of Holland State Park, 1870 Ottawa Beach Rd.; telephone: 399–9120. Entertainment, water view. Closed Sun.

Ottawa Beach Inn
2155 Ottawa Beach Rd.; telephone: 399–9220. Closed Sun.

Point West
West on 16th St. to end of Lake Macatawa; telephone: 335–5894. Tops! Spectacular view of water.

Prince's
174 River; telephone: 396–8193.

Wooden Shoe Restaurant
U.S. 31; telephone: 396–4744. Some authentic Dutch recipes.

SCHOOL

Hope College & Seminary
265 College; telephone: 392–5111. An integral part of community. Michigan Historic Registry.

SHOPPING

Uppatree Handcrafts
30 1/2 W. 8th St., 2nd floor; telephone: 392–1175. Mon.–Sat., 11–5 PM; Mon. and Fri. 7–9 PM

Dutch Village
1 mile north of Holland on U.S. 31; telephone: 396–1475. Highly commercial, but buildings have Dutch flavor.

Bulbs

Nelis Nurseries
Lakewood Blvd.; telephone: 392–6051. Spectacular fields of 157 varieties of tulips alone.

Veldheer's Tulip Gardens
4 miles north of town on U.S. 31; telephone: 399–1900.

Wooden Shoes

Fred Oldemulder
U.S. 31 by-pass at 16th St.; telephone: 396–6513.

DeKlomp Wooden Shoe Factory
257 E. 32nd St.; telephone: 396–2292. Mon.–Sat., May 1–October, 9–5:30; Tulip Time, 8–10 PM; closed Sun. and holidays.

SPECIAL EVENTS

Ottawa County Fair
Last week in July.

Tulip Time Festival
Book early! For help with reservations, call: 396–4221. Second week in May.

THEATER

Hope Summer Repertory Theater
12th at Columbia; telephone: 392–1449. July 7–September 2, 8:30 PM.

Saugatuck

Population: 1022   Area Code: 616   Zip Code: 49453

Douglas

Population: 943   Area Code: 616   Zip Code: 49406
Chamber of Commerce: Village Hall (Butler Street); telephone: 857-5801.
Mon.–Fri., 10–4; Sat., 9:30–4:30.

The twin villages of Saugatuck and Douglas might be described as Provincetown, Mass., without Portuguese. While the combined full-time population hovers at around 2000, from May to October the head count reaches carnival proportions as crowds jam the shops (some very creative), the galleries, the cruise boats and ice cream parlors. There are yachts everywhere. And ducks. And artists. The latter began coming 100 years ago, to study, teach, show, and hold fairs. They were right. Crowds or not, the place is paintable, perched on the Lake and bisected by the Kalamazoo River, and blessed with some of the highest sand dunes on the coast.

In the beginning too the area was lively, for it was chief village of the Potawatomi and the Ottawa who were ousted from Green Bay by the Iroquois (the Indians wintered here and moved up to Mackinac in the summer). The first white settler to arrive was a Connecticut Yankee named William Butler, who with his wife, built a log cabin, ran a thriving trade center, and platted the village. The main business street is named for him.

There were lots of complaints in the early settlement about the ague. Life was divided between "well days" and "ague days," and everyone planned schedules accordingly. Ministers delivered sermons when they had "shakeless days," and young blades left their courting to "well nights." But ague or no, the lumberman and trappers and tanners arrived, as they did in so many other Lake communities. Of course, they helped cut the boards that rebuilt Chicago after the Great Fire. Saugatuck was a big boat-building center with three shipyards, and between 1880 and the turn of the century 190 craft skidded into the river, baptized with wine, blessed with prayers, and cheered by the endless visitors who came to watch. Douglas had a big basket factory at that time, for this was the period of the great peach bonanza. Hundreds of thousands of bushels of peaches were raised in the area, loaded onto the Chicago and Milwaukee boats that docked daily. No one used spray then; the orchards were treated like pasture, and pruning was left to the cattle. But in 1906 a great freeze brought the peach heydey to its end. There was another flourishing town in that era, the hell-raising Singapore. It had three mills, two hotels, and a lot of lumbermen. But when the white pine was raped, the residents left, and Singapore became a ghost town, eventually buried under dunes. In 1945 a Chicago importer of exotic oils bought up the site of Singapore and turned its 402 acres into a wildlife sanctuary.

Saugatuck has had its share of shipwrecks. The municipal flagpole is made out of the masts of two of them. It's been the inspiration for a book: James Fennimore Cooper's *Oak Openings.* But the real boom began in the late 1880s when the side paddlewheelers, *Cities of Saugatuck* of *Grand Haven* and *Holland* made regular runs to its docks. The city slickers arrived then. They were met by gentlemen in high silk hats whose brightly colored wagons were pulled by black geldings, and they were taken to town and to the huge new pavilion with its 66,000-square-foot dance floor. Some of the visitors came from as far as Cincinnati and St. Louis, and they decided to stay and build summer homes. "I got me three damn fools," one farmer said. "They want to pay $500 for a pile of sand in my cow pasture, and I want to close the deal before they back out." He closed. There are fine houses along the Lakeshore now where the great-grandchildren of those early slickers still come. And though the dance pavilion burned, the Lake excursions stopped, and the lumbering is long gone, the artists and the antiquers, the yachtsmen, and the ice cream freaks come each year in ever increasing numbers, for they too like the Provincetown of the Midwest.

ARCHITECTURE AND HISTORIC SITES

Chain Link Ferry, 1838
In park on Water St., Saugatuck. Used to cross the channel.

Octagon House
Randolph and Mixer, Douglas. Used to be referred to by old timers as "house mitt da steeple."

Old Grist Mill
844 Holland St., Saugatuck.

ART CENTER

Oxbow
Telephone: 857–5818. Sixty-eight-year-old art school. Visitors should call for appointment to see painting, print making, sculpture classes. Summer only.

MUSEUMS

Saugatuck Historical Museum
403 Lake. Sat., 10–5; Mon.–Fri., and Sun., 12–4.

S. S. *Keewatin*
Tower Marine. "Last of the classic steamships of the Great Lakes." A 1907 coal-burning passenger vessel now serving as a preserved and living marine museum. Daily, May 1–Oct. 1, 10 AM–4:30.

ORCHARDS

Crane Orchard and Cider Mill
M-89, 1 1/2 miles west of Fennville, telephone: 561–2297. Light lunches. Great homemade pies. Daily, year round, 10–5; Sun., 12–5.

David Babbit Orchards
Blue Star Highway, Ganges-E on 119th St.; telephone: 543–4272. Pick your own strawberries; fruit stand. Daily, summer, 8–6 PM.

PARKS

Allegan State Game Preserve
10 miles south of the Lake, between Fennville and Allegan (I-196 via Glenn exit to M-89, which crosses park); telephone: 673–2430. 45,000 acres; campgrounds; hiking; snowmobiling; cross-country skiing; birding; residence for thousands of Canada geese October to March; short season of wild turkey and deer hunting.

Thousands of Canada geese have established residence in the
Allegan State Game Preserve near Saugatuck-Douglas, Michigan.
Edgar G. Mueller

Cook Memorial City Park
River Rd. (runs along channel). Picnicking, ducks.

RECREATION

Beaches

Douglas Public Beach on Lake
Near foot of Center St., Saugatuck. No charge.

Oval Beach
On Lake Michigan. Take A-2 to blinker, right on Center St., right on
Ferry Street to Oval Beach Road.

Boat Rides

City of Douglas
Tower Marine, Saugatuck; telephone: 857-2151, ext. 26. Cruise to
Lake Michigan or Kalamazoo River. Sails at 1, 3, and 7 (about 1 1/4
hours); summer.

The Queen of Saugatuck
650 Water St.; telephone: 857-9973. Scenic river trip. Daily, summer,
1, 4, and 7 PM.

Boating

Gleason's Marina (rentals)
650 Water St.; telephone: 857–9973.

Dancing

Square Dancing
On Saugatuck tennis courts. May–Sept., last Saturday evening of each month.

Dune Rides

Dune Schooners
Exit 41 off I-196; telephone: 857–2253.

Charters

First Choice
Telephone: 857–9973 or 857–4558.

Schippa-Hoy
Telephone: 857–4558 or 857–9973.

Happy Retreat
Telephone: 857–4558 or 857–9973.

Can't Miss
Telephone: 857–4481 or 857–9973.

Golf

Clearbrook Country Club (18-hole)
Blue Star Highway to 135th Ave.; telephone: 857–2000.

Westshore Golf Course (18-hole)
Ferry St., Douglas; telephone: 857–2500.

Music

Band Concerts
At band shell in park along channel, Saugatuck. Summer, Sun., 3 PM and 8 PM.

RESTAURANTS

The Butler
End of Butler St.; telephone: 857–3501. II AM–I:30 AM.

Elbow Room
200 Holland Rd.; telephone: 857–2691. Mon.–Thurs., 7–3; Fri.–Sat.,
7 AM–8 PM; Sun., 7 AM–5:30 PM.

Embassy
215 Butler; telephone: 857–4315. Daily, noon–10 PM; closed Mon.

Tara
200 Center St., off U.S. 31; telephone: 857–1441. Mon.–Sat., II:30 AM–II
PM; Sun., noon–10 PM.

SHOPPING

Bell of the Reef
119 Butler; telephone: 857–5581. Nautical. Daily, 10–8.

East of the Sun
252 Butler; telephone: 857–2640. Antiques and brass. Daily, 10–5:30.

Just Christmas
Butler St.; telephone: 857–4642. Just what it says. Daily, 10–5:30.

Prajna Gallery
134 Butler; telephone: 857–7861. American art. Daily, April–Labor
Day, II–5.

Valleau Studio
3534 63rd St.; telephone: 857–2128. Brass sand-casting. Year round,
9–3.

SPECIAL EVENTS

Antique Show
Second weekend in July.

Arts and Crafts Fair
Last week in August.

Flea Market
64th St. Sat. and Sun. all summer.

Outdoor Art Show
Last three Sats. in July.

Venetian Festival
Last Sat. in July.

THEATER

Red Barn Theater
Telephone: 857–3601. June 25–Sept. 4, Mon.–Sat., 8:30; Sun., 7:30; Wed. & Sat. matinee at 2.

TOUR

Lloyd J. Harris Pie Plant
350 Culver; telephone: 857–2171. Call to arrange.

South Haven

Population: 6500   Area Code: 616   Zip Code: 49090
Chamber of Commerce; 535 Quaker Street; telephone: 637–1450

Some people come to South Haven to fish for coho and trout (and the catch is great), others to pick fruit (and it's abundant), or to enjoy the biggest blueberry festival in the country (85 percent of Michigan's crop is grown within a radius of 12 miles of this little town of 6000 people). But there was a time, in the 1920s, when 250,000 people vacationed in South Haven every summer. There were Lake steamers in those days, bringing some folks for a day's outing and others for a week's vacation "in the country." Seventy-five family resorts opened their doors to the visitors (mostly Jewish residents of the Chicago ghetto), and the town boasted a casino, a dance pavilion and an opera house. It all ended when the Jewish community became more affluent and began vacationing elsewhere. Only four of the old resorts remain, and even some of them are building and selling condominiums where the famous old hotels once stood.

Boats have always played an important part in the life of South Haven, and even the town's name is a reminder that it has been a safe

Pier fishing in South Haven, Michigan. *Michigan Travel Commission*

harbor for Lake sailors from the beginning. Though few Indians ever lived in this area, there was a time when a flotilla of 100 canoes, (each carrying a Potawatomi family) paddled into the port. The biggest ship owner in the world today, billionaire Ludwig, was a South Haven boy who got his start by dredging up a sunken freighter and restoring it to working condition. As a matter of fact, C. P. Ludwig, the billionaire's grandfather, had a pier 4 miles south of town. In 1874 he commissioned a schooner that he called the *Mary Ludwig* in honor of his wife, which he used for commercial purposes. In that period, before the resorts, schooners would wait at the piers for the farmers to bring their apples and peaches and blueberries for transport to cities around the Lake.

Since 1852, when the first apple orchard was planted, fruit also has played a vital part in the life of the community. The town developed a basket company for packing the produce, and in 1871 organized the Pomological Society to study ways to grow a better apple. In 1879 the manufacture of fruit packages began in South Haven, and within twenty years more than 2 million packages were sold annually. In that same era the South Haven Agricultural Experiment Station began its cooperative work with Michigan State College on the cultivation of better orchards. Small wonder then that the town's most famous native was Liberty Hyde Bailey, the great horticulturist, who went on to head Cornell University's renowned agricultural school. His boyhood home is a museum now and, like the coho and the fruit, still a part of the town's pride.

MUSEUM

Liberty Hyde Bailey Museum
903 S. Bailey Ave.; telephone: 637–2991. Birthplace of famous horticulturist. A good look at the life of an 1850s family. Michigan Historical Registry. Tues. and Fri., 2–4:30; or by appointment.

ORCHARDS AND FARMS

Adkin Brothers
65th, between 103 and 106th; telephone: 637–5740. Apricots, all tree fruits in season. July 15–Oct. 1.

Vincent Degrandchamp
Blue Star Highway and 14th Ave.; telephone: 637–3915. Pick your own blueberries.

South Haven Agricultural Experiment Station
802 St. Joseph St. For interested agronomists only. Famous for work on Red Haven peach — now most popular variety.

PARKS

Covert Township Park
County 378 at Lake, 6 miles south of South Haven. Camping, swimming, hiking.

Van Buren State Park
Ruggles Rd. at Lake Michigan, 5 miles south of South Haven. 250 campsites, trails, good beach, snowmobiling.

RECREATION

Beaches

South Beach
Foot of Michigan Ave.

North Beach
Oval off North Shore Beach.

Packard Park
Off North Shore Dr.

Charters

Nichols Landing
South Haven Charter Boat Headquarters, 600 Williams St. Telephone: 637–2507.

Captain Don Buckberry
Telephone: 543–4540.

Captain Fernan Gruber
Telephone: 637–4241.

Captain Al Holmes
Telephone: 637–1643.

Captain John Tiggelman
Telephone: 637–1548.

Golf

Glenn Shores Golf Club (9-hole)
Blue Star Highway, 5 miles north of South Haven; telephone: 227–3226.

South Haven Country Club (18-hole)
Blue Star Highway, 3 miles north of South Haven; telephone: 227–3226.

Marinas

All Seasons Marina
231 Black River St.; telephone: 637–3655.

Georg Marina
280 Oak St.; telephone: 637–4302.

Municipal Marina
Telephone: 637–5211.

RESTAURANTS

Holly's Suburban Restaurant
Blue Star Memorial Highway at M-140; telephone: 637–2707. Year round, Sun.–Thurs., 6:45–8; Fri.–Sat., 6:45–9.

Marge's Restaurant
524 Phoenix; telephone: 637–6742. Daily, 7–7.

The Mariner's Inn
38 North Shore Dr.; telephone: 637–1360. Expensive. Great river view. Bar. Summer, Tues.–Sat., 5:30–10 PM.

Plantation Pancake House
51 North Shore Dr.; telephone: 637–9020. Summer only (not part of a chain).

SHOPPING

The Antique Shop
Dyckman at Williams; telephone: 637–1932. A bit of everything, housed in an old depot. Daily, 1–5; closed Sun.

SPECIAL EVENT

National Blueberry Festival
Call Chamber of Commerce for details. Parade, queen, pie-eating contest, baking contest, even blueberry soap! Mid-July.

TOUR

Black River Orchids, Inc.
77th St., Box 110; telephone: 637–5085. 400 varieties of orchids. Big color in spring and fall. Mon.–Sat., 9–4.

Benton Harbor

Population: 15,894   Area Code: 616   Zip Code: 49022

St. Joseph

Population: 11,262   Area Code: 616   Zip Code: 49085
Chamber of Commerce: 777 Riverview Drive, Benton Harbor; telephone:
925–0044

St. Joseph, the third oldest settlement in Michigan, was first visited by Pere Marquette in 1675. It was here in 1679 that LaSalle waited for his ship, the *Griffon,* the first sailing ship on the Lake and subsequently the first shipwreck too. When it failed to arrive, LaSalle set off on foot for Canada; the first white man to take the overland route through dense forest. LaSalle returned to the area later and established Fort Miami, a trade center which flourished for more than 100 years. In 1800 when the federal government wanted to garrison the area, the Indians objected, and instead Fort Dearborn in Chicago became the official military center.

For early sailing ships that moved up the Hudson, through the Erie Canal, and into the lakes, St. Joseph was a vital stop. Until 1843 it handled more wheat and flour than Chicago. The big boats docked and reloaded smaller boats, which then carried supplies inland for 150 miles.

St. Joseph, incorporated in 1834, was built on high ground on the west side of the St. Joseph River. In the 1860s a new canal created a Lake connection and harbor, and Benton Harbor grew on the east bank.

The two towns feuded for years, but eventually built a bridge that connected St. Joseph's Wayne Street with Benton Harbor's Main Street, and they found common bonds in their orchards, their shorelines, as well as mutual benefits from their tourists and manufacturing. Today the area is the manufacturing center for Southwest Michigan. Clark Equipment Company has its headquarters here. So does Whirlpool. The area's industries make forgings, travel trailers, and there is a great fruit processing center. The House of David, a religious cult, flourished here early in the century, becoming locally famous for their beards and baseball, as well as their piety. They also owned land at High Island in the Beaver Archipelago. Although some claimed they used this as a penal colony for miscreants, the facts are they timbered and farmed up the Lake.

ART CENTER

St. Joseph Art Center
600 State; telephone: 983–0271. Art exhibits, monthly change, supplemented by annual July Art Fair. Tues.–Fri., 10–4; Sat.–Sun., 1–4.

MUSEUM

Josephine Morton Memorial House, 1849
501 Territorial Rd.; telephone: 925–7185. Groups must be scheduled ahead. Period rooms and historical exhibits. State Historical Marker in front yard. Thurs., 1–4; Sun., 2–4; June–October. Free admission.

ORCHARDS

Lowell Jasper
622 W. Marquette Woods Rd.; telephone: 429–9305. Peaches. August.

Nye's Apple Barn
4716 Hollywood, I-94, exit 27, St. Joseph; telephone: 429–0595. Tour orchards and buy apples. Sept.–Nov.

PARKS

Lake Bluff Park
Lakebluff Ave. Park and State sts., St. Joseph. Fort Miami marker commemorates spot where LaSalle waited in vain for ship *Griffon,* and where he built first fort in lower peninsula, 1679. Opposite Hotel Whitcomb.

Sarett Nature Center
2300 Benton Center Rd., Benton Harbor, 49022; telephone: 927–4832. Nature area on Paw Paw River flood plains (off the beaten path). Field trips, lecture, hiking, tours. Special. Tues.–Sat., 10–5; Sun., 1–5.

RECREATION

Canoe Rental

Wolf Enterprises
1207 Ann St., St. Joseph; telephone: 983–1008.

Boat Trips

Float your way down the St. Joseph for 22.8 miles. Sixteen public access sites between Berrien Springs and St. Joseph. Charter or bring your own.

Charters

Harold Beutseu
Telephone: 429–1387.

Guy Berley
Telephone: 925–7738.

Donald Buckberry
Telephone: 543–4540.

James A. Faultersack
Telephone: 925–9765.

Walter Fisher
Telephone: 429–5533.

Glen Kimmerly
Telephone: 683–5760.

William Klemm
Telephone: 925–2558.

Ken Neidlinger
Telephone: 983–7816.

Walter Olmstead
Telephone: 429–4834.

Donald Radde
Telephone: 663–2234.

Ted Ryznar
Telephone: 983–6268.

Roy Wiest
Telephone: 429–5033.

Ben Yacobozzi
Telephone: 429–9512.

Golf

Blossom Trail (18-hole)
1565 Britain, Benton Harbor; telephone: 925–4591.

Lake Michigan Golf Course (18-hole)
2520 Kerlikowske, Benton Harbor; telephone: 849–2722.

Paw Paw Lake Golf Course (18-hole)
Paw Paw Ave., Watervliet; telephone: 463–3831.

Pipestone Creek Golf Course (18-hole)
Naomi Rd., Eau Claire; telephone: 544–1611.

Wyndivicke Country Club (18-hole)
3711 Niles Ave., St. Joseph; telephone: 429–6210.

Marinas

Benton Harbor Boat Ramp
Riverview Dr.; telephone: 925–7061.

Benton Township Ramp
1725 Territorial Rd.; telephone: 925–0616. Access to Lake Michigan.

Lighthouse Marine
Industrial Island, St. Joseph; telephone: 983–3681.

Pier 1000
1000 Riverview Dr., Benton Harbor; telephone: 927–4471.

West Basin Marina
273 Prospect, St. Joseph; telephone: 983–5432.

Whispering Willow Marina
2383 Niles, St. Joseph; telephone: 983–9963.

Music

Band Concert
Lake Bluff Park, Lakebluff Ave., St. Joseph. Summers, Sun., 2:30 PM
& 7:30 PM.

Skiing

Royal Valley Ski Resort
R.R.#1, Box 457, Main St., Buchanan; telephone: 695–3847. Snow
Festival, second weekend in January. Daily, Thanksgiving–March 15.

Swimming Beaches (north to south)

Rocky Gap Park
Benton Harbor

Jean Klock Park
Benton Harbor

Tiscornia Park
St. Joseph

Silver Beach
St. Joseph

RESTAURANTS

Captain's Table
655 Riverview Dr.; telephone: 927–2421. Daily, breakfast, 7–12; dinner, 5–11; Fri. & Sat., 5–12; Sun., 5–9.

Holly's Landing
105 N. Main, on the river, St. Joseph; telephone: 983–2334. Mon.–Sat.,
11–midnight; Sun., 12–12.

Bill Knapp's
139 at I-94, Benton Harbor; telephone: 925–3212. Mon.–Thurs., &
Sun., 11–10; Fri. & Sat., 11–12.

SHOPPING

Harbor Fruit Market
1891 Territorial Rd.; telephone: 925–0681. Largest noncitrus cash to

grower market in world. Open daily during production season, Mon.–Fri., May 1–Nov. 1.

Heath Company Factory Store
Hilltop Rd.; telephone: 983–3961. Country's largest manufacturer of electronic kits. Mon.–Fri., 8:30–5; Sat., 9–3.

SPECIAL EVENTS

Blossomtime Festival
Telephone: 983–7383. May 1 is Blessing of the Blossoms. Third week in May is grand floral parade (very colorful).

Fort Miami Day
St. Joseph Lake Bluff Park; telephone: 983–1375. Sponsored by the Fort Miami Heritage Society, this day celebrates the old days! Home tours, band concerts, ice cream social, antiques display. Mid-August.

St. Joseph Annual Art Fair
Telephone: 983–0271. July.

Tri-State Regatta
Labor Day weekend. Boats arrive in early hours of Saturday; Sunday to Michigan City. Gorgeous to watch activities and start of race to Michigan City and back to Chicago.

Annual Western Amateur Championship
Point O' Woods Country Club (18-hole), 1516 Roslin Rd.; telephone: 944–1433. Watch great golfers! Late July or early August. Daily admission fee.

THEATER

Twin-City Players
3101 Lake Shore Dr. St. Joseph; telephone: 983–7394. Amateur — call Chamber of Commerce for schedule.

TOURS

Bronte Winery
M-152, Keeler 49057; telephone: 621–3419. Tour lasts about twenty-five minutes (children welcome). Watch and taste great variety of wines! Year round, Mon.–Sat., 10–4; Sun., noon–4.

Whirlpool
Upton Rd., Benton Harbor 49022; telephone: 926–5000. Appliance company can be toured. Call in advance.

Stevensville

Population: 1070   Zip Code: 49127

Bridgman

Population: 1621   Zip Code: 49106

Sawyer

Population: under 200   Zip Code: 49125

Harbert

Population: under 200   Zip Code: 49115

Lakeside

Population: under 200   Zip Code: 49116

Union Pier

Population: under 200   Zip Code: 49129

New Buffalo

Population: 2784   Zip Code: 49117

Grand Beach

Population: under 200   Zip Code: 49117

Long Beach, Indiana

Population: 2740   Zip Code: 46360

Stevensville

As early as 1867 Stevensville had a pier for schooners to load lumber and later fruit for the Chicago markets. In 1884 a Niles, Michigan, banker platted the square-mile village and named it for himself. Today Stevensville is known for its Grand Mere Preserve, which has drawn national attention because of the conservation battle fought to keep it an ecological study area for the state of Michigan.

ORCHARD

Henry Writzke
I-94, Stevensville Exit to Washington Ave. to John Beers Rd.; telephone: 429–9317. Strawberries.

PARKS

Grand Mere Nature Preserve
c/o Grand Mere Association, Box 140, I-94 to Thornton, Stevensville. Beach, woods, old lake bed, hemlock swamp. Great birding (thousand of goldfinch in October). Water fowl. Area has three inland lakes, cranberry bog. Wishart Road in Grand Mere proposed as southwest Michigan's only scenic road. Write to association for tour information.

North Lake Park
West of Grand Mere Preserve. Swimming, beach, picnicking.

RESTAURANTS

Tosi's Restaurant
4337 Ridge; telephone: 429–3689. Italian food. Bar. No reservations, but crowded. Very good. April 1–Dec. 31; Mon.–Fri., 5–11; Sat., 5–12.

Win Schuler's
5000 Red Arrow; telephone: 429–3273. Bar. Old English motif, including waitresses' dresses. Very good. Mon.–Fri., 11–11; Sat., 11–midnight; Sun., 10–10.

SHOPPING

A-Bit-of-Swiss Bakery
4337 Ridge; telephone: 429–1661. Connected with Italian Tosi's German-run restaurant.

Mr. Don's Hobby Shop
5806 St. Joseph Ave.; telephone: 429–8151. Wide variety of hobby kits.
Shop is housed in an old country church. Daily, 10–6; closed Sun.

Bridgman

When the first visitors came into this area in 1843, it had high dunes
and great herds of deer. One early hunter bagged sixty in a single
winter. Those who followed bagged the rest, and equally zealous
lumbermen stripped the woods. There was a mill, connected to a Lake
pier by a small railroad that spanned the gorgeous ravines and tun-
neled through the dunes to the beach. Early settlers came from Massachusetts, many on horseback, and one of them, George Bridgman,
platted the village. During the first two decades of the century Bridgman was a secret rendezvous spot for the Wobblies, the international
workers of the world. Today it is resort country and a thriving nursery
center.

PARK

Warren Dunes State Park
Red Arrow Highway, north of town; telephone: 426–4013. Camping,
picnicking, trails, beach. Fine hang gliding at Tower Hill.

RECREATION

Golf

Pebblewood Country Club (18-hole)
9794 Jericho; telephone: 465–5611.

Swimming

Weko Beach
Lake St. at Lake Michigan. Municipal beach with boat launch.

RESTAURANT

Hyerdall's
Red Arrow Highway; telephone: 465–5546. Simple and nice. Lunch,
11:30–3; dinner, 5–8; closed Mon., and Jan., Feb., March.

SHOPPING

Midwest School of Hang Gliding

U.S. Moyes, Inc. (manufactures hang gliders), 11522 Red Arrow Highway, Bridgman 49106; telephone: 426–3100. Tours available at plant. School opens for lessons during summer and early fall.

TOUR

Cook Nuclear Center

Red Arrow Highway at Livingston Rd.; telephone: 465–6101. The Indiana and Michigan Electric Company explains to the public how nuclear energy provides power. Jan.–May, Mon.–Fri., 10–5; Sun., 11–5; June–Nov. Wed.–Sat., 10–5; closed Dec. and holidays. Free admission.

Sawyer

Sawyer, early known as Troy Station, once was mostly timber and a deep swamp. When the timber was cut, and the swamp drained, cattle raising took over, cowboys and all. For many years Sawyer rivaled Bridgman as strawberry plant center of the world. Today it is a thriving summer community, many of whose residents are descended from old Swedish families who have been coming here for years. But increasingly new year-round residents are settling here, many of them commuting to jobs in Benton Harbor.

ORCHARD

Richard Soper Blueberries

Holloway Dr., 1/2 to 3/4 mile west of Red Arrow Highway; telephone: 426–4521. Buy or pick your own. Daily, July–Labor Day, 10–6.

SHOPPING

Haalga's Gift Shop

Red Arrow Highway and Lake Shore Dr.; telephone: 426–4233. Unusual selection of gift items. Daily, 10–6; closed Thurs.

Harbert

Harbert was once called Greenbush because of a small swamp that kept its vegetation green all summer. Railroad officials named it Harbert in honor of a Chicago capitalist. It is an old summer colony and, like Sawyer, has many residents of Swedish descent. Carl Sandburg spent some summers here, and the Prairie Club, a Chicago hiking association, has its summer colony in the town.

SHOPPING

Harbert Fruit Market
Red Arrow Highway (in town). Complete line of locally grown fruit and vegetables in season.

Swedish Bakery
13746 Red Arrow Highway; telephone: 469–4202. Excellent homemade Swedish goods. Summer, daily, 7 AM–6 PM.

Lakeside

The Chikaming tribe of Indians once powwowed in this section of the shoreline. Later the local town square was known as Horse Thief Park. Stolen horses were cached in the nearby Galien woods, their hair was dyed, and then they were resold. When local vigilantes discovered the horse thieves, they hung them in the park. Lakeside got its start as a summer resort in the early 1890s. The first visiting Chicagoans lived in tents, the later ones in substantial homes. The Lakeside Inn, still standing but no longer in service, employed waiters who worked the winters at the Palmer House in Chicago. Many early residents came from the University of Chicago. The most famous vacationer was Jane Addams, but a favorite was radio newsman Clifton Utley who golfed during the tense pre–World War II days with a portable radio to keep abreast of the news.

TOUR

Lakeside Vineyard
1358 Red Arrow Highway; telephone: 469–0700. Taste and watch

wine made. March–December, Mon.–Sat., 9:30–3:30; May–December, Sun. also, noon–4 PM.

Union Pier

Cheek by jowl with Lakeside is Union Pier, which got its name from a long (and long gone) loading pier extending into the Lake. Its summer colony was Jewish for two generations, and is now a mix of Lithuanian and black.

PARK

Warren Woods Park
East off Red Arrow Highway on Warrenwoods Rd. Over 300 acres of virgin forest of beech maple. Named for E. K. Warren who donated it as a permanent park and natural laboratory. River; natural springs; picnicking. Once Potawatomie encamped here to tap maples. Spectacular.

RECREATION

Swimming

Lake Michigan Beach
End of Town Line Rd. at Lake.

SHOPPING

Union Pier Bakery
Town Line Road and Red Arrow Highway; telephone: 469–1010. Summer, daily, 7 AM–6 PM; winter, Fri., Sat., 7 AM–1 PM.

New Buffalo

In 1834 Captain Wessel Whittaker's ship *Post Boy,* en route to Michigan City, was washed aground during a terrible Lake storm. He walked across the Galien River where it joins the Lake, and was so impressed by the potential for a natural harbor that he went back to Buffalo, New York, gathered some friends, and came to lay out this southernmost of Michigan towns. He was sure it would outstrip Chicago, but shifting sands constantly closed the harbor. The town flourished as long as it was the terminus of the Michigan Central Railroad and passengers had to be moved onto Lake boats to complete their journey to Chicago. But once the track was completed into the city, the competition was over. (Bearing no grudge to its big cousin, New Buffalo sent a pumper to help fight the great Chicago fire of 1871.) For years New Buffalo has been a summer resort for Chicagoans. In 1974 its harbor was rebuilt, and now offers first-class boating and fishing facilities.

MUSEUM

LaPorte Historical Steam Society
Exit 49 on I-94, south on Highway 39 to County 1000 N, east on 1000 N. for 2 miles, LaPorte, Indiana. Antique steam power of all kinds. 2-mile steam train ride. Memorial Day–Labor Day, Sat.–Sun., 1–6 PM; Labor Day–Oct., Sun., 1–6 PM.

RECREATION

Birding

Harbor, Galien River area, Beach
All can be reached by taking Whittaker St. to Lake Michigan.

Boats

Oselka Snug Harbor
514 W. Water; telephone: 469–2600. 525 slips. Complete boat service.

Public Ramp
Red Arrow Highway north of New Buffalo at Galien River.

Fishing

New Buffalo Charter Service
Telephone: 469–4510. Fishing at Lakefront and Galien River.

Swimming

Lake Michigan Beach
End of Whittaker St. at Lake. Admission fee for nonresidents.

RESTAURANTS

Hesston Bar and Grill
4 miles east on County 1000 N.; telephone: 778–2938. Daily, 5 PM–11 PM; closed Mon.

Little Bohemia
115 S. Whittaker; telephone: 469–1440. Bohemian foods a specialty. Daily, lunch and dinner; closed Mon.

Skip's Other Place
Red Arrow Highway, 2 miles north of New Buffalo; telephone: 469–3330. Prime rib a specialty. Daily, 5 PM–11 PM; closed Mon.

TOUR

Ban Holzer Wine Cellars
Exit 49 on I-94 at Highway 39 and County 1000 N, New Carlisle 46552, telephone: 778–2448. Tour and taste wine from locally grown grapes. April 1–Jan. 1, Mon.–Sat., 11 AM–5 PM.

Grand Beach, Michigan, and Long Beach, Indiana

Strung along the Lake south of New Buffalo is a row of popular residential and summer colonies: Grand Beach; Michigan Shores; Michiana; Duneland Beach; and Long Beach, Indiana. The Grand Beach claim to fame was its most celebrated householder: the late Chicago mayor Richard J. Daley. Michiana, which borders the Indiana line, is a cluster of log-cabin-type homes, and Long Beach is largely a suburb of Michigan City, Indiana. A Lake road, with bus service, weaves in and out of the suburban-type communities, giving one quick glimpses of the shore and the waves.

Indiana

FROM
MICHIGAN CITY
TO
HAMMOND

LAKE MICHIGAN

MICHIGAN

• Chicago

ILLINOIS

Indiana
Harbor

Indiana Dunes National
Lakeshore Park

• Michigan City

Whiting •

• Beverly Shores

East Chicago •

Ogden Dunes

• Dune Acres

Hammond

• Gary

Burns
Harbor

• Chesterton

Portage

INDIANA

SANDERSON

Michigan City

Population: 41,000   Area Code: 219   Zip Code: 46360
Chamber of Commerce: 711 Franklin Square; telephone: 874–6221

Michigan City is a big-little town of 41,000 people at the mouth of Trail Creek. The area figured notably in early exploration of the country when Father Marquette met here with the Potawatamis in the 1670s. After Indiana became a state in 1816, the Trail Creek outlet to Lake Michigan was developed and a road built from the harbor all the way to the Wabash River. Michigan City was not only a port for schooners, but the end of the overland trail for the pioneers coming from the East in wagons.

When Michigan City was incorporated in 1836, many people, including Major Elston, its founder, expected it to outstrip Chicago in size. It was important for Indiana to have a city on the Lake and even Daniel Webster lobbied in Congress for money to dredge and enlarge its harbor. But as the years passed, the Michigan Central Railroad reached Chicago and Lake shipping could no longer compete with the faster freights.

The waterfront has remained important to Michigan City, however. Oldsters remember when 100 families made their living from fishing, and fish were "shovelled out of their boats as farmers fork out hay." Today only two commercial fishermen remain, but charter boats and sports fishermen have taken over. One recently described seeing coho salmon 3 miles offshore "in such numbers they reminded me of a herd of buffalo." Although all the eastern towns on the Michigan coast claim to be the coho capital, perhaps Michigan City's claim is strongest for it is at the southernmost point of the Lake where the water is warmest.

There was a time when Lake schooners brought wheat into town, took out tons of fish and lumber, the sailing vessels so thick "that they had to be double parked in order to unload." At a bend in the harbor still stands the old lighthouse, constructed in 1858 by the U.S. government, whose beacon shown brightly on Great Lakes sailors for a century. Today's harbor is jammed with all manner of pleasure craft and involved in two great Lake races, the Tri-State and the Chicago-

Michigan City. The shorefront Washington Park covers 90 acres of wooded picnic grounds, flower gardens, tennis courts, playgrounds, fine beaches, and a bandshell where concerts are well attended during summer months. The most outstanding feature of Washington Park is the zoo, the oldest in the state, which raises more Bengal tigers than any other zoo in the country. Today citizens are urged to "adopt" specific animals and provide for their feeding.

Michigan City was noted for the great sand dune that dominated its Lakeshore. One was the Hoosier Slide, a 184-foot mountain of sand which from 1890 to 1920 was totally destroyed to make Ball fruit jars, auto windshields, farm equipment, and landfill for the Illinois Central's right of way in Chicago. Today the Northern Indiana Public Service Company stands in its place, its gigantic cooling tower an awesome guardian of the waterfront.

Michigan City was once host to summer excursion boats bringing tourists across the Lake to enjoy the park and to dance at the Oasis Ballroom where all the big bands used to play. A kid in knee pants named Benny Goodman once worked the pleasure boats with his wicked clarinet.

One of the great historic events in the life of the town was the arrival of the Lincoln funeral train. The ladies of the community entertained passengers and the crew at lunch, where, sensing the history of the moment, they used their best china and linen. A little boy, knowing that children were forbidden to view the body of the martyred president, found his way inside by ducking under the hooped skirt of an unsuspecting lady. It was fitting that the funeral train carried the first Pullman car, because Michigan City was the home of a major railroad car factory eventually bought by the Pullman empire. The son of one of the founders of the Haskell-Barker Car Company, John H. Barker, made many generous gifts to the city and his magnificent thirty-eight-room turn-of-the-century mansion now belongs to Michigan City, which uses it as a civic center and opens it for public viewing.

Always part of the transportation pattern of the country, first as a harbor, then as a stagecoach stop on the Detroit-Chicago run, finally as a rail center, Michigan City attracted many early manufacturers because of the lure of cheap labor from the nearby Indiana State Prison. Manufacturers of shoes, cigars, bicycles, and overalls had contracts with the prison until a law passed in 1904 forbid the practice.

Today extensive redevelopment is going on near the neglected harbor area. Handsome public buildings are being erected, including the prize-winning Michigan City Library, which has been internationally admired for its innovative architecture. The old downtown area has been enlivened by a little mall, at one end of which is the Canterbury Theater complex, an attractively remodeled 100-year-old church and school that maintains a semiprofessional stock company in the summer.

Today Michigan City has sixty-one manufacturing plants, among them Dr. Scholl's, Jay-Mar Ruby, Joy Manufacturing, and Sullair. Development at the south end of town revolves around a large covered shopping center, Marquette Mall, which serves a considerable area in northwest Indiana.

ARCHITECTURE AND HISTORIC SITES

Brewery
E. Michigan Blvd. An old brewery put to new and imaginative use.

* Barker Mansion
Civic Center, 631 Washington; telephone: 872–0159. Home of one of Michigan City's early millionaires, this is a splendid English manor house with marble and walnut, handcarved teak. Beautiful gardens. Presented to city by Barker's daughter as a cultural center in his memory. Mon.–Fri., 10–3; Sat. & Sun., 11–3. Group tours by arrangement.

Michigan City Public Library
C. S. Murphy, Architects
100 E. 4th; telephone: 879–4561. Kalwall exterior (plastic with fiber glass fill), exposed pipes in brilliant colors. Indiana local history collection. Audio-visual equipment superior. Call for calendar of events. Mon.–Thurs., 9–9; Fri. & Sat., 9–6; Sun., 1–5.

Moslem Mosque
Islamic Center of Michigan City, Brown Rd.; telephone: 879–9667. Sun., 10:00–12:00.

Mullen School
Architects, Shaver Partnership
100 Manny Ct.; telephone: 872–5783. Lovely school nestled in the dunes.

Waterford Inn
Johnson & Wozniak Rds., I-94 overpass. Now a home, but was a stagecoach stop on the Chicago-Detroit journey.

ART CENTER

John G. Blank Community Center for the Arts
(Old Michigan City Library), 8th St.; telephone: 872–6829. Lessons, exhibits.

MUSEUM

Lighthouse Museum
At bend of harbor on Washington; telephone: 872–6133. Once a guide-post for ships. Now a museum for early Michigan City books, maps, and other memorabilia. Summer, Tues.–Sun., 1–5; winter: Tues.–Sun., 1–3:30.

ORCHARDS

Arndt Orchards
Wozniak Rd. and 200 N.; telephone: 872–0122.

Garwood Orchards
421 south to U.S. 2, east to 500 W. and follow signs; telephone: 362–4385. Raspberries, apples, vegetables, cider mill.

John Hancock Fruit Farm
U.S. 20 east for 7 miles beyond I-94 overpass to Fail Road, then left 3 miles; telephone: 778–2096. Apples, peaches, perennial plants.

PARKS

International Friendship Gardens
Liberty Trail Rd.; telephone: 874–3664. 100 acres of variety in gardens from everywhere. Memorial to world peace. Daily, 9–dusk.

Washington Park
Pine Ave. at Lake Michigan. Beaches, boating, picnicking, tennis courts. Weekend charges for entrance to park and parking in summer.

Washington Park Zoo
In Washington Park, Franklin at Lake. Seventy species of birds, fish, animals. Summer, daily, 10:30–8.

RECREATION

Charters

Dick Shapanski
Michigan City Charter Boat Association; telephone: 872–3977. Clearinghouse for twelve fishing charter owners.

Golf

Michigan City Municipal Golf (18-hole)
Wolf Ave. and Michigan Blvd.; telephone: 872–2121.

North Golf Course (18-hole)
Warnke Rd.; telephone: 872–3478.

Marinas

B & E Marine
Washington Park; telephone: 879–8301. Private, but has gas.

Michigan City Municipal Marina
Washington Park Ramp; telephone: 872–1712.

South Lake Marine
6th St. Bridge; telephone: 872–7201. Private, but has gas.

Sprague Marina
E. 8th St.; telephone: 879–4300. Public launch ramp, gas.

Music

Band Concerts
Band shell in Washington Park. Summer, Thurs., 8 PM.

RESTAURANTS

Benny's
3101 E. U.S. 12, north of Michigan City; telephone: 872–8621. Daily 11:30–2 AM; closed Sun.

Duneland Beach Inn
311 Potawatomi Trail, Duneland Beach; telephone: 874–7729. Special Sunday brunch, 10–2; in summer, sandwiches and ice cream are served on the porch; make reservations after May 15; closed Nov.–March.

Hoe Choy Restaurant
110 W. 9th; telephone: 874–6251. Tues.–Thurs., 11:30–9:30; Fri. & Sat., 11:30–10:30; Sun., 12–9; closed Mon.

Holiday Inn
5820 S. Franklin St., U.S. 421; telephone: 879–0311. Daily, 6 AM–10 PM.

Maxine & Heine's Tavern
521 Franklin Square; telephone: 879–9068. Bar. German cooking; gargantuan portions. Vast collection of decorative whisky bottles provides setting. Daily, 4–12 PM; closed Sun.

Rodini Restaurant
5518 U.S. 421; telephone: 879–7388. Bar. Greek food a specialty. Mon.–Fri., 11–11; Sat., 4–11; Sun., 4–9.

SHOPPING

Furness Fisheries
River at 2nd St. Bridge, Rt. 12; telephone: 874–4761. Take good fresh fish home, even if you haven't caught any. Mon.–Thurs., 9–5; Fri., 9–7; Sat., 9–5.

Ritters Fish
517 E. 4th; telephone: 874–7635. Mon.–Sat., 8:30–5; Fri., 8:30–7.

SPECIAL EVENTS

Miss Indiana Scholarship Pageant for Miss Indiana
Call Chamber of Commerce for time and date. June.

Summer Festival
Call Chamber of Commerce for details. Great drum and bugle corps contest. Indiana's second-largest parade. July.

THEATERS

Canterbury Playhouse
907 Franklin; telephone: 874–4269. Summer stock in restored 102-year-old church.

Dunes Art Foundation Summer Theater
Oakdale Road, Michiana Shores; telephone: 879–9782. Children's plays and classes in theater and arts. July and August, summer stock.

Beverly Shores

Population: 946   Zip Code: 46301

Half the homes in this small town are owned by Lithuanian families who settled here because it was so reminiscent of the Baltic coast. Beverly Shores is an area of splendid beaches (in low-water years), dunes (many of them now hidden under heavy vegetation), woods, and marsh. Quiet country roads wind about for miles, and pheasant (and occasional deer) are to be seen.

Beverly Shores was once used for intensive cranberry and blueberry farming. In the 1920s, Frederick Bartlett, a Chicago realtor, bought up thousands of acres of land. He built his own house (with a private zoo) high on a dune, and wooed carloads of Chicagoans with Sunday excursions on the South Shore Railroad. Many of his customers bought parcels of land, but the building boom went up in smoke during the Depression.

Since then other Chicagoans have arrived, many of them professionals, most of them to summer in the area. Beverly Shores has been caught in the battle for the National Lakeshore Park for years. Today, everything but a small island in the center of town is included, although the battle in Congress goes on each year. (For National Park facilities in the area see Indiana Dunes National Lakeshore Park.)

ARCHITECTURE AND HISTORIC SITES
All of the following are world's fair houses, brought from 1933 Century of Progress in Chicago.

Old North Church (Unitarian)
Beverly Dr., west of Broadway.

House of Tomorrow
Lake Front Dr., west of Broadway.

Paul Revere and Ben Franklin Houses
Pearson St.

RESTAURANT

Red Lantern
Lake Shore Dr. at Broadway; telephone: 874–6201. Bar. Gorgeous view. On clear nights, one can see the tall buildings and lights of Chicago. Daily, 4–10; Sun., noon–6.

SHOPPING

Save the Dunes Council Shop
Rt. 12 and Broadway; telephone: 879–3937. Local artists, etc. Run by the famous conservation group to support Indiana National Lakeshore Park, lobbying and education. Mon.–Sat., 9–5:30.

Chesterton

Population: 6000   Area Code: 219   Zip Code: 46304
Westchester Chamber of Commerce: 135 S. Calumet, P.O. Box 591; telephone:
926–5513. (Includes Tremont, Furnessville, and Porter.)

Chesterton is a charming Indiana town, with more than its share of churches, good shops, and streets lined with maple trees that blaze every autumn.

It bills itself as the Gateway to the Indiana Dunes, and indeed the great Indiana Dunes National Lakeshore as well as the State Park are both nearby. Chesterton (originally Coffee Creek, then Calumet) also claims to be the only incorporated town with that name anywhere. In 1952 when it celebrated its Centennial, the Lord Mayor of Cambridge, England, came to visit. He said that Britain too had had a Chesterton but that it had been annexed to Cambridge. "You alone," he said, "bear this name. Let no one take it away." It is improbable that anyone will, for each time the subject of merging with the nearby town of Porter arises, an irate citizen reminds his townsfolk that whatever the advantages, the town's identity as well as its name might be lost.

The identity began with the earliest settler in the area, a Frenchman named Joseph Bailly who settled down with his Ottawa Indian wife and traded with the Potawatomi. In 1833 three brothers named Morgan rumbled in from Ohio over the Sauk Trail. They built cabins, farms, businesses, and a bank, and the house of Morgan still holds a fine reign over the town. One member, interested in aesthetics, planted the maple trees that line the streets, and an earlier Morgan, more interested in law and order than nature, started the Morgan Prairie Anti–Horse Thief Association.

After the Ohioans came Scandinavians, Germans, and Poles to farm, and Irishmen to help lay the track of the Michigan Central Railroad. At one time twenty-four trains rumbled over those tracks each day, and the delighted farmers, eager for markets, brought their wheat and corn to town as well as stacks of wood to keep the hungry engines fueled. Railroad Park, now Thomas Centennial Park, is today a lovely area of flowering trees with a charming band shell. Four freight lines still run through town, but passenger service was abandoned long ago.

Chesterton was at one time a stop on the Underground Railroad; at another a place where several gangland shootings took place in its dunes. Early in this century it began attracting artists and craftsmen, and it still has one of the best summer art fairs in the region. Its newest attraction is a series of creative shops for people interested in antiques, ceramics, jewelry, dolls, paintings, toys, natural foods, and magnificent ice cream. It also has more than a dozen light industries.

For the sake of simplicity Tremont, Furnessville, and Porter are treated here as part of Chesterton.

ARCHITECTURE AND HISTORIC SITES

Augsburg Svenska Skola, circa 1880
Oakhill Road, 2 miles east of Mineral Springs Rd. Early church of Swedish settlement; seats seven; cemetery believed on Indian mound. Private property, no trespassing.

Holmes-Brown House
700 Porter. New headquarters for Duneland School Corporation.

ART CENTER

Chesterton Art Gallery
115 Fourth St.; telephone: 926–4711. Exhibits of area artists. Classes. Gallery of miniature paintings. Tues.–Sun., 2–5; closed Mon.

CEMETERY

Furnessville Cemetery
Furnessville Road, off Rt. 20 and County 275 East. Charming old cemetery (across from the Schoolhouse Shop).

PARKS

Indiana Dunes State Park
Take Rt. 49 (accessible from I-94, U.S. 12, U.S. 20) to its end; telephone: 926–1215. A gorgeous 2182-acre park with ten trails (maps available at entrance gate). Camping, beach house, miles of beach, cross-country skiing, picnicking, grocery store.

This park is heavily used and supports the whole Indiana state park system. One can see every sort of habitat: high dunes, low marshes, tree graveyards, blow outs. A birder's paradise; a painter's delight; a hiker's nemesis on its more rugged trails. Park has been used to begin training Himalayan climbers. Memorial Day–Labor Day, 7–11; fall, 8–6; winter, 8–4:30. Free admission in winter.

RECREATION

Music

Band Shell
Railroad Park, Calumet and Broadway. Call Chamber of Commerce for summer schedule.

RESTAURANTS

Magnificent Obsession
225 S. Calumet Ave.; telephone: 926–4568. Charming ice cream parlor. Tues.–Sat., 11–10 PM; Sun., 12–6; closed Mon.

The Spa
Mineral Springs Rd., south of Rt. 20; telephone: 926–1654. Beautiful setting. Feeders for raccoons. On site of old mineral springs. Once area had race course and baths. Mon.–Thurs., 11 AM–10 PM; Fri. & Sat., 11 AM–11 PM.

SHOPPING

Antique Shop
105 W. Porter Ave.; telephone: 926–1400. Tues.–Sat., 10–5; Sun., 12–5.

Carol's Antiques
119 Broadway; telephone: 926–4757. Daily, 10–5.

Five Gables' Antiques
500 S. Calumet Ave.; telephone: 926–7411. Daily, 10–5.

Freight Station
123 N. 4th St.; telephone: 926–6030. Interesting shopping in the old New York Central Station. Paintings by local artists, crafts, art supplies, plants. Tues.–Sat., 10–5; Sun., 12–5; closed Mon.

Gem Tree Rock
Highway 12, Porter; telephone: 926–1919. Call in advance.

The Jeweled Gazebo
132 S. Calumet Rd.; telephone: 926–2555. Daily; closed Sun. and Mon.

Marc T. Nielsen Interiors/Lower Barn Antiques
Take 49 south, go east on U.S. 6 for 2 miles, take Old Suman Rd. 1 mile (beware dangerous railroad tracks). Top-notch European and Oriental antiques; yearly buying in Europe. Mon.–Fri., 9–4:30; closed weekends.

Pottery ETC Etc.
910 Broadway; telephone: 926–4358. Shows works of many regional potters, and pots herself. Daily, 10–5:30; Sun., 12–5; closed Mon.

Schoolhouse Shop
Furnessville Rd., off U.S. 20; telephone: 926–1875. One of the top browsing gift shops anywhere — clothes, toys, china, glass, and the world's best smell. Daily, 9–5; Sun., 12–5; closed Mon.

Upstairs, Downstairs Antiques
402 Grant; telephone: 926–3894. Mon.–Sat., 10–5; Sun., 12–5.

VMS Hannell Pottery
Furnessville Rd., off U.S. 20 and County 275 East; telephone: 926–4568. A charming old pottery shop beautifully located in deep woods. Ring if no one there, or leave message on blackboard.

Yellow Brick Road
762 Calumet Ave.; telephone: 926–7048. Dolls, doll houses, and miniatures. Run by eleven women, each with a special doll mania. Daily, 9:30–5:00.

SPECIAL EVENTS

Chesterton Art Fair
St. Patrick School grounds. Run by the artists and craftsmen of Porter County to support their gallery, and to further the arts generally. Juried; supervision for children. A gala. First weekend in August.

Duneland Folk Festival
Westchester Public Library; telephone: 926–7696. Genuine folk festival in collaboration with Indiana National Lakeshore Park. Begins after July 4.

Indiana Dunes National Lakeshore Park

Kemil Road and U.S. 12 (well marked)
Visitor's Center: telephone: 926–7561.
Zip Code: 46304
Mailing address: Indiana Dunes National Lakeshore Park, 1100 N. Mineral
Springs Road, Porter, Indiana 46304
Summer: 8–8   Winter: 8–5
Rangers available for information. Exhibits, lectures, written programs. Every
Monday evening, 7–7:30, is movie night; many other evening activities sched-
uled. Hikes leave from various points throughout the park. Monthly
schedules are available, and include owl hunts, sand castle contests, swamp
tromps, etc.

When the glaciers first began moving south some 15,000 years ago to gouge out Lake Chicago (the far larger grandfather of Lake Michigan), it was as though the earth crunch was a call for battle: first, wave against wind in the creating — and then the blowing out — of great sand formations; then species against species in the struggle for survival and succession; then man against man for establishing ownership and use.

The idea of the park started fifty years ago, championed by Stephen Mather (first director of the National Parks) and the Chicago Prairie Club, but the outbreak of World War I halted action. In 1923 the Indiana State Park at Tremont was established, and in the 1940s rumors began that the best of the remaining dunes were being sold for a steel mill. On that note, citizen action began as a number of housewives organized the Save the Dunes Council, the conservation group which to this day keeps watch over the whole area.

After years and years of patient lobbying, and the active support of the late Senator Paul H. Douglas of Illinois, an Indiana Dunes National Lakeshore Park was authorized by Congress in 1966. The rumors about steel mills turned out to be true, and the same Congress authorized establishment of a Port of Indiana for use by the mills. In 1972 the park was dedicated, a compromised reality. Today it is a magnificent 12,000 acres of sun-flecked woods, marsh, bog, lagoons,

Sunset from Mt. Baldy, Indiana Dunes National Lakeshore Park.
Indiana Dunes National Lakeshore Park

high dunes, and 20 miles of beach. The first urban park in the United States, it is being planned for the enjoyment of the people of one of the nation's most populous areas. Its boundaries to the east are the outskirts of Michigan City; to the west, with the 1976 legislation, the park now extends into Gary to the road that separates Indiana's Lake and Porter counties; on the north, the Lake itself. Its southern boundary is gerrymandered so that it skips from U.S. 12 to U.S. 20, skirts the mills, pops in and out of exclusive settlements, and reaches out to four very special sections: Hoosier Prairie, the Blue Heron Rookery, Pinhook Quaking Bog, and nearby Cowles Bog (the latter two so unusual that they are listed as Registered National Landmarks).

These dunes are not as tall as those at Sleeping Bear and other Michigan locations, but they stretch miles farther inland. Their base is sand rather than glacial till. The prevailing northwesterly wind and currents bring sand down the Lake from communities as far north as Waukegan, and sweep it into this southernmost point on the shore.

All dune areas follow a pattern of natural succession from the newly formed storm beach, back to the foredune, then the pine forest (in Northern Michigan, red pine; in Indiana, jack pine), and finally to the oldest, most established area, the climax forest. New theories suggest that Michigan's climax forest of beech and maple is probably older than Indiana's of oak and hickory.

It was in the dunes area that the late great Henry R. Cowles did his studies, which led to theories of plant and earth succession and to the science of ecology itself. Cowles, on his way to a meeting at the University of Chicago, looked out the window of his train near the site of the present Dune Acres and saw a community of plants from varied habitats growing next to each other. Intrigued, he got off at Gary, hired a buggy, and went back to study. He severed his eastern academic connection, and became a scholar at the University of Chicago and the savant of the bog. Today, from Cowles's work, we know that the 2 1/2-mile landscape from Mt. Baldy (the highest moving dune in the park), over the Lake and treetops to a series of ridges to the south represent 15,000 years of botanical and geological history.

Climatic zones for many birds and animals as well as plants meet in this dune country, so one can see cactus hobnobbing with arctic bearberry or tropical orchids. The dunes are also a birder's delight. With binoculars, addicts can study some 200 species that live in the

Dune grasses in Indiana Dunes National Lakeshore Park. *Bob Daum*

various habitats of the area, or that migrate through in season.

The dunes had bison and black bear, cougar and wolves, until they were hunted out. It now has small game and some deer. It had Indians too (the Miami and then the Potawatomi), but they too were hunted out, and in a sad rout (known as The Trail of Tears) were shipped to a Kansas reservation under President Jackson's administration.

The Bailly Homestead, now being restored, is a reminder of what life must have been like 150 years ago when the Potawatomi lived in the area and did business with fur trapper and first settler, Joseph Bailly, and his part-Indian wife, Marie.

The Cowles Bog, named for the good doctor, can be seen on ranger-led hikes on weekends. Pinhook Bog, a genuine quaking bog of 120 acres with huckleberries the size of grapes, is extremely fragile, and is now open to students of science on request. It is hoped that in the near future some sort of boardwalk will be built so that visitors can examine this unusual habitat. At present, however, except on rare occasions, hikes don't go into the bogs; they can only be viewed from the wetlands.

The Hoosier Prairie as well as the Blue Heron Rookery, both far removed from the park, are also now out of bounds to visitors.

This is a park in search of a personality, trying to find in what ways it can best serve a metropolitan area of some 10 million people and still maintain its fragile base. Enjoy this lovely gift of the glaciers.

ARCHITECTURE AND HISTORIC SITE

* Bailly Homestead, Cemetery, Chellberg Farm, Trail
Howe Road and U.S. 20. House built in 1830s by pioneer fur trader Joseph Bailly. Fur house, chapel, and kitchen have tapes describing the life of the era. 2-mile trail goes to cemetery. Summer, daily, 10–8; winter, daily, 10–6.

RECREATION

Bicycling

Calumet Trail
Starts parallel to the South Shore railroad track in Dune Acres and continues to Rt. 12 near Mt. Baldy at the edge of Michigan City. 9 1/2 miles. Maintained by state and federal governments.

Boat Launches

See Michigan City and Portage.

Camping

See Chesterton, Indiana Dunes State Park

Hiking and Cross-Country Skiing

Ly-Co-Ki-We
(see Horseback Riding).

Calumet Trail
(see Bicycling).

Bailly Trail
(see Architecture and Historic Site).

Horseback Riding

Ly-Co-Ki-We Horse Trail
U.S. 20 and County Road 275 East. Bring your own horse. 3 1/2-mile trail winds through beautiful dunes and woods. Parking lot for trailers and cars. 6 AM–dusk.

Swimming (east to west)

All beaches between Mt. Baldy and Bethlehem Steel Mills are now public. You can swim where you like. Parking is a major problem, except on beaches listed below.

Mt. Baldy
Rt. 12 and Rice Street, 6 miles east of Visitor Center. Parking. Marvelous moving dune, beach, chemical portable toilets. No policy on hang gliding.

Central Avenue
2 1/2 miles west of Mt. Baldy, off Beverly Dr. Parking, beach, portable toilets.

State Park Rd.
1 mile north of Visitor Center. Beach, swim, toilets.

Porter Beach
End of Waverly Road. Private, admission charge for parking. Area of fine dunes and swimming.

West Beach
U.S. 12 and County Line Road (west of Ogden Dunes). 9 AM–8 PM. Huge parking area, new beach house, concession, guarded beaches. Most developed facility in the park. New picnic shelters with toilets. West Beach Trail, 3 miles of dune and marsh hiking. Long Lake. Lifeguards in summer.

Miller Beach and Marquette Beach
Both Gary facilities. Fine park, lagoons, easy parking.

SPECIAL ATTRACTION

Four very special areas are not open to the general public: Cowles Bog, Pinhook Bog, Hoosier Prairie, Blue Heron Rookery.

Every Saturday and Sunday a five-hour tour of Cowles Bog begins at 11:45 from the Visitor's Center, led by a trained ranger. The other facilities are seldom listed because of their fragility. If you wish to see them, write to the Visitor's Center, Rt. 12, Box 139 A, Kemil Rd. and U.S. 12, or phone: 926–7561.

TRANSPORTATION

South Shore Railroad
The South Shore and South Bend Railroad, last electric interurban, which leaves from IC Station at Randolph in Chicago, makes routine stops at Dune Acres, Tremont, and Beverly Shores. If requested they will now stop at Kemil Road (Visitor's Center), or at U.S. 12 near Mt. Baldy (1/2-mile walk to the high dune). The South Shore, at present, has no facility for carrying bicycles.

Johnson Beach

Population: under 200   Zip Code: 46304

Dune Acres

Population: under 200   Zip Code: 46304

Johnson Beach or Porter Beach

The Johnsons were commercial fishermen who worked this area and ran an inn until their fishing beach was absorbed into the Indiana Dunes State Park in 1923.

The Johnson Beach area today is a cluster of small homes along the Lake and some very fine new ones high up on the great dunes. The old inn is now a bar in summer, where for the price of parking, guests can swim in the Lake (no beach house or bathroom facilities). The eastern section of the settlement is now in the National Park; the western portion, contiguous to Dune Acres, is not. (Approach Johnson Beach via Waverly Road, a north turn from U.S. 12.)

Dune Acres

Dune Acres is a private preserve of expensive homes settled among and atop fine dunes. A guard at the gate keeps trespassers out. The settlement includes the great Cowles Bog, where modern ecology was actually born (see Indiana Dunes National Lakeshore Park). The bog can be visited on regularly scheduled hikes with park rangers, but because the area is so special and so fragile, no visitors are permitted on their own. Ironically, this tight little island of affluence now finds itself squeezed between the new mills of Bethlehem Steel Company and the far more plebian Johnson or Porter Beach.

Portage

Population: 24,800   Area Code: 219   Zip Code: 46368
Chamber of Commerce: Portage Mall; telephone: 962-1383

Starting at Dune Acres on the east and running 3 miles to Ogden Dunes, is a sprawling industrial colossus that includes the Bethlehem Steel Company, the new Port of Indiana, Midwest Steel, and Burns Ditch.

This area was the vortex of a controversy that raged for a generation, pitting growth versus nature, development versus dunes. In 1966 the U.S. Congress finally compromised with enough votes for both a port and a park and funding for each. Glorious dunes were mined to build the new shipping facilities, and much of the sand was carted across the Lake to build the addition to Northwestern University's Evanston campus.

Midwest Steel Company began operating in 1957, producing a variety of cold steel rolled products, and Bethlehem in 1964 launched the nation's most modern steelmaking facilities. Ore arrives at the company docks on the east side of the port, undergoes a series of steps in the steelmaking process, and emerges as steel slabs, which in turn are converted into numerous products.

The population of the Portage area is exploding as facilities expand and employment possibilities increase.

ORCHARD

Johnson's
Rt. 6 at I-130; telephone: 962-1383. Pickers taken by truck to raspberries, strawberries, vegetables, with stops at each crop. Pick your own.

RECREATION

Charters

Bob Cash
Telephone: 938-2839.

Jim Oursler
Telephone: 462-0366.

Marinas

Burns Harbor Marina
1700 Marine; telephone: 762–2304.

Doyne's
Burns Ditch, off Rt. 249; telephone: 938–3551. Ramp.

Lefty's Coho Landing
Rt. 12; telephone: 762–1711. Ramp.

SCENIC INDUSTRIAL DRIVE

U.S. 12, starting at Dune Acres and running through Portage and Gary gives an awesome view of industrial might. This area and the stretch through East Chicago, Whiting, Hammond, and South Chicago is the Ruhr Valley of the United States.

TOUR

Bethlehem Steel Company
Rt. 12; telephone: 787–3241. Occasional large group tours. Arrangements must be made well in advance.

Burns Waterway Harbor

Ogden Dunes

Population: under 200   Zip Code: 46368

Burns Waterway Harbor (Port of Indiana)

In 1816 when Indiana gained statehood, the territorial government pleaded with Congress to set boundaries so that the fledgling state would have one port on the Lake. To oblige, Congress set aside the 10 miles running north of the Lake's southern shoreline. Fifteen decades later, the Burns Waterway Harbor opened, an old dream finally realized.

The harbor, 30 miles east of Chicago, is Indiana's only deep-water port and the newest and busiest trade center on the Great Lakes. It is within twenty-four-hour reach of 160 million Americans by truck or rail, and within 300 miles of many basic ingredients for our complex society: coal, limestone, iron ore, oil, slag, and scrap.

The port is manmade, the only facility built especially to handle St. Lawrence Seaway traffic. Unlike most harbors (including Illinois's Calumet Harbor) it has an open-water approach with no channels to maneuver, no bridges to clear. Although tugs are available, they are seldom needed. A 4600-foot breakwater protects incoming vessels with drafts up to 28 feet. Seven modern ships can berth at once, and the harbor has facilities for self-loaders as well as containerized cargo. Everything is handled, from a crate of grandma's heirlooms to giant 40-foot containers, and the vessels come from Europe, India, Asia, Latin America, and the third world countries of Africa. A complex of railroads lies nearby, and major highways running north and south, east and west make truck hook-ups simple. Barge traffic moves in and out, year round, connecting the Lake with the Ohio and Mississippi rivers. There is no better place on the Lake to grasp the flow of waterway traffic and the connection of Escanaba, Port Inland, and the Soo with this great industrial complex of the Calumet.

TOUR

Burns Waterway Harbor (Port of Indiana)
Make arrangements for viewing by writing to: Mr. Ralph B. Joseph, Indiana Port Commission, P.O. Box 189, Portage 46368; telephone: 787–8638. Exciting view of Lake, vast mills, great ore, coal, slag mounds among great dunes.

Ogden Dunes

As in Dune Acres, there is a guard at the entrance of Ogden Dunes, and a similar air of exclusion. The community is entirely residential and outside the National Park, although some of its residents have been working for years to extend the park through their Lakefront area.

Started by Gary realtors, who understood the desirability of a suburban community on the Lake and near the mills, the town has been flourishing for half a century. There is good architecture, including a Frank Lloyd Wright house. There also was Diana of the Dunes, often called Dunehilda, a lady hermit who chose to live a life of primitive simplicity in the lonely woods near the shore.

Gary

Population: 175,000   Area Code: 219   Zip Code: 46402
Chamber of Commerce: 538 Broadway; telephone: 885-7407. (Includes Miller.)

Gary, third-largest city in Indiana, was an industrial miracle of the twentieth century: a whole city built in one period and designed to house, service, and employ more people than any other town its size in the century. The man responsible was Judge Elbert Gary, then chairman of U.S. Steel Corporation. The task was to build the largest integrated steel mill in the world, and to do that 12,000 acres of dunes were leveled, $100 million was spent, and within a decade, starting in 1906, a town of 53 square miles was booming on the south banks of the Grand Calumet River.

As in East Chicago, immigrants came from all over Europe and were ultimately joined by blacks, Appalachian whites, and representatives of the Hispanic world: a giant workforce, which turns out 8 million tons of ingots yearly. Before long other mammoth concerns settled in too, among them American Sheet and Tin Plate, American Bridge, and Universal Atlas Cement.

Gary's period as a company town ended with the CIO's struggle to organize the mills and with the signing of union contracts in the 1930s. In 1969 Gary elected its first black mayor, Richard Hatcher. Gary's slogan, "City on the Move," has proved sadly prophetic, for in recent decades there has been a mass exodus of whites to other towns in Lake and Porter counties, an outmigration that has left the city poorer despite massive efforts at urban renewal.

Miller, the residential section of Gary situated on the Lake, is struggling to develop a racially integrated community. In the past it was a fishing and ice mining center. It was here in 1896 that Octave Chanute made the first successful flight in a heavier-than-air craft, a feat that made possible the Wright Brothers' flight four years later and is commemorated in Miller's lovely Marquette Park.

ARCHITECTURE AND HISTORIC SITES

Al-Amin Mosque   (Turkish & Arab Mosque)
3702 W. 11th; telephone: 949–1854. Serving area's Lebanese, Arabs, Turks, and Egyptians. One of largest mosques in U.S.

Doll House, circa 1930
5th Avenue and Pierce. Fire station built to look like doll house.

Frank Lloyd Wright House
Northeast corner 7th and Van Buren.

ART CENTER

Gary Artists' League Gallery
400 S. Lake (in a church); telephone: 938–3356. Changing shows; by invitation. Sun. 1–5.

CEMETERY

Cemetery of Pioneer Settlers of Gary Area
Grant at 19th.

PARK

Marquette Park
Grand Blvd. and Forest Ave. Urban park designed by landscape architect Jens Jensen. Fine beach, lagoons, pavilion. Memorial commemorating Octave Chanute's experiments with gliders.

RECREATION

Golf

N. Gleason Park (9-hole)
3200 Jefferson; telephone: 944–0607.

S. Gleason Park (18-hole)
3400 Jefferson; telephone: 944–6417.

Swimming

Lake Street Beach
Lake at Lake Michigan, Miller. Also boat launch, ramp.

RESTAURANTS

Golden Coin
Rt. 20 and Clay St., Miller; telephone: 938–5357. Bar. Entertainment. Mon.–Sat., 11 AM–midnight.

Ming Ling Chinese Restaurant
566 S. Lake; telephone: 938–6617.

SHOPPING

The Barn
East 33rd; telephone: 962–9697. Antiques.

Wilco Store
6300 Miller; telephone: 938–6631. Great supermarket, with excellent Greek bakery.

East Chicago and Indiana Harbor

Population: 46,980   Area Code: 219   Zip Code: 49829
Chamber of Commerce: 2001 East Columbus; telephone: 398–1600

As you drive along I-94, the twin cities of Indiana (East Chicago–Indiana Harbor) look menacing. Trucks lumber, grime blows, smokestacks belch, and 38 miles of railroad track crisscross the towns, dividing them into a jumble of faded and aging neighborhoods.

If you turn off at Indianapolis Boulevard you will be surprised to find an area of many churches, a park with a splendid lake view, good down-to-earth restaurants, and one of the first company towns in the U.S.

The Indians named the land at the bottom of the lake the Calumet because it resembled their peace pipe in shape. Today the Calumet area stretches from the Illinois line to Gary, and includes East Chicago–Indiana Harbor among its four cities.

East Chicago is the Ruhr Valley of America, with one of the great integrated economies of the world. It is the center of the country's largest steel complex, and its port, the Indiana Harbor Ship Canal, is one of the busiest harbors on Lake Michigan.

The twin cities cover 11 square miles, contain fifty-seven industries, employ 50,000 workers. Fifty-nine European and Middle Eastern nationalities have contributed skills to this mighty labor force. When the bishop of the Catholic archdiocese was planning for this ethnic mix back at the turn of the century, he set up seventeen churches, fifteen of them with foreign language services, to ease the adjustment for the new immigrants. The workers arrived in Indiana alone, and lived in hotels for men. When the day's work ended, they congregated in saloons, many of which have added restaurants now. When the beer stopped flowing at 7 PM, they grabbed their guns in pursuit of wolves, then abundant in the area.

The grandchildren of those early Poles and Croatians, Turks and Welshmen, have been joined by southern blacks and Mexicans, and in such numbers that the towns are now one-third black, one-third Latino, and one-third white. As their grandparents before them, these people make and process steel, fabricated metals, chemicals, industrial diamonds, tank cars, and dozens of other products.

Joseph L. Block, newest ore boat in the Inland Steel Company's fleet, docked at Inland's Harbor Works, East Chicago, Indiana. *Inland Steel Company*

The growth of the twin cities was not sudden, for the area was an unwanted no-man's land for 250 years after the French explorers first saw it in 1600. Swill, swale, marshland, and dune: the Indians looked and wanted higher ground; the farmers looked and wanted better soil; the missionaries looked and wanted more souls. The early visitors, bound for Chicago, pulled on their hip boots and cursed as they struggled for six days to cover the final 40 miles of their trek. In the 1830s, however, an imaginative engineer named George Clark looked at the area and decided that the introduction of good transportation could cause a boom for this swamp so close to Chicago. He bought up vast acreage, and started a sawmill and lumber business. Later his heirs supplied a good part of the lumber needed to rebuild Chicago after the fire of 1871.

Clark gave the area a boost, and soon the northern tip, called Poplar Point, was dredged and became a thriving harbor. That done, men talked and dreamed of a shipping canal. By 1909 those dreams became reality with a canal extending a mile inland from the Lake. Today the canal divides all east and west street numbers in the twin cities. The harbor is a 1500-acre manmade peninsula reaching 2 miles into the Lake.

The great push toward development came when a Cincinnatian named Joseph Block stopped in the area on his way to the Columbian Exposition in Chicago in 1893. Impressed, he decided this was the spot for the scrap steel business he had started in Chicago Heights, Illinois. When the developers of the area offered him 50 acres of land (20 of them still under water), he found seven partners, borrowed $65,000, and went off to New York to make plans for transporting skilled immigrants to his brand-new Inland Steel Company. The men came. The first steel ingots were turned out in 1902; a blast furnace was built in 1906. Today Inland is the seventh-largest steel mill in the country.

But Inland today is only one of many companies in the twin cities. U.S. Gypsum, City Service, Atlantic Richfield, Jones and Laughlin, and American Steel Foundries are only a few of the top plants that make East Chicago a hub of industry. In fact 70 percent of the city is industrial, making it number 1 in America for the concentrated use of land. For a swamp, that's truly a switch.

ARCHITECTURE

Marktown
Dickey and Riley Rds., off Indianapolis Blvd. This model community was built in 1917 for the workers of the Mark Steel Company (Jones and Laughlin). It was designed by Chicago architect Howard Van Doren Shaw to show an overall unity in architecture, at the same time using a variety of housing types. The slightly faded homes are no longer owned by corporations, but belong to individuals. Marktown has Indiana Historic Registry standing.

PARKS

Jeorse Park (Lakefront Park)
Michigan at Indiana Harbor. City marina, ramp, beach, picnicking. Excellent view of giant Inland plant and ore boats out in Lake waiting to enter dock on opposite side of mill.

Washington Park
142nd and Grand; telephone: 392–8320. Conservatory, tennis, ice-skating, flower show at Easter time.

RECREATION

Todd Park and Golf Course (9-hole)
140th and Indianapolis Blvd.; telephone: 398–4200, ext. 264.

RESTAURANTS

Big John's
2014 Columbus; telephone: 398–9803. Croatian. Marvelous lamb barbecue on Saturday noons, with mostly male mix of laborers, police, politicos. Mon.–Sat., 9 AM . . .

Casa Blanca
4616 Indianapolis; telephone: 397–4151. Good Mexican food. Daily, 7:00 AM–midnight

Danny's Lighthouse
1208 Carroll; telephone: 398–1010. Owner consults astrology and schedules special events six times yearly, such as Tahitian night, Greek nights, with special foods, music, dancing. Mon.–Fri., 11–11 (bar till 2 AM); Sat. 5–11 (bar till 2 AM); closed Sun.; kitchen closed Mon. evening.

Jockey Club
Elks Building 4624 Magoun; telephone: 398–2353. Bar; weekend entertainment; steaks. Interesting because grew out of saloon era when sportsmen gathered to relive athletic events over a drink. Every neighborhood had sports clubs. Football was so popular in this area that the National Football League really developed here. Mon.–Fri., 11–3 AM; Sat., 5 PM–3 AM.

SPECIAL EVENT

Mexican Independence Day
A true gala with parades, dancing, ethnic foods. Call Chamber of Commerce for date. Early Sept.

TOURS

Amoco Oil (Whiting Refinery)
2815 Indianapolis Blvd.; telephone: 473–3093. Group tours for from four to forty can be arranged; minimum age: eighteen. Advance book-

ing necessary. Tour includes slide presentation and drive through refinery.

Inland Steel

Plant 2 South Gate (foot of Michigan Ave. near Lake); telephone: 392–1200. Wear low, closed shoes; long sleeves; no cameras. Check with company about specific transportation and insurance regulations. Two-hour tour begins at 9:30 AM; must be booked in advance. Minimum age, sixteen.

Whiting

Population: 7247   Area Code: 219   Zip Code: 46394
Chamber of Commerce: 1200 119th Street, P.O. Box 350; telephone: 659–0292

Whiting calls itself the Gateway to the Calumet Region. Its 970 acres are squeezed between Hammond to the west and the other cities of the Calumet to the east. Amoco, the largest oil refinery in the world, is here as are divisions of Union Tank Car, Lever Brothers, Boise Cascade, American Maize Products, and the American Smelting Company.

For thousands of years the Whiting area was a rugged stretch of dunes and swamp. In 1847, with an eye to the future, George Roberts bought 500 acres of this land. He knew that the coming of railroads would revive the area, and sure enough between 1852 and 1874 three railroads laid track, connecting Chicago with the East. One of the trains had a wreck, and the little settlement where it occurred became known as Whiting's Crossing, and later Whiting, after the conductor in charge.

In the meantime the Standard Oil Company built a pipeline from its oil fields in Lima, Ohio, to Chicago, hoping to capture the midland markets (kerosene was then the product refined from oil; gas, a useless by-product, was dumped in the streets and burned). When the citizens of Chicago's South Side objected vociferously to the smell of the new refinery, the company was forced to look elsewhere along the pipeline. Whiting looked promising, with plenty of water from the Lake, several railroads, and a growing city to the west. So it was here, as the country's need for gasoline grew, that Standard Oil established its refinery and developed the thermal cracking process by which large amounts of gas could be derived from crude oil.

Whiting, unlike East Chicago and Gary, never became a company town. Today its small residential section has a generous ethnic mix, including the largest Turkish settlement in America.

ARCHITECTURE AND HISTORIC SITE

Memorial Community House

1938 Clark; telephone: 659–0860. J. D. Rockefeller and Standard Oil contributed in 1923. Center of community life. Swimming pool.

PARK

Whiting Municipal Park

117th St. at Lake Michigan; telephone: 659–0860. Tennis, fishing, picnicking, baseball, pistol range, and trapshooting.

RESTAURANTS

Condes Restaurant and Lounge

1440 Indianapolis Blvd.; telephone: 659–6300. Greek food. Daily, 11 AM–1 AM.

House of Yung #2

1423 Indianapolis Blvd.; telephone: 659–7770. Lunch and dinner daily.

Vogel's

1250 Indianapolis Blvd.; telephone: 659–1250. Tues.–Sat., 11–11; Sun., 11–10.

THEATER

Marion Theater Guild

1844 Lincoln; telephone: 659–2368. Good community group; weekend shows; dinner theater in spring and fall; call for schedule.

TOUR

Amoco Oil Company

(Whiting Refinery) 2815 Indianapolis Blvd.; telephone: 473–3093. Arrangements must be made two to four weeks in advance. No children under sixteen. Film and drive-through tour.

Hammond

Population: 108,000   Area Code: 219   Zip Code: 46320
Chamber of Commerce: 429 Fayette Street; telephone: 931–1000

As early as 1780 the French and English battled each other as well as irate Indians in the dunes of the Hammond area. In time the bickering ended as the participants began to realize that trade accomplishes more than tomahawks.

Originally named Hohman for an early resident, the town was incorporated in 1883 and rechristened Hammond for an enterprising citizen named George Hammond who was the inventor of the refrigerated rail car. In time, and with the help of four rail lines, Hammond prospered. However when fire destroyed the slaughterhouse and meat packing moved on to Chicago, great unemployment set in for a while. Determined to diversify its industry, Hammond eventually attracted plants that produced corn syrup, steel and soap, and the modern industries today include Rand McNally, Pullman Standard, and Clark, Shell, and Mobil Oil.

Hammond was the home of the nation's first professional football team. Its First Baptist Church boasts the largest sunday school in the world. And probably its most illustrious native was a watchmaker named Roebuck who teamed up with a salesman named Sears to sell goods by mail.

ART CENTER

Northern Indiana Art Center
5446 Hohman; telephone: 931–0018.

PARK

Harrison Park
Waltham and Hohman Ave.; telephone: 853–6378. Greenbelt with tennis, ball park.

RESTAURANTS

Cam-Lam
132 Sibley; telephone: 931–5115. Mon.–Sat., 11–9; closed Sun.

Freddy's Steak House
165th and Kennedy; telephone: 844–1500. Bar. Wall-to-wall politicians. Daily, 11–12 AM; Sun., 2–9 PM.

McGee's
142 Rimback; telephone: 932–4600. Bar; restaurant; discotheque with mirror globes that spin and gel lights. The restaurant is in an old union hall, refurbished to the tune of $1 million. Fun. Mon.–Fri., 11–3 AM; Sat., 5–3 AM; closed Sun.

Phil Smidt & Son
1205 North Calumet; telephone: 659–0025. Deluxe fish house. Mon.–Thurs., 11:15–9:30; Fri. and Sat., 11:15–10:30; closed Sun.

SHOPPING

Indiana Botanic Gardens
626 177th; telephone: 931–2480. Begun in 1910. Second generation. Herbs unlimited — domestic, imported, fragrant.

SPECIAL EVENT

International Cultural Festival
7047 Grand Ave.; telephone: 931–5100. Weekend after Labor Day.

Past and Present Lake Michigan Terms

Lake Michigan Statistics

U.S. Coast Guard Stations

Harbors and Marinas

State and National Parks with Camping Facilities

Index

Past and Present
Lake Michigan Terms

Amen corner. Corner in bunkhouse where old-timers reminisced.

Bare-back boat. Stripped down and rented without any extras.

Bell ox. A lumber foreman.

Black robes. Indian name for early French Jesuits.

Black water diving. Diving in Lake Michigan; so called because of murky water.

Boat. On the lakes, all vessels are boats — never ships.

Bo jo. A greeting; derived from early French voyageurs' use of *bon jour.*

Breath dish. A dish of coffee beans used by sailors on pay day to freshen breath before returning home.

Bubble boat. A boat that stays in water all winter, because water flows around it.

Cackleberry. Lumber camp lingo for an egg.

Camp. Upper Peninsula lingo for any recreational facility, grand or not, outside of town.

Chart. A nautical map.

Chautauqua. An organization that brings moral uplift and lectures to smaller communities; a poor man's university (after the Chautauqua Assembly, formerly held in summer in Chautauqua, New York).

Draft. The vertical distance from the water line to the bottom of a floating vessel.

Finglish. The dialect spoken by Finnish Americans.

Fresh (or *pond*) *sailors.* Lake Michigan sailors. In winter, called "hard water sailors."

Fulgerite. Small pieces of tubelike glass formed by lightning striking sand on beach.

Going down below. Mackinac expression for going south.

Gone to the breakers. Descriptive term for a dismantled boat.

Island goat. Sailor who has been in twenty-five Mackinac races.

Keenaw nips. North country socks; squares of cloth wrapped around feet diaper style.

Laker. Huge ore boat — up to 1000 feet long.

Mackinac boats. Flat-bottomed boat, with a sharp prow and square stern, propelled either by oar or sail.

Mackinaw coat. Coat originally sewn from Mackinaw blankets to protect soldiers on the island.

Mayday. A distress signal (like SOS), derived from the French *m'aider*, "help me."

Mirage or *looming.* A special Lake phenomenon where objects seem to be distorted or appear to be upside-down.

Pasties. Food eaten by Cornish miners in the Upper Peninsula (somewhat like a cold ravioli or a "tired egg roll").

Peanut cruise. A Lake cruise that is so short you don't have time to eat a bag of peanuts.

Racine feet. New feet sewn onto old stockings

Racon-radar transponder beacon. A device that extends the range and utility of shipboard radar units (used in the Mackinac Straits).

Rip-rap. Stone used to stop erosion along Great Lakes shoreline.

Seiche. Great Lakes tidal wave caused by sudden changes in barometric pressure.

Short ton. A commercial measure; 2000 pounds.

Sun dogs. A partial rainbow.

Taconite. Low-grade iron ore.

Tip-up towner. An ice fisherman.

Upper lakes. Lake Superior and the northern parts of lakes Michigan and Huron.

Voyageur. Person employed by fur companies to transport supplies to and from their distant shores.

Wampus cat. An imaginary animal who makes night noises around a lumber camp.

Wannigan. A floating (usually on a wood scow) eating house used in lumber camps.

Wickiup. A bark wigwam.

Wood pecker. A poor chopper of wood.

Yap. A crazy lumberjack.

Lake Michigan Statistics

GENERAL DESCRIPTION

Age: 4500 years old.

Size: covers 22,400 square miles, third largest of the Great Lakes; 578.8 feet above sea level, 21 feet lower than the surface of Lake Superior. Division of Lake Michigan territorially: Illinois 7 percent, Wisconsin 33 percent, Michigan 59 percent, Indiana 1 percent.

Average depth: 276 feet (deeper end is north of Milwaukee, Wisconsin, and Grand Haven, Michigan (923 feet at deepest point off Manistee, Michigan).

Length: 304 miles at longest point.

Average width: 76 miles (118 miles at widest point).

Volume: 1165 cubic miles (complete changeover of water in Lake Michigan [with its main outlet at Lake Huron] takes 100 years compared to only 2 1/2 years for Lake Erie).

SHORELINE

Population: 13.5 million people live in the Lake Michigan Basin, most at southern end of Lake. Two thirds of this population uses Lake Michigan for drinking water. The 13.5 million figure represents: one third of total Illinois population, one fourth of total Wisconsin population, one thirtieth of total Michigan population, one thirteenth of total Indiana population.

Coastline: 1,661 miles including islands. Shoreline usage: 487 miles, residences; 367 miles, forests and undeveloped land; 283 miles, agricultural; 151 miles, recreational (Lake Michigan has one half of the recreational area on the Great Lakes); 93 miles, industrial (forty-five thermal power plants are located on Lake Michigan and use its water).

Ownership: 1,117 miles, private; 220 miles, state and local government; 25 miles, federal government.

One hundred rivers and streams empty into Lake Michigan. There are approximately 400,000 registered pleasure craft on Lake Michigan.

ISLANDS

There are thirty-nine islands in Lake Michigan (many still unsurveyed).

Location: two are in the straits, sixteen are in Beaver Archipelago, eighteen are in Green Bay area, three are north of Green Bay toward Garden Peninsula.

Ownership: six privately owned, six inhabited and can be visited by excursion boat, twenty-seven uninhabited (more than half of which are publicly owned); most can be visited by private boat for fishing and/or picnicking.

WEATHER

Precipitation: Two thirds of Lake Michigan's precipitation rises back into atmosphere through evaporation; its 22,400-square-mile surface daily releases the energy of 7000 atomic bombs.

Rainfall: averages 26 to 35 inches annually (60 percent of which falls during May-to-September growing season).

Snowfall: averages 20 to 120 inches (worst storms in November).

Ice coverage: 40 percent normal, 80 percent severe, 95 percent winter of 1978–79.

Windscale:

Term	Miles per hour	Wave height
light winds	0–7	1 foot
gentle winds	8–12	2 feet or more
moderate winds	13–18	5-foot rollers
fresh winds	19–24	crested rollers
strong winds	25–40	small-craft warnings

Weather forecast: radio — PSB band, 162.55 MHz, KWo39 (Illinois, Wisconsin, Michigan, Indiana); phone — (312) 936–1212, Chicago area; marine radio — channel 16, distress signal to U.S. Coast Guard.

Light stations (formerly called lighthouses): Thirteen stations still on Lake Michigan (only three manned year round). One hundred and fifty smaller (pierhead) lights. Lights are identified individually by differences in color, frequency of flash, or groupings (as lighted buoys).

Old sailors' weather chanteys:

Evening red and morning gray,
Will send the sailor on his way.
But evening gray and morning red
Will bring rain down upon his head.

When clouds appear like rocks and towers,
You may expect light wind and showers.

Rain before wind, take your topsails in,
Wind before rain, hoist 'em up again.

Here's an old Lake chantey from the late 1890s that was sung by the hands on the schooner *E. C. Roberts,* an ore boat that made the run from Escabana, Michigan, to Chicago:

Some sailors got shovels and others got spades,
And more got wheelbarrows — every man to his trade.
We looked like red devils; our fingers got sore;
And we cursed Escanaba and her damned iron ore.

SHIPPING INDUSTRY

There are twenty-eight harbors on Lake Michigan for big boats (to accommodate big boats, harbor depth must be minimum of 25 1/2 feet).

Illinois: Calumet Harbor, Chicago, Waukegan.

Wisconsin: Kenosha, Racine, Milwaukee, Port Washington, Sheboygan, Manitowac–Two Rivers, Kewaunee, Sturgeon Bay, Green Bay.

Michigan: Menominee (Marinette, Wisconsin), Escanaba, Port Inland, Petoskey, Traverse City, Frankfort, Manistee, Ludington, Muskegon, Grand Haven, Holland, Benton Harbor-St. Joseph.

Indiana: Burns Harbor, Gary, Buffington, Indiana Harbor.

Approximately 300 boats handle 112 million tons of cargo annually on Lake Michigan carrying the following basic resources: agricultural products, iron ore, limestone, lumber and paper products, salt, gravel, coal, fuel oils, and even fish. Lake boats range in size from a 45-foot boat for commercial fishing to a 1000-foot ore boat.

SHIPWRECKS

There have been 4000 known shipwrecks on Lake Michigan with some maps charting as many as 170 identified remains. Lake chanteys, popular among sailors' hangouts, commemorated shipwrecks, as in the disappearance of the steamer *W. H. Gilcher* with all hands lost off South Manitou Island in a severe night storm late in the season of 1892:

On October twenty-eight,
Oh, how the wind did scream!
The last time the *Gilcher*
And crew was ever seen.

Of death these jolly lads
Never once did dream
As routed for Milwaukee
They from Port Huron steamed.

It was a fearful night,
The *Gilcher* should turned-to,
But she held to her course
'Till off the Manitous.

Says a sailor's hurried note
That later came to light,
They were breasting mounta'n'us seas
At nine o'clock that night.

Lost in Lake Michigan
They did not reach the shore,
The gallant ship and crew
Will sail the Lakes no more!

FISHING

Coho salmon, chinook salmon, steelhead, and smelt are the most sought-after of the thirty-seven varieties of fish in the Lake. Between 1966 and 1977 Lake Michigan was stocked with 100 million fish. Fish must be replenished annually because no spawning habits are yet present. (Approximately thirty-one communities around Lake Michigan have some commercial fishing, most in very small amounts, representing about 33.5 million pounds of fish annually.)

U.S. Coast Guard Stations on Lake Michigan

All stations may be toured upon request.

ILLINOIS
Wilmette Harbor
312–251–0185

WISCONSIN
Kenosha
414–657–7651
Milwaukee
414–224–3167
Sheboygan
414–452–5115
Two Rivers-Kewaunee
414–793–1304
Sturgeon Bay
414–743–3366
Plum Island
(Washington Island)
June to September only
414–847–2215
Green Bay
June to September only
414–435–7042

MICHIGAN
St. Ignace
906–643–9191

Charlevoix
616–547–2541
Frankfort
616–352–4242
Manistee
616–723–7412
Ludington
616–843–9088
Muskegon
616–759–8581
Grand Haven
616–842–2510
Holland
616–335–5871
South Haven
616–637–2208
St. Joseph
616–983–6114

INDIANA
Michigan City
219–879–8371
Calumet Harbor
312–768–8000

Harbors and Marinas*

Marinas or Harbors	Public	Private
CHICAGO**(from south to north)		
Jackson Park Harbor	*	
312–363–6942		
59th St. Harbor	*	
312–493–8704		
Burnham	*	
312–294–4614		
Monroe	*	*
312–294–4612		
Diversey	*	
312–327–4430		
Belmont	*	
312–281–8587		
Montrose	*	
312–878–3710		
ILLINOIS		
Wilmette Harbor	*	
312–251–4234		
Waukegan Harbor	*	
312–662–5222		*

*In emergencies all harbors are available. Since berth figures vary from one year to the next, they are not included.

**Harbor Master of Chicago Park District (312–294–2271) operates these harbors.

Marinas or Harbors	*Public*	*Private*
WISCONSIN		
Trident Harbor		*
(at state line)		
414–694–1200		
Kenosha Harbor	*	
414–656–6151		*
Racine Harbor		*
414–633–8883		
Milwaukee Harbor	*	
414–273–5224		*
Port Washington Harbor		*
414–284–5585		
Sheboygan Harbor	*	
414–459–3366		*
Manitowoc Harbor	*	
414–684–3325		*
Two Rivers Harbor	*	
414–793–1191		*
Kewaunee Harbor	*	
414–388–2670		*
Algoma Harbor	*	*
414–487–2163		
Sturgeon Bay		*
414–743–3311		
Baileys Harbor		*
414–839–3311		
Sister Bay		*
414–854–2124		
Ellison Bay		*
414–854–2006		
Gills Rock		*
414–854–2606		
Washington Island		*
414–847–2526		
Ephraim	*	*
414–854–2041		
Fish Creek		*
414–868–3226		

Marinas or Harbors	*Public*	*Private*
Egg Harbor		*
414–868–3000		
Green Bay	*	*
414–497–3265		
Oconto		*
414–834–9973		
Marinette shares with Menominee		
Harbor.		
MICHIGAN		
Menoninee Harbor	*	
906–863–8498		
Escanaba Harbor		*
906–786–9614		
Gladstone Harbor		*
906–428–9924		
Manistique Harbor		*
906–341–6841		
Naubinway Harbor	*	
906–477–6312		
St. Ignace	*	
906–643–8131		
Mackinac Island Harbor	*	
906–847–3561		
Mackinaw City Harbor	*	
616–436–5269		
Harbor Springs Harbor	*	
616–525–5355		
Petoskey Harbor	*	
616–347–6691		
Charlevoix Harbor	*	
616–547–9752		
Beaver Island Harbor	*	
616–448–2252		
Boyne City	*	
(near Charlevoix)		
616–582–2232		

Marinas or Harbors	Public	Private
Elk Rapids	*	
(near Traverse City)		
616–264–9920		
Traverse City	*	
616–947–3371		
Suttons Bay	*	
616–941–1800		
Northport Harbor	*	
616–386–5411		
Leland Harbor	*	
616–256–9132		
Frankfort Harbor	*	
616–352–9051		
Arcadia	*	
616–352–7571		
Manistee	*	
616–723–6491		
Pentwater	*	
616–869–8301		
Muskegon	*	
616–722–3361		
Grand Haven	*	
616–846–5590		
South Haven	*	
616–637–3171		
St. Joseph	*	
616–983–5432		
New Buffalo	*	
616–469–2600		
INDIANA		
Michigan City Harbor	*	
219–872–1712		*

State and National Parks
with Camping Facilities*

Parks	Towns	Acres	Camp Sites	Swim- ming	Boat- ing	Fish- ing	Hunt- ing
ILLINOIS							
Illinois Beach 312–662–4811	Zion	2485	161	*	*	*	
WISCONSIN**							
Harrington 414–285–3015	Belgium (north of Port Washington)	636		*		*	
Kohler-Andrae 414–452–3457	Sheboygan	750	105	*		*	
Kettle Morraine Forest 414–626–2116	Campbellsport (west of Sheboygan)		391	*	*	*	
Point Beach Forest 414–794–7480	Two Rivers	2770	149	*		*	
Potawatomi 414–743–5123	Sturgeon Bay	1126	125		*	*	
Whitefish Dunes 414–823–2400	Sturgeon Bay	647		(being developed)			
Peninsula 414–868–3258	Fish Creek	3763	466	*	*	*	
Rock Island 414–847–2235	Washington Island	900	40	*	*	*	

*Where acreage is not included, the park is a small part of a large forest or National Lakeshore.

**There are Wisconsin communities along Lake Michigan with public hunting grounds not included in the above. For exact locations call Department of Natural Resources in Madison, Wisconsin, 608–266–2621).

Parks	Towns	Acres	Camp Sites	Swim- ming	Boat- ing	Fish- ing	Hunt- ing
Newport 414–834–2500	Ellison Bay	2017	13	*			
MICHIGAN							
J.W. Wells 906–863–9747	Cedar River (north of Menominee)	974	155	*	*	*	
Fayette 906–341–6917	Fayette (Garden Peninsula)	365	80	*	*	*	
Portage Bay 906–341–6917	Fayette (Garden Peninsula)		18	*	*	*	
Indian Lake 906–341–6917	Manistique	567	300	*	*	*	
Big Knob 906–477–6262	Engadine (near Naubinway)		23	*	*	*	
Little Brevort 906–477–6262	Brevort		32	*	*	*	
Straits 906–643–8620	St. Ignace	174	318	*			
Wilderness 616–436–5381	Carp Lake (near Mackinac City)	7514	210	*	*	*	*
Petoskey 616–347–2311	Petoskey	305	90	*		*	
Young 616–582–6681	Boyne City (near Charlevoix)	563	293	*	*	*	*
Bells Bay Forest 616–582–6681	near Charlevoix	2200	41	*		*	
Beaver Island Wild Life Area 616–582–6681			25	*	*	*	
Traverse City 616–947–7193	Traverse City	39	330	*		*	
Leelanau 616–947–7193	Northport	1044	42	*		*	*

Parks	Towns	Acres	Camp Sites	Swimming	Boating	Fishing	Hunting
D.H. Day, Sleeping Bear Dunes National Lakeshore 616–334–4017			100	*			
Platte River Campground, Sleeping Bear Dunes National Lakeshore 616–334–4017			150	*			
Interlochen 616–276–9511	Interlochen	187	550	*	*	*	
Orchard Beach 616–723–7422	Manistee	201	175	*		*	
Ludington 616–843–8671	Ludington	4156	398	*	*	*	*
Mears 616–869–2051	Pentwater	50	179	*		*	
Silver Lake 616–873–3083	Mears	2685	249	*	*	*	
Muskegon 616–744–3480	Muskegon	1125	357	*	*	*	
Hoffmaster 616–798–3711	Muskegon	1043	333	*		*	*
Grand Haven 616–842–6020	Grand Haven	48	170	*	*	*	
Holland 616–335–8959	Holland	143	342	*	*	*	
Allegon State Game Reservation 616–673–2430	Allegon, near Saugatuck	1000	147	*			*
Van Buren 616–637–2788	South Haven	326	205	*			*
Warren Dunes 616–426–4013	Sawyer-Bridgman	1502	249	*			*
INDIANA							
Indiana Dunes 219–926–1215	Chesterton	2182	311	*			

Index

Acme, MI, 286, 288–89
Algoma, WI, 161–65
Arcadia, MI, 324

Bailey's Harbor, WI, 177–79
Bay View, MI, 271
Beaver Island, MI, 282–85
Benton Harbor, MI, 376–82
Beverly Shores, IN, 399–400
Bower's Harbor, MI, 299–300
Bridgman, MI, 383, 385–86
Brussels, WI, 195–96
Burns Waterway Harbor, IN, 415–16

Cedar Grove, WI, 135–36
Charlevoix, MI, 277–81
Chesterton, IN, 401–4
Chicago, IL, 3–11
    architecture and historic sites,
        14–21
    art (indoor and outdoor), 21–26
    entertainment, 26–33
    recreation, 33–39
    restaurants, 39–41
    shopping, 41–44
    sources of information, 11–14
    tours, 44–46
    vistas, 46–47
Cross Village, MI, 263–66

Door County, WI, 173–75
Douglas, MI, 364–70
Dune Acres, IN, 412

East Chicago, IN, 420–24
Eastport, MI, 286–87
Egg Harbor, WI, 194–95

Elberta, MI. See Frankfort-Elberta,
    MI
Elk Rapids, MI, 286, 287–88
Ellison Bay, WI, 181–83
Empire, MI, 308, 313
Ephraim, WI, 189–91
Escanaba, MI, 226–32
Evanston, IL, 48–51
    architecture and historic buildings,
        51–52
    museums, 52
    orchards and gardens, 52–53
    parks and nature centers, 53
    recreation, 53–54
    restaurants, 54–55
    scenic drive, 55
    shopping, 55–56
    source of information, 51
    special events, 56
    theater, 57
    tour, 57

Fairport, MI, 235, 240
Fayette, MI, 235, 238–40
Fish Creek, WI, 192–94
Fort Sheridan, IL, 77
Frankfort-Elberta, MI, 314, 317–23

Garden Peninsula, MI, 235, 237–
    38
Gary, IN, 417–19
Gill's Rock, WI, 183–85
Gladstone, MI, 233–34
Glen Arbor, MI, 308, 310–13
Glencoe, IL, 67–69
Grand Beach, MI, 383, 390
Grand Haven, MI, 349–54

Great Lakes Naval Training Center, IL, 84
Green Bay, WI, 197–202
Gulliver, MI, 245–47

Hammond, IN, 427–28
Harbert, MI, 383, 387
Harbors and marinas, 439–42
Harbor Springs, MI, 267–70
Highland Park, IL, 70–74
Highwood, IL, 75–76
Holland, MI, 355–58
  architecture and historic sites, 358
  cemetery, 358
  museums, 358–59
  orchards and farms, 359–60
  parks, 360
  recreation, 360–61
  restaurants, 361–62
  school, 362
  shopping, 362–63
  special events, 363
  theater, 363
Horicon Marsh, WI, 133

Indiana Dunes National Lakeshore Park, IN, 405–11
Indiana Harbor, IN, 420–24

Jacksonport, WI, 175–76
Johnson Beach, IN, 412

Kenilworth, IL, 62–63
Kenosha, WI, 97–99
  architecture and historic sites, 99
  museums, 99
  park and nature center, 100
  recreation, 100–102
  restaurants, 102
  shopping, 103
  special event, 103
  tours, 103
Kewadin, MI, 286, 287
Kewaunee, WI, 157–60

Lake Bluff, IL, 82–83
Lake Forest, IL, 79–81
Lakeside, MI, 383, 387–88
Leland, MI, 305–7

Long Beach, IN, 383, 390
Ludington, MI, 332–37

Mackinac Bridge, MI, 248, 252–53
Mackinac Island, MI, 248, 255–58
Mackinaw City, MI, 259–62
Manistee, MI, 326–31
Manistique, MI, 241–43
Manitou Island, North, MI, 308–9
Manitou Island, South, MI, 308, 309–10
Manitowoc, WI, 148–50
  architecture and historic sites, 150–51
  museums, 151
  parks, 151–52
  recreation, 153–54
  restaurants, 154
  shopping, 154–55
  special events, 155
  tour, 155
  transportation, 155
Marinas and harbors, 439–42
Marinette, WI, 213–18
Menominee, MI, 221–25
Michigan, Lake, statistics about, 433–37
Michigan City, IN, 393–98
Milwaukee, WI, 111–15
  architecture and historic sites, 115–16
  art centers, 116
  museums, 117
  music, 117
  parks, 119
  recreation, 119–23
  restaurants, 123–24
  scenic views and drives, 124–25
  shopping, 125
  special events, 126
  theaters and civic centers, 126
  tours, 127
Muskegon, MI, 342–43
  architecture and historic sites, 343–44
  farms, 344
  museums, 344
  parks, 345–46
  recreation, 346–47

Muskegon (*cont.*)
  restaurants, 347–48
  shopping, 348

Nahma, MI, 235, 237
New Buffalo, MI, 383, 388–90
North Chicago, IL, 85
Northport, MI, 299, 303–4

Oconto, WI, 206–9
Ogden Dunes, IN, 415, 416
Old Mission Peninsula, MI, 299,
  300–301
Omena, MI, 299, 303
Onekama, MI, 324–25
Oostburg, WI, 135–36

Parks, state and national, with camp-
  ing facilities, 443–45
Pentwater, MI, 338–41
Peshawbestown, MI, 299, 302–3
Peshtigo, WI, 210–12
Petoskey, MI, 271, 272–76
Portage, IN, 413–14
Port Washington, WI, 128–32

Racine, WI, 104–5
  architecture and historic sites, 106
  art center, 106
  museums, 107
  music, 107
  parks and nature centers, 107
  recreation, 107–9
  restaurants, 109–10
  special events, 110
  theater, 110
  tours, 110
Rapid River, MI, 235
Rock Island, WI, 188

St. Ignace, MI, 248–50
St. Joseph, MI, 376–82
Saugatuck, MI, 364–70
Sawyer, MI, 383, 386
Sheboygan, WI, 137–39
  architecture and historic sites,
    139–40
  cemetery, 140
  museums and art centers, 140–41

orchard, 141
  parks, 141–43
  recreation, 143–45
  restaurants, 145
  shopping, 145–46
  special events, 146
  tours, 147
Sister Bay, WI, 179–81
Sleeping Bear Dunes National Lake-
  shore Park, MI, 314–16
Soo Canal, MI, 248, 251–52
South Haven, MI, 371–75
Stevensville, MI, 383, 384–85
Stonington Peninsula, MI, 235, 237
Sturgeon Bay, WI, 166–72
Suamico, WI, 203–5
Suttons Bay, MI, 299, 301–2

Thompson, MI, 235, 240
Traverse City, MI, 290–98
Traverse City Bay, MI, east arm of,
  286
Traverse City Bay, MI, west arm of,
  299
Two Rivers, WI, 148–50
  architecture and historic sites,
    150–51
  museums, 151
  parks, 151–52
  recreation, 153–54
  restaurants, 154
  shopping, 154–55
  special events, 155
  tour, 155
  transportation, 155

Union Pier, MI, 383, 388
U.S. Coast Guard Stations, 438

Washington Island, WI, 185–88
Waukegan, IL, 86–89
Whiting, IN, 425–26
Wilmette, IL, 58–61
Winnetka, IL, 64–66
Winthrop Harbor, IL. *See* Zion and
  Winthrop Harbor, IL

Zion and Winthrop Harbor, IL,
  90–94